ALL THE LONELY PEOPLE

ALL THE

PEOPLE

Robert Hamburger

L O N E L Y

Life in a Single Room Occupancy Hotel

Ticknor & Fields / New Haven and New York   1983

Library of Congress Cataloging in Publication Data

Hamburger, Robert, 1943—
    All the lonely people.

  1. Poor—United States—Case studies.
  2. Lodging-houses—United States—Case studies.
  3. Single people—Housing—United States—Case studies. I. Title.
HV4045.H35 1983   305′.90694   82-19128
ISBN 0-89919-159-2

Printed in the United States of America.

S 10 9 8 7 6 5 4 3 2 1

The tape-recorded interviews, transcriptions, and manuscript drafts of this book have been placed in the permanent collection of the Schomburg Center for Research in Black Culture, a branch of the New York Public Library system. These materials are available to all interested readers and scholars.

The author appreciates permission to quote from the following sources:

From *The Member of the Wedding* by Carson McCullers. Copyright 1946 by Carson McCullers. Copyright © renewed 1974 by Floria V. Lasky. Reprinted by permission of Houghton Mifflin Company.

"Another Brick in the Wall." Copyright © 1979 by Pink Floyd Music Publishing, Ltd., London. Published and administered in the U.S.A. by Unichappell Music, Inc. International copyright secured. All rights reserved. Used by permission.

"Game Satirizing Life on Welfare Draws Criticism, but Sells Well"—November 30, 1980. Copyright © 1980 by The New York Times Company. Reprinted by permission.

Book design by David Ford.

For my grandparents

Minnie and Bernard Epstein
Harriet and Arthur Hamburger

... But alas! this was a time when every one's private safety lay so near them that they had no room to pity the distresses of others; for every one had death, as it were, at his door ... and knew not what to do or whither to fly.... There were many instances of immovable affection, pity, and duty ... but in general, the danger of immediate death took away all bowels of love, all concern for one another.

Daniel Defoe, *A Journal of the Plague Year*

CONTENTS

Preface   xvii
Acknowledgments   xxi

W I N T E R

Informer   3
The Man who Shot Frank Sinatra   4
Easy Money   8
Flying with Doobie   12
Three Signs   14
Movie Star   14
The Hostage Situation   19
Righteous High   20
Fortune   21
Overflow   21
A Death   22
A Proper Bostonian   24
Muriel Berry's Story   26
Do I Have a Story!   42

SPRING

A Nice Day 45
Brothers 47
Bobby Carman's Story 49
Doug's and Bobby's Room 54
Doug Carman's Story 55
Mr. Winslow 69
Ironsides 70
Primary Day 72
Arthur Moore 73
Loner 73
David Torres's Story 76
Street Scene 90
Shit 90
Check Day 92
Books 93
Family 94
Mother's Day 96
Arguments 99
Door Signs 102
Snapshots 102
Bobby Carman's Story 104
Doug Carman's Story 107
Paris 112
A Death 113
Kind of a Letdown 115

SUMMER

Summer Song 119
Breaking Away 120

Sunday Afternoon 122
Two New Watches 124
Lost Energy 124
Gerry 126
Geraldine Footé's Story 127
A Death 136
Lloyd Smith's Room 136
Lloyd Smith's Story 137
David's Rough Month 147
Friday the Thirteenth 156
In the Hole 159
Mourning 160
Candy Man 161
Getting Back 161
Fed Up 162
Independence Day 162

H E A T W A V E

A Wonderful Afternoon 167
Coming Apart 168
Poker Game 169
White Pussy 172
Fire Sale 173
Yvonne Smith's Story 175
House of Death 183
Coming Soon 184
The Glendale 184
Daddy's Coming 187
My Brother's Keeper 188
Too Many Thoughts 189
Breakfast at the B-way 190

Help   191
Runaround   195
Home   200
A Matter of Pride   201
Good Impression   202
To Keep a Man   202
Three Fine Girls   203
Missing   204
High Summer   204
Death Rattle   206
People's Convention Parade   206
Bliss on Broadway   207
Swami   208
Shipwreck Park   209
The Last of Candy   211
Garbage Symphony   211
Birthday   212

AUTUMN

Change of Weather   221
Suitor   222
School   223
Youngblood   224
Youngblood's Story   225
Yoga   236
Mess   237
October Buttons   240
A Face like Charles Bronson's   240
Sweet Face   242
Flying   242

Disorganized   243
Wages of Sin   243
Close Shave   245
David's Movie   246
Frustrated   247
Sign   249
November 4: Bad Weather   249
The Morning After   253
Youngblood's Postmortem   253
New Regime   255
A Rare Joke   257
Return of the Bishop   257
Frying Pan   258
Captive TV   259
Uptown   261
November 18: Greensboro   262
Too Violent   263
Discouraged   263
Rough Birthday   265
Slow   266
Bad Elements   267
Thanksgiving   269
Lost   271

HOLIDAY SEASON

Fun and Games   277
R.E.A.C.T.   278
The Sunday Program   279
On Doc's Case   280
Run Down   282

Youngblood's Analysis   283
Duran Postmortem   284
A Suitor, a Black Moment, and the Energy Crisis   284
Too Warm   286
Christmas Is Coming   287
A Lotta Hate   288
Another Death   288
Haircut   289
Cold Snap   290
Cornucopia   290
All the Girls   291
Scary Sunday   292
Six Days till Christmas   292
Hole   297
Magic   298
Power Source   298
Sibling Rivalry   299
Christmas Letter   300
Reflections on a Golden Arm   302
Emergency Power Source   306
The Bishop Splits   306
Hunger   307
An Age of Miracles   310
The Gospel According to Youngblood   312
Street Preacher   313
The Bishop's Blessing   314
Doc's Christmas Eve   315
Christmas   317
One Last Thing   317
Graduation   320
Reunion   325

Friends   326
Safe   328
Year's End   329

Epilogue: The Following Year   329

PREFACE

Single room occupancy hotels (SROs, they are commonly called) are residential hotels where each person lives in a tiny, sparsely furnished room. Many SRO residents receive some form of economic assistance, and many of those who don't live off those who do. SRO residents who depend on economic aid have usually passed through mental hospitals, prisons, or drug and alcohol addiction programs before some social service agency directs them to an available room in an SRO. A New York State Assembly report presents this somber picture of the SRO population:

The typical SRO hotel is a cross section of mental, physical and social pathology. Studies have indicated that at least three-fourths of the residents suffer from major chronic diseases such as heart disease, tuberculosis, cirrhosis of the liver, diabetes, and blindness. In some SRO hotels, over half the tenants are alcoholics and as many as sixty percent have histories of psychiatric problems.

It costs the state between $1000 and $2000 per month to maintain someone in prison and $3000 per month for each mental hospital resident. SRO residents receive $300 per month to live on, but thrift is rarely used to justify SROs. Theory holds that they are residential stations where vulnerable people who are "well" enough to live apart *from institutional supervision can begin the process of reentry into community life.*

Some SRO residents have their own refrigerators, stoves, and bathrooms, but most live in "units" separated from the main corridor by a door that may or may not lock. Each unit has three or four separate rooms as well as cooking and toilet facilities, which are shared by the unit's occupants.

A few hotels, particularly those with large numbers of former mental patients, have outreach clinics that give city social workers and medical teams a chance to deliver desperately needed services. But these offices are there at the sufferance of hotel management, a situation that hampers the city from bearing down on negligent treatment of SRO tenants.

A few SRO residents hold down regular jobs; others receive Social Security or payments from the Veteran's Administration. But by far the largest source of income maintenance is Supplemental Security Income (SSI), which is given to people whose ability to support themselves has been judged to be permanently impaired. SSI recipients receive about $300 per month in New York State; $180 pays for a room. That leaves $120, or four dollars a day, for food, laundry, transportation, clothing, and other expenses. These people subsist, but barely.

SROs exist in most American cities; they are concentrated in the hard-pressed urban centers of the Northeast and the old industrial belt. Until recently, there were close to 70,000 SRO residents in New York City alone, but a wave of real estate speculation and building conversions has driven tens of thousands of these people into the streets, where they face an even harsher struggle for survival.

This book records the passage of a year in the lives of the residents of a New York SRO. "Hotel Walden" is a fictitious name, and I have changed the names of some residents, but otherwise this book is true. The life stories come from tape-recorded interviews, and the many episodes and snatches of conversation that make up the rest of the book come from notes I took on the spot. A few times I have entered the unspoken thoughts and feelings of people; but with these exceptions, I have depicted life as I found it.

ACKNOWLEDGMENTS

This book was made possible by a research grant from the National Endowment for the Humanities. For their strong support of my NEH proposal I want to thank Susan Davis, Professor Stanley Kutler, and Professor Jacqueline Hall. During the early stages of my work Bill Stamp, Belle Cogdell, and Ethany Braithwaite were enormously helpful. They introduced me to many of the people in this book, and they offered heartfelt encouragement to my research. I have the greatest admiration for Bill, Belle, and Ethany — for their professional competence and their active sympathy for SRO residents. I also received generous advice from Tom Faison, Ken Quagenti, and Howard Marcus. I depended on their good sense and drew upon their remarkable stamina more than they realize.

I consider myself extremely fortunate to have had Peter Matson support this book as my agent and to have had the benefit of James Raimes's tactful, intelligent editorial guidance. I also want to thank Elizabeth Torrey West and the Ossabaw Island Project for allowing me to work on my manuscript at their splendid artists' retreat. There's no way I can adequately acknowledge the great boost I received from those friends who advised and encouraged me during the making of this book. They have my thanks and my love — and now they have this book.

Finally, I want to express my deep gratitude to the people of Hotel Walden. They trusted me enough to share their time with me, and eventually their thoughts and feelings. I have given a hard two years to SROs, but these people are giving their lives.

WINTER

INFORMER

You an informer! An informer, hear? You come in an get a book outa us — the people that don't need it, read it; the people that's against us keep on keepin on. You an informer! You ain't gonna be president. You ain't gonna change nothin. Reagan ain't gonna read your book. But say one of his peoples reads it — you think that's gonna help?

See, you conscientious — I ain't sayin you ain't. You come in here to learn an maybe you come out with some understandin. But the others — Reagan an his gang — they the ones that gonna do the damage. They read what you gotta say — how you think it's gonna go down with em: "Look here! Lookit what this guy says about this hotel — this dude's sellin food stamps for a pint of Night Train; this one's runnin numbers; she's selling Valiums or somethin the doctor give her cause she needs the money an she's tired of turnin tricks." You think tellin the truth's gonna do some good, but you informin on us. All they gonna see is a buncha run-down niggers who ain't worth the taxpayers' money. They jus lookin for a reason to cut back on us.

Tell me this — why we got all these fuzzy-wuzzies runnin the country, an other peoples got Mao an Castro an that black dude in Rhodesia? I'll tell you — it's cause no one here wants to look at the real information. What I'm sayin is *we're* the real information — this hotel, an all the garbage out there, an this young girl over here, who don't know how to take care of herself. What's she doin here? Welfare's supposed to mean *helpin people,* don't it?

You gonna be an informer — you tell em what you see aroun here, tell em how they put this whole deal together, tell em about all the lonely people. But I'm tellin you, they ain't gonna listen, they don't wanna know — cause if people could see, there'd be a revolution. There'd have to be.

THE MAN WHO SHOT
FRANK SINATRA

It's way too warm in here. Mildew and unbathed bodies. Thirteen men and women, eleven of them black, are seated on folding chairs along the wall. Television on a table. Wild, off-color images — green Rock Hudson, orange Doris Day. Everyone's eating from sagging paper plates — franks and beans or ice cream and cake. Fat Edna pigging out, shovelling beans with fingers, stuffing her face, scarfing franks in a single mouthful, mindless of the globs of food she fails to swallow. Fat legs spread apart, unmatched shoes, grubby layers of dresses and sweaters. She shuffles out and returns with ice cream and cake.

Beside her, a black man with a pleasant face. Hunched over, all attention on his hands. Constant rubbing, as if to keep warm. Hard work. A time-consuming project — his preoccupation, his mission, his necessity. He looks up for one stolen moment — face sweet and vulnerable — then his hands draw him back to his task.

"Are you a doctor?" A perky black woman with short hair is speaking to me from the center of the room. Alert and intelligent-sounding. Her tone demands an answer.

"No, I'm just visiting."

"Well, what do you do? Are you a social worker?"

"No." I didn't want to begin like this. I guess I hoped I'd pass unnoticed.

"Well, what do you do?" A few people are listening, but most seem preoccupied by their respective obsessions.

"I write."

"Are you gonna write about us?"

"Do you write fiction or nonfiction?" A stately white woman asks. Her voice excudes courtesy like a proper Bostonian's. She sits upright, holding a black cane. Clothes loose fitting, carefully arranged. Lost elegance — an heiress who went astray.

"What I do is make books where the people in them have a chance to speak. I may do a book about single room occupancy hotels, and if I — "

"What's that?" the perky woman asks quickly.

"Places like this. Where each person has a small room to live in."

"What for? I don't wanna read a book like that!"

"Well, I think many of you have had interesting lives. If you had a chance to tell me your stories, it could be a good book."

"Isn't that nice!" the proper Bostonian observes. "Fiction's my favorite!"

"What's that?" the other asks.

"Stories," she explains. "If you tell a story, it's fiction."

"How do you know?" the perky woman asks.

"It's what the words mean," I explain. "If you tell about your life, that's nonfiction."

"But I could be telling a story to fool you!"

"I suppose."

"So your nonfiction would be my fiction." She folds her arms in triumph.

A new voice chips in. "How much ... how much ... uhhh ... hey, can you tell me how much you make?" Shaky young guy with darting eyes and full beard. Army surplus fatigue jacket. He smiles when he's not talking.

"Not much," I tell him.

"This book ... this book ... hey, you writing this book yourself?"

"Nonfiction!" the perky woman snaps in my behalf. "He don't write nonfiction by himself. He needs people to tell him things."

The shaky guy checks his watch, sweeps a hand across his forehead, then rushes to the door. "I got the ... I got the ... the ... the. ... Hey, I got the doctor now."

A teenaged boy with a tired face slips into his seat and begins scratching his chest and arms. He yanks up his sleeve, tearing at the needle marks up and down his vein. Scratching, scratching till the tired skin is grey.

Fat Edna smoking a Kool. Gobbling smoke. No one saying much. Rock and Doris do all the talking.

A kid in thick glasses enters. Half-inch lenses magnify his eyes so they seem to burst froglike from his head. He blows his nose energetically, very publicly, with enormous gusto. He grins at me as though we'd both witnessed some third person's loutish impropriety. "I intend to fill it up," he says nodding at his handkerchief. "All she can take."

Someone tells him I'm a writer. "I like that," he says with conviction. "Me, I think about writing. I think a lot, think all the time, but I ain't got me no woman — so I guess thinking ain't good for everything. But now you take writing. Can't be a writer till you can spell, ain't that right?"

"Sort of."

"Well, spelling just comes natural to me. You take a long word — take *international,* okay? I-N-T-E-R . . ." He rushes through the prefix, then pauses like a game-show contestant. "N-A-T-I-O-N-A-L." He doesn't wait for my praise. "See, I can take on big words cause I know how to break it down. I did all right in school. Almost went to college."

"Why didn't you go?"

He leans forward confidentially. "I shot Frank Sinatra. Couldn't stay in school after that. I didn't want to shoot him. Honest, I didn't. The elders, they made me do it — said I had to or they'd come after me. But I didn't want to. I left him spread out on the living-room floor. Mafias standin guard all around the house, but I gave em the slip. . . . After I done it, I felt bad. He never done nothin to hurt me."

"You're lucky you didn't kill him," I say.

"Them who live by the sword must die by the sword. . . ." He stares at the television. William Holden riding a red horse. Green clouds. Blue Mexicans. "You seen *Crazy Horse?* That's my favorite. It's got Victor Mature. Now that's some movie! He leads his people off the reservation, but then somebody sticks him an he dies at the end. Real sad. . . ."

A young guy in good new sneakers sashays into the room and slaps five with the tired boy who's been scratching his tracks for forty minutes now. "Say Slater, whatchya watchin, man? This a gangster or a western?"

"I don know. I jus been here a while."

Edna sets her head on the table, directly in front of the TV, and falls asleep instantly. Four dessert plates, puddled with ice cream, at her feet. "Here comes the birthday girl!" a social worker announces from the doorway. She leads Sadie into the room — white woman with disheveled hair, coughing and spitting into a handkerchief. Sadie takes a seat while the social worker prepares a portion of ice cream and cake. "It's Sadie's sixty-fifth birthday!" the social worker announces gaily. Sadie smiles shyly and pokes at her plate until the social worker leaves. She slides her plate aside and stares across the room. An old black man in two dark sweaters and a tattered sports jacket ambles to her side and clasps her hand gallantly. "You the birthday gal?" he says, patting her hand. "I'll tell you a little secret — I'm gonna be twenty-four myself next week."

Off in the corner a massive black man stirs to life. His huge belly and bulging thighs make his head and feet appear tiny, like a genie freshly squeezed from his bottle. He wears a soiled red baseball cap, red gym sneakers like a little boy's, and minuscule dark glasses with lenses the size of quarters. For an hour he's sat there unchanged — arms folded, legs poking stiffly ahead, head tilted in sleep. Now he props his arms on his knees and bellows loudly. "I'm fuckin tired of yuh! FUCKIN TIRED." He glowers directly at someone near me. His voice is so belligerent, his outburst so abrupt and histrionic, that his rage seems to rush right past us towards some private, unnameable nemesis. "FUCK YUH! FUCK YUH!" he says bestowing his curse on each one of us.

Edna is snoring now. Dress hitched above her knees. Mottled bruises all over her legs.

"FUCK YUH! FUCK YUH!"

Sadie raises a handkerchief, demurely patting her mouth as her turn approaches. And the man who shot Frank Sinatra waits expectantly — a bright child at a spelling bee.

EASY MONEY

The clock in the outreach clinic waiting room shows 7:20. It's just after noon. A World War II espionage film this afternoon — *St. Joan of Paris*. Drizzling, cobblestone streets, Nazis on motorcycles, trench coats, clandestine meetings in dark churches. Television watchers staring with no curiosity — more a tropism towards sound and movement than a conscious choice. Fat Edna slurping peaches. Mr. Winslow, the enormous man, is dormant. An attractive woman named Rita is talking with a lean young man in laceless black sneakers.

Two months ago, her husband jumped out their fifth-story window — high on angel dust. She says how he tried to jump a few times before, how she caught him once on the rooftop, half over the edge, yanked him back somehow; how he would seem just fine and suddenly he'd be plagued with nightmarish fears — guns aimed at him from neighboring buildings, people listening at his door, unthinkable forces lurking inside the room, already triumphant, jeering at his futile resistance. "I couldn't stop him," she says. "I got him that one time on the roof, but I couldn't hold on to him every minute. It was late at night. We was in bed, and he'd been drinkin and had some of this angel dust, and he gets up while I'm sleepin. I heard him in the other room, and when I got there he was gone. . . . His brother says I shoulda saved him. It was my fault, he says. But how could I watch over him every night?"

"Your husband was paranoid!" A thin black man with lively eyes leans towards her from across the room.

"Paranoid?"

"Paranoid's when your mind ain't right. Fear takes you over an you lose control. You don't see nothin the way it is; all you see's your own mind, stuff you're scared of. You so messed up you do anything to get away from it." His thin, sad face comes alive as he talks. Rita listens intently.

"His brother's a priest," she says, "and he tells me he knows I coulda saved him. They was twins — sometimes he could be right inside my husband's mind. At least that's what he says. Like when my husband was kissin me, this priest brother-in-law of mine dreamed he was kissin me too. The night my husband died, his brother dreamed he was fallin."

"You know about twins?" the thin man asks her.

"It's when one egg splits in two, an they both gets the same genes."

"That's right! They each gets half of what they's supposed to, an they — "

"No, they don't get half," she says. "It ain't like that."

"What I mean to say is twins sometimes *think* like they only get half — that the other, he's takin somethin from him. It can mess with your mind, make you think you ain't a whole man."

"I'm fuckin tired of yuh! Fuckin tired! FUCKIN TIRED!" Mr. Winslow has come uncorked. "FUCK YOU! FUCK YOU!" His pants are halfway down over his buttocks. A little white suitcase sits between his outstretched legs — something a child would take to a pajama party. "FUCK YOU! FUCK YOU! FUCK YOU!"

"Gilligan's Island." Yellow-green faces pursued by flickering red ghosts.

Later, the thin-faced man moseys into the waiting area outside the medical care office. "Hey Thurman!" he says to a man about his age, "You know what you look like there? The Thinker!"

Thurman raises his chin from his bent arm. "Shit, Youngblood, I ain't made of stone! I ain't constipated either. That Thinker, he sits there like that cause he can't get off the pot."

They both laugh.

"That was good!" Thurman adds. "Now you didn't think I was gonna come back with something sharp like that."

Youngblood takes a seat beside him. "Speakin of constipation, I was hospitalized a ways back, an just before I'm gettin ready to go home the doctor asks me what my stool looks like. I seen a bit of blood that mornin, just a spot really, but I told him. . . . Now why I gone an done that? They took me in the test laboratory an stuck a microscope right up my ass!"

"You gotta keep your mouth shut an yer pants up when you aroun doctors. They listen when you talk, waitin till you tells em somethin wrong. Then in they go, pokin equipment where they ain't got no business, cuttin yuh up — turn you inside out if yer not careful."

"Here now, I'll put it for you in a proverb." Youngblood pauses for effect. "Speech is silver," he says deliberately, "but silence is golden."

"Uh-huh! You hear a man or woman talkin an talkin, never stoppin, an I'll show you someone makin no sense. . . . What's the word I'm lookin for?"

"Blabbermouth."

"*No sense,* I mean. When you makin no sense."

"Nonsense!"

"You got it! Jus slipped my mind when I come up on it."

"I love semantics. All those objects an pronouns an predicates," Youngblood says. "You can do anything with words if you know how."

"An if you don't know how," Thurman adds, "you talkin NON-sense!"

They lapse into silence for a few minutes.

"Hey Youngblood, you know what I'd do if I could get around better? I'd get me some underwater divin gear an go find me them Spanish galleons. Now there's a way to make some easy money! All that gold sunk off Cape Hatteras somewhere."

"Yeah, an you know whose gold it was? Who found it an dug it

up? It was them Indians. Aztecs an Incas. Had so much gold they
didn't think nothin of it. Spanish come in an kills em all off. Didn't
have to dig for it or nothin — jus load it on their ships an turn
aroun fer home."

"The one thing I'd worry about is sharks — sharks an that
moray eel. You divin fer gold, you better keep yer eyes open."

"That's right! But now say a shark's comin — you just hit it on
the nose an he'll turn away. They're scared of people; I read that.
I'll tell you, boa constrictors an pythons — that's what scares me.
Wrap aroun an crush every bone in your body."

"DOCTOR! I need a doctor!" A man lurches into the room. "I
been stabbed! Where's a doctor?"

The male nurse remains cool. "Where'd this happen?" he asks
from his chair.

"Seventh floor. I jus come from there." He jerks open layers of
sweaters and shirts as he speaks.

"What were you doing there?"

"I live there."

"You know who did it?"

"Sure I know him. He's my best friend. Took four dollars from
me and stuck the knife in here." He pulls up his thermal undershirt
to show the wounded flesh. A mean little cut, maybe an inch
deep — flesh torn apart, caked brown blood smeared across his
chest. The knife struck his rib cage. A different angle of entry and
the man might be dead.

The nurse gets to work dabbing the wound with disinfectant.

"You come back here with your Spanish gold," Thurman says to
Youngblood, "an we got people ready to stab you for four dollars."

"His best friend," Youngblood muses. "Seems like a friend
ought to fetch a higher price."

FLYING WITH DOOBIE

Room 408. Shock of rancid air seals my nostrils. I fight off nausea and breathe through my mouth. The bathroom's crowded with medical apparatus I don't understand. Arthur Moore planted in his wheelchair in the center of the bedroom. He's in his sixties, bald, with the peculiar look of fatigue one sees in those who have spent their lives at physical labor. Powerful neck. Thick arms gone slack. Below the waist something terrible has happened. Everything swollen, blown out of proportion like a parade float. Impossibly huge legs ending in bulging feet the size of hams. One massy foot sprouts a tuberlike growth which might have been a toe. The other foot shows five toes, curled like fat red slugs. Arthur Moore's body has gotten away from him — as if some curse has seized his lower body, holding the human remnant captive. His face is kind. Gentle washed-out aspect in his gaze. His time is spent meeting the simple demands of daily living — wheeling himself about to make his bed, opening a can of soup to heat on his small burner, sitting by his dirty window looking down on the busy street.

When he was young and fit he worked for the old Chesapeake and Ohio Railroad as a cook, crisscrossing the Northeast, having his share of adventures, seeing a bit of the country.

I try one slow breath through my nose. I cannot do it. It is not the small inconvenience of breathing through my mouth that bothers me. It's the disgust I feel, the loathing I don't want to feel, for the ruined body, for its grotesque proportions, for Arthur Moore's acquiescence. Breathe slowly, naturally, I tell myself. But I cannot.

"Romper Room" on television. Doobie, a surprisingly ugly, rather slapdash bee with a round Mickey Mouse head, prances onto the screen to discuss gravity with a mob of predictably precocious kids.

"Where is gravity?" the hostess asks.

Doobie unfolds his arms in an all-embracing gesture. "Everywhere!" the kids squeal.

"What does it do?" she asks.

Doobie flops to the floor. "Makes you fall down!" they yell.

"Can you see gravity?"

Doobie shakes his head, "NO-O-O-O-O!"

A knock on Arthur's door.

"Come in!"

A hip-looking guy in a leather cap saunters into the room. "Excuse me," he says checking me out. "Hey, no offense, man. No offense."

Arthur gives the man an inquisitive stare.

"Excuse me," he repeats. "See, I was lookin fuh my friend, an I must've got off on the wrong floor." His arms swing as he talks. "Excuse me, brother. Excuse me." He backs up towards the door. "See, I got the right apartment but the wrong floor."

The guy splits, and Arthur turns his wheelchair to face the TV. The bratty kids are writhing through an impromptu ballet, flapping their arms, high-stepping behind Doobie the bee. Arthur watches the screen with the same indifference he trained on the suspicious visitor.

"Wasn't it fun to fly with Doobie!" the hostess declares. "And you know, we'd all fall from the sky if we didn't flap our wings."

THREE SIGNS

> Please Do Not
> Knock On The
> Door!!! Don't Want
> to Be Disturbed
>   Thank You

> Don't Knock th
> God Damn Door
> Mother Fucker
>   C.J.

> Knock! Call Out
> Your Name in a
> Respected Way and
> Step Back Three (3) Feet
>   Thank You

MOVIE STAR

Sugar Blue. Loveable, crazy Sugar Blue. He was wearing an old melton topcoat and a yellow scarf tied over his head the first time I met him at the outreach clinic. "Sugar, what's that poking out from your scarf?" Bill, the head nurse, asked.

"My curlers." Sugar Blue is handsome, light-skinned, with fine angular features, gentle dark brown eyes, and a wry smile, trusting and amused.

"Sugar! You can't go around with everything hanging loose!" Bill told him.

"I know, Mr. Bill, but I can't think of everything all at once." It's as if he met some crushing defeat early on, without even knowing it. He shows no tension, no anxiety, yet he's always around the clinic, welcoming Bill's gentle reprimands with a charming, be-mused smile.

After our first meeting Sugar Blue seems ubiquitous. I see him on the street dribbling a basketball, spinning it on one finger, not a care in the world. I see him by the carry-out place on Ninety-eighth Street and down at McDonald's on Ninety-sixth. Here in the hotel, he's in and out of the TV lounge all day long. Everyone knows him. There's always some message he's got to deliver or re-ceive, or some crazy plan to undertake like rushing off to check some savings account in a Bronx bank twenty minutes before clos-ing time. I get used to his worn melton topcoat, but also to his blue satin basketball jacket, and a brown and green striped corduroy sports coat. Each outfit suggests the existence of a slightly different person, yet Sugar Blue is always Sugar Blue. On the wall of the TV lounge is an article about SROs torn from the *Times* magazine sec-tion. It includes a portrait of Sugar in which his hair is cropped close to the skull; his face appears gaunt, his eyes empty — the vic-tim of some unthinkable atrocity. It isn't him so much as a per-formance in which he portrays one of his many versions of himself. Yet of course that *is* him, that's very much who he is.

In the clinic again.

"Sugar," Bill says, "I want you to wash that grease outa your hair before I see you tomorrow."

"Okay, Mr. Bill." He grins obediently, like a child who knows he will be tucked in bed when his day's chores are over.

"Sugar, what's that on your collar?"

"Ohhhhhh," he beams, "I'm savin my gum."

Bill begins pulling the glop from Sugar's clothing. "Mr. Bill, I saved a woman's life! In the elevator! She was havin — what you call that? — she started shakin and went stiff."

"A seizure."

"That's it! She was havin a seizure in the elevator, an I stuck my finger in her mouth so she wouldn't swallow her tongue. She bit me — look at this here — an today she didn't even remember."

"That's okay, Sugar. People often don't remember what happened in a seizure."

Sugar Blue's relieved; you can feel his spirits rise. "I'm gonna clean my hair, Mr. Bill, I'm gonna clean it for tomorrow. But you know, I been studyin an I didn't have the time. I took books outa the library an I'm studyin to be a doctor."

"I thought you wanted to be a nurse."

"First a nurse," he says with conviction, "an then I go on to be a doctor . . . . The trouble is, I can't read so good."

"Well, wash your hair, Sugar. Tonight! Wash it good with lots of soap."

Sugar Blue picks up his basketball. "I was coachin a team," he says, "teachin kids how to play for the Olympics. But I don't have time no more, not with my studyin."

The following day in the TV lounge.

"Victor Mature! It's Victor Mature!" Sugar Blue is grooving by the television. He waves at me and tips his head toward the old movie. "They got him playin an old man."

"You washed your hair," I say.

"I got to." His face opens in a perfect smile. "I'm gonna be a movie star!"

"I thought you were studying to be a doctor."

"They're makin a movie of me," he says. "I been singin songs for em; they brought a camera right in my room an they're gonna put me on television."

Fat Edna is sobbing. A little black man beside her has fallen asleep.

I wander into the hallway and find it cluttered with lighting equipment, a sixteen-millimeter camera, a tripod, and assorted paraphernalia. "What's going on?" I ask a tall bearded guy who's watching over the equipment.

"BBC documentary—outpatient care for the mentally disturbed." He puffs distractedly on a Camel. I have the feeling he wants to break someone's neck.

A few minutes later, one of the outreach clinic social workers explains the problem. The BBC crew had come to them with their
proposal, and everyone had been anxious to help them get their
footage. Even hotel management had given its consent. Only two
rules: no filming after five (when most of the clinic personnel are
gone) and no interviews with former mental patients unless a
member of the outreach medical staff is present off-camera. Yesterday the director broke both rules at once. Having decided that
the staff was determined to interfere and keep him from the *real*
story, he went to Sugar Blue's room in the early evening and encouraged him to do his thing. The cameras rolling, Sugar Blue
showed off his extensive collection of dirty magazines. Then, sens-
ing a movie career within his grasp, he sang a few hymns and
topped off his performance with "The Star-Spangled Banner."
When the clinic staff heard about the incident, they told the film-
maker to pack up and leave. "Sugar's so prone to suggestion," a
staff member said. "He'll do anything to please. I know the film
crew didn't trick him or force him to do this, but there it is, right?
People in Europe are going to turn on their television and see this
poor guy sitting in his little room singing the national anthem un-
derneath a pile of sex magazines. He's taking his cue from them,
giving them what he thinks they want. It's not right to exploit
people like that."

Back in the hallway, I strike up a conversation with the director.
He's German, a bearish version of Allen Ginsberg — bearded,
metal-framed glasses, long uncombed hair ringing his bald pate.
He's sick of bureaucrats, he tells me. He says his cameras weren't
even loaded when Sugar Blue sang but that the clinic is all pan-
icked because the scene might have placed the national anthem in
compromising circumstances.

Sugar Blue spots us and rushes up with a friendly smile. "Did he
tell you about our movie?" he says to me. "I sang, an they had
cameras in my room, and I'm gonna be a movie star!" It's too
much for the discouraged director. He hauls his equipment to the
elevator and heads downstairs.

I run into the director once again on my way out. All the equipment is stacked in the hallway while he waits for his assistant to
come around with the car. "If it wasn't a rush job," he says, "if I
had two months here, I could produce a full-length feature."

"Get that camera outa here!" A tall black queen has just come
in off the street, and she is angry. "Don't take no picture of me!"

"Don't get excited," he says contemptuously. "We don't want to
film you."

"Don't tell me what you want to do!" She strides right at him.
"You point that thing at me an I'll sue!" By the time she reaches
us, the director has pivoted his camera to face the wall, but this
fails to reassure her. "Get it outa here!"

"That's exactly what we're doing, my friend." I think he almost
wants to antagonize her.

"Why you come in here to take my picture?"

"We're filming a documentary for British television."

"Not in here you ain't!"

"I know. I know."

"Well, I'll just help you pack up!"

"Now listen," the director says, stepping into her path, "we'll be
out of here in ten minutes. My assistant will load the car and we'll
drive away. There's no film in the camera. We're done — look!"
He unscrews the camera from the tripod and sets it down carefully.
The queen watches suspiciously, arms folded.

A few minutes later, the van is almost loaded. "You get out too!"
she says to me.

"I'm not with them," I answer.

"What are you?" She presses closer. She's a good five inches
taller than I am.

"A writer."

"Get out! Get out! We don't need any of you!"

For the next week Sugar Blue spends his days in the TV room,
watching the screen with little interest, then flicking the set from

station to station after each show ends. "I was stupid," he says. "I shoulda asked him what time they was gonna play my movie."

THE HOSTAGE SITUATION

Dittsey is short, dark, and cute. Usually she's out in the hallway or downstairs in the entrance area, half dancing as she moves about with the flow of conversation and booze. Today she makes a grand entrance into the TV lounge, one hand on her hip. "Mister Lee, Mister Lee, ooooh Mister Lee, Mister Lee, Mister Lee, ooooh-ooooh-ooooh Mister Lee," she sings. "Hey Mister Lee! Now tell me what's happenin!"

Nobody moves. The television is tuned to a midday news report, but most eyes are fixed on some invisible point in the empty center of the room. I've never noticed it before, but almost half the people here are clutching room keys in their hands like penitents. Fat Edna sits with her legs apart, cheap wig all tousled and sliding perilously down her forehead. Incongruous pale blue knee socks. She sucks her gums and stares at nothing, fingering her dime-store key chain.

Their rooms are dishevelled, their walls blank and beds unmade. Their movements are listless. Deprived of stimulation and contact with the flow of life, some appear relatively emotionless while others are agitated and display classical symptoms of anxiety and confinement. Even after their release, many of these hostages are certain to bear the scars of their captivity for life.

"Come on now Mister Lee, talk to me. You been in de-tox, ain'tchya?"

"Don't let em send ya to St. Luke's," a middle-aged guy responds. "They don't do nothing but keep ya sittin there. I been to a good place on Fifty-seventh and Sixth. You tell em to take you there."

Dittsey listens intently and nods at his words. "I gotta stop drinkin," she says. "I been gettin sick. I can't keep drinkin."

"Sick! Sick! I'm SICK!!!" An old lady in the corner explodes from her lethargy. "I'm SICK! I'm SICK! Her keys fall from her lap, and she fumbles on the floor to recover them.

Dittsey leans forward toward her friend, face tightened in concentration. 'Now what you saying Mister Lee?"

"St. Luke's makes you sit around no matter what your condition. You tell em to — "

"I'm SICK! SICK!"

"Look," Dittsey says to the old lady, "we all concerned together, but we can't all speak together. Now *please* — you let me talk here with Mister Lee."

"I'm SICK. I been here two weeks an I'm gettin worse." She is not speaking to anyone. "The doctor says I'm sick." She subsides into silence.

They have been forced to live under severe mental stress. Regardless of their actual physical treatment, American psychologists who have seen this latest footage of the hostages remind us that the strain of confinement often manifests itself in physical symptoms.

"Fuckin doctors! Fuckin hospitals!" Dittsey's eyebrows knit, her lips tighten, her eyes brim with tears. "Look at this finger!" She pops from her chair and crouches before her friend. "Look at this Mister Lee! Does that look like they fixed it right?"

Mister Lee shakes his head.

"Eight stitches! Eight stitches they gimme, an it ain't held properly. I'm gonna tell em, I'm goin in there an tell em to send me to Mister Lee's hospital."

RIGHTEOUS HIGH

Soft drizzling day. Thurman wobbles along the curb — one foot on the sidewalk, one foot splashing in the gutter. Eyes glazed and peaceful. When traffic clears he drifts onto the street, stamping each puddle gleefully — a mischievous child who couldn't care less about getting his feet wet.

FORTUNE

Someone working behind the front desk has taped a fortune-cookie message to the plate-glass window

> Fortune is like glass. The more it glitters the easier it breaks.

OVERFLOW

Broken glass. Screams. Godforsaken moans. "No! NO! NO! AAAARRGGH!" I'm here in my apartment. Terrified screams bursting forth from a neighboring brownstone. I've called the police.

I see a young woman swaying by her window, rubbing her arm against shattered glass. I yell down to her. No response. She's holding a telephone now, stooping by the window, cradling the receiver like a child with a small pet, sobbing and moaning.

Miserable day. Cold gusting rain. A torn yellow curtain slaps through the broken window. "AAArrgghh!"

A cop is on the roof now; I point out the apartment to him. He can't get in. Heads poke out of windows all around the rear courtyard. People yelling into the rain, exchanging plans to rescue her. The woman has disappeared from the window. Now the cop disappears. Neighbors tuck their heads back inside. The courtyard is silent.

She's at the window again. This time she pulls it open and leans out, body rocking, arms hanging loose at her sides. Quivering. Face empty. "Get back! Get outa there!" I'm screaming to her at the top of my lungs. She sways in the gusting rain like a sleepwalker, then glides out of sight.

Sharp crash. Another scream. Breaking glass from inside her apartment. The yellow curtain is pulled back inside and a cop pokes his head out and waves. All is well.

Youngblood shrugs his hunched shoulders when I tell him about it. "She'll be here before too long," he says. "They'll run her over to Bellevue for ten days, an let her out. She's probably on narco or somethin. This happens a few more times — she won't make her rent an they'll send her over here. See, we're gettin the overflow on this welfare thing. This girl, a lotta people, they can't take it. No work. No money. Pressure builds up till you're just crazy. You gotta get high to get your head straght. See, that's what all these peoples is tellin theirselves. Soon the police is leavin em off at Bellevue.

"See, with this welfare, you got these guys makin money on oil and banks and ownin buildins. They're doin fine an everyone else is lookin for work. Now what you gonna do with the overflow? They got no use for em, you see. They put em up an give em their little bit of welfare money an some food stamps. Hand out pills to keep the noise down. Main thing is to keep em outa the way. You parta the overflow an you can't take it? —you be here before too long."

A DEATH

"Thurman's dead!"

"Thurman?"

"They found him this morning. . . ."

He looked fine when I saw him last week. Drunk but full of talk, eager to have me sit down and speak with him. "Did someone beat him up?" I ask. "Did he jump out a window? What happened?"

"Nothing. Apparently, he just died. . . ."

Frankie, the desk clerk, is hanging around in the entrance corridor when I arrive — a bustling little man with sad eyes. "I was sorry to hear — " I begin, and already he's nodding sympathetically, "about Thurman."

"Yeah," he says.

"He was a nice man."

"It happens." He looks at his watch. "They took him outa here an hour ago."

Familiar faces in the TV lounge. I sit down beside Youngblood. Joan Crawford in *The Woman Is Dangerous*. No one is watching:

"*I wish I were back in the hospital. I'm not ready for this reality.*"

"*You'll be all right. You need time and fresh air. . . .*"

"Thurman died," I say to Youngblood.

"Yeah." He shifts in his seat without looking at me. "They took someone outa here this mornin."

"I thought you knew him pretty well."

He shakes his head slowly and stuffs his hands between his knees. "I didn't see him. I was in here when they took him away."

I remember them talking and laughing together, swapping stories, using language with a playfulness I had not expected here. "He must've been about your age," I say. "He drank a lot, didn't he?"

"Yeah, alcohol musta killed him."

After Youngblood leaves, I take a seat beside Muriel Berry, the proper Bostonian. "How are you?" I ask.

"How are *you*?"

"Sad," I say. "I heard Thurman died. I liked him."

"Ohhhh, *yes!*" Her tone is so peculiar — someone in a light comedy recalling a forgotten acquaintance. "Why they were talking about that this very morning!" She pauses. Her hasty enthusiasm vanishes utterly. "I'll bet he wasn't taking his medication. He was diabetic, you know. I'll bet he wasn't taking his insulin. You've got to take your medicine."

"Isn't there someone to check up on people?"

"I broke my hip when I stopped my medication. It's not a hospital here — you've got to take care of yourself."

"Don't the doctors — "

"The social workers will ask you sometimes, but there's nobody to check you every day. It's up to you. You forget and — my Lord, it's certainly happened enough times to me — you can get hurt. Doctors come once a week and they're very sweet, but it's not a hospital here. That man who died forgot his insulin. You've got to take care of yourself."

A PROPER BOSTONIAN

"I was playing solitaire when you knocked," Muriel Berry says to me. "I play it a lot." She grins, then laughs — that peculiar air that led me to imagine her as a missing heiress. She still gives that impression: a sophisticated eccentric who took a wrong turn somewhere, a bad reversal that sent her off course.

Six print dresses are bunched on the bed where she sits. Sheets and blankets heaped in a pile. On the splotchy linoleum floor are a tin ashtray and a roll of toilet paper. A dish with butter sits on the window sill, and on the floor (cracked wood where the linoleum has peeled away) are a hotplate, red kettle, and ancient electric heater. Her dresser is covered with cosmetic jars and medication. Also, there are three books: Morris West's *Salamander*, a leather-bound pocket volume of Edna St. Vincent Millay, and *The Best* — a novelty item of a few years past that guides its readers to the best ice cream, the best tennis racket, the best Caribbean island, the best ocean liner, etc. Muriel tells me it is an interesting book. She has no clear recollection of how it got here.

Green walls soiled with years of city grime and cooking fumes. Two "Thinking of You" greeting cards taped on the wall. Muriel keeps a box of them in her dresser, but with the exception of Jack and Nora, her two friends, there is no one out there to send them to. A post card showing a yellow map of Cape Cod is taped over her bed. Behind the wooden chair where I sit is an Exxon street map of the New York metropolitan area. ("Look behind it!" she

tells me later. I peel the map away to uncover a gaping hole filled
with broken plaster. "My head did that!" she says with her odd
whimsical chuckle. "My last seizure.") Other decoration: a match-
book cover from a restaurant called the Blue Goose, and below it, a
tiny red applique of a raspberry.

Muriel spends about twenty hours a day in this little room. The
rest of her time is spent upstairs in the TV lounge. When she had
her last seizure, she fell and broke her hip. She has not ventured
outdoors in weeks. Her single window opens on a cramped courtyard. Scrawny city tree reaching upward — a black tee-shirt and
some yellowing newspaper stuck among its branches. That is
her prospect. Across the courtyard, just fifteen feet away, I can
look into a pleasantly furnished apartment. Bookcases crammed
with paperbacks. A stack of hi-fi equipment and lots of records. A
young couple doing dance exercises. That is all there is to see —
that and the changing daylight which gives a rough sense of passing time.

As we're talking, Muriel crosses the room to show me something.
With her broken hip she has to pull herself about in little awkward
skips. It is almost too much to look at — she seems so injured when
she moves. And out across the courtyard a young woman stretches
before a tall mirror, arms raised, checking her lines. She kicks a leg
upward and spins and spins till she topples off balance into her
lover's arms . . .

Muriel's Dream

"I was outside an old building and some man came up to me and invited me in. This building wasn't much from the outside, but it was big,
very big inside. It surprised me. There were antiques everywhere. Beautiful things. It astonished me to see so many of them. From the outside
of the building you wouldn't have thought you could find all this in
here. The man told me to look around; he said I could pick out whatever I wanted. It was so interesting! I went all around and found more

and more beautiful old things. It wasn't like a dream. It was like it really happened."

Her glasses slide off her nose as she talks, hanging from one ear just below her mouth. "Oh, my goodness!" she says when she discovers them. "They'll turn up anywhere. A will of their own. . . ."

MURIEL BERRY'S STORY

Wild flowers and wild fruits. Blueberries. Raspberries. I gathered them all as a child — quite different in taste from the cultivated. And I can remember Grandmother Berry used to gather blackberries along the railroad tracks and make jam out of them. . . . A wonderland. That's what the Cape was while I did my growing up. Back then, during the Depression, fresh fruits, vegetables, meats — what would ordinarily be on the table, we couldn't afford. But the seashore offered us food. I remember clamming with my dad — setting lobster traps — and my mother making clam chowder. Lobster was rather commonplace — all that lobster, but butter was a luxury. And look over there — that stick of Hotel Bar butter on my windowsill — now I've got butter but nothing to go with it. . . . They say those were hard times, but I can't ever remember being hungry. All those peanut-butter-and-jelly sandwiches we made for my dad's lunch box and for my brother's and myself's. How many selfs have I got? One is too much sometimes. . . .

Things vanish. And when they're gone — just snapped away — I've got to ask myself if maybe it was all a very real kind of dream. Like Frisky. There was a wealthy family by the name of Snow, and they had a small airfield and a plane and a lot of ponies. I would walk the distance from our house, probably half a mile, and just go to the barn. The stablekeeper got to know me and he would say, "Would you like to ride one of the ponies today? They can use some exercise." Frisky was black as coal and well named. I mounted him and we went shooting across the airfield and — he wanted to be a loner, I guess. "I don't want anybody on my back," he said and sssssssp! Away he went.

My brother used to love coming round that airfield. He was interested in airplanes all his life. He decided that he would become
a pilot at the start of World War II, and he was on his last solo
flight before graduating . . . his very last. I don't know exactly what
happened. He crashed in the plane. Burned up. Eighteen years old
and he came home in a sealed casket. . . . How can you ever know
when things will change? How can you believe it? It broke my
mother's heart. She just devoted herself to the graveyard. Every
morning — to the graveyard. Every evening before bedtime — to
the graveyard. She planted a garden to be certain there were fresh
flowers on the grave at all times.

I painted and tried to make my mother happy. There was one
watercolor my mother loved — a house that was sort of built on a
sandbar. It was pink, pink and stucco. Looked like a little castle.
Mother was so fond of it that I decided — well, Mother's Day is
coming up so I'll have it framed for her. She was tickled pink —
tickled pink with the pink house. Maybe she even forgot my dead
brother for a few minutes. I couldn't have given her anything that
would have pleased her more. . . . And here's another thing — I've
lost all my paintings. I don't know what happened to my portfolio. . . .

The constant mourning — it was reaching me, sort of destroying
my life. One day I made up my mind. We were having supper and
I said, "I'm going to art school!"

School in Boston, home for the weekends — how I loved it! And
then another strange thing — you wonder if you really can remember, or if you dreamed it. After my first semester at school, I came
home to the Cape to spend the summer. There was a big regatta
and I thought, "Gee, I wish I could be in that regatta! How in the
world can I do it? I don't have a boat." And right off our shore was
the *Fleetwing*. Teak deck. Mahogany keel. I thought, "Boy, that
would be perfect! I'd love to get my hands on that!" So I swam out
and climbed aboard. But the regatta wasn't important enough for
me to steal the boat. "Why should I steal it?" I said. "For heaven's
sakes — I can't even sail!"

I swam back. I didn't know I was being observed. On shore a man approached me. "I noticed you were swimming out to the *Fleetwing*," he said. "What were you thinking about?"

I said, "It would be awfully nice if I owned it. Then I could join the regatta."

"Oh, you like to sail, eh? I just had a birthday a short while ago and my mother gave me a boat yard."

I wondered who I was talking to. "My name is Muriel Berry," I said. "Would you introduce yourself, please?"

"My name is Robert Parkinson." And, oh my Lord, my father was his mother's chauffeur! This is a millionaire family! "What are your plans now?" he asks me. I said I must go home and not be late for supper. "But you'd like to have a boat, wouldn't you?"

"Oh, yes!"

"Well, if you must be home, supposing I drive you home?" A Cadillac. I couldn't resist. My father had, not a Model-T Ford, but it was something similar. "Your name is Muriel Berry," he said. "Does your father's name happen to be Alton?"

"Yes."

"Well, for heaven's sakes! Your father was my mother's chauffeur. Hop aboard. We'll go home and I'll say hello. I haven't seen your dad for quite some time." So here I am — after trying to steal a sailboat I'm riding home in a Cadillac!

My dad is out working in the garden and my mother's preparing supper when I drive up in this Cadillac. "Oh, Bobby!" Dad said. They were so pleased to see one another. My mother looks a little astonished. She's not able to put it all together. "I had the table set," she says. "You know how I feel about being prompt for meals. What have you been doing all afternoon?"

"Swimming around."

"Around those boats out there?"

I said, "Yes." My dad was looking at me with a sort of challenging look. Wondering what I'm going to come up with for why I'm late.

So Bobby said, "My mother just purchased a boat yard. Gave it to me for my birthday."

"That's nice! That's fine!" My dad was very pleased about it.

"I'd like to take your daughter out to dinner some evening," Bobby said to him. Dad looks at my mother to see if she approves. Well, why should she say no?

"You go up and dress," my mother says. "She'll be ready in an hour," she tells Bobby. They were all excited about this multimillionaire boyfriend of mine. Especially my father. I could hear him talking away while I was getting dressed upstairs. Anyway, Bobby came back. I'm all dressed up, and he takes me to this home that they owned. The place was something else! Enormous. It just sort of flowed. I don't know how many rooms — forty, I guess. A beautiful place. Bobby introduced me to his mother, Polly — Pauline Parkinson. I'd heard a lot about Polly from when my father was her chauffeur. Oh, she was a handsome woman! A real knockout. One of these proper Bostonian types. I was nervous. Can't remember what we had for dinner — just this long, long dinner table. Served by servants, of course. A luxurious meal. It wasn't baloney and Campbell's mushroom soup!

It's been so long since I've thought about this. It's like a dream — this part anyway — it takes a little while to bring it back.... After dinner we sat by the fire and — oh, we had cordials! It was quite exciting. I didn't want it to end but I'd promised to be home at a reasonable hour. "It's getting late," I said. "I must be getting home."

"All right," he said. "And by the way, are you interested in music?" At one time I played the violin and loved music. Well, here I am being invited to the Boston Symphony concert with Serge Koussevitzky conducting. I thought I must be dreaming.

My mother decided that I needed a special dress, a new gown for the occasion. We went to New Bedford and selected a very elegant dress. The most expensive thing I'd worn. And after the concert there was a reception for Koussevitzky. A very charming man —

wasn't impressed with himself at all. Very dignified, of course, but he didn't think he was anything special. Bobby knew him very well.

I've got to pinch myself to make sure I'm not dreaming this. . . . My mother was sitting up all excited when I came back home. Wanted to know all about it. My father was tired after a hard day's work and was upstairs sleeping. He didn't inquire about my date until the next morning. "That was awfully nice for Bobby to see you again. Did you have a nice time?"

"Oh, yes!" I said. "Very nice."

"What kind of music did you hear?"

"Symphonic."

"What kind of music is that?" If I had said cowboy music he would have known what I was talking about. "You enjoyed it?"

"Oh, yes! Very lovely!" My mother's busy packing his lunch — peanut butter and jelly sandwiches with a banana for dessert and a thermos of coffee — and here I'd been dining on lobster Newberg with Bobby.

Then Bobby called again. "I have something for you."

Hmmmm, I wonder what he's got for me. "Oh, yes?" I said. I'm all curiosity, you know. All eyes and ears.

"I have a boat that needs a little work done on it. A sailboat. I thought perhaps that you might like to have it." I'm dreaming, you know. This can't be real. "If you're willing to do the extra work on it," he says, "when they have the next regatta you'll be all set. You'll have your own boat."

I thought I was living in a dream. I'm going to wake up and find that's all it is. Just a dream. Every morning I'd get up when I heard Dad's alarm go off. I'm so enthusiastic I'm preparing his breakfast instead of my mother. Letting her sleep late. Every morning I'd take my pal Teddy down to the shore with me. Teddy was my Belgian sheep dog. He'd lay in the sand and watch me working on this boat. I could see his mind working — "What in the world is she doing?" Once in a while he'd chase a seagull or something, but he was very patient with me. He'd be right back there to make sure I was on the job, I guess.

Then one morning, I was going down to the shore with Teddy as usual to work on the boat. . . . My God! What in the world's going on? The boat's not there!

I'm fifty-six now, and to this day I still don't know what happened to it. I couldn't believe! Still can't believe it to this day. I didn't hear anything more from Bobby either. "Muriel," my dad said, "I'm afraid there probably is some feeling about the fact that we are poor and they are extremely wealthy. Probably, his mother interfered. Polly must've stepped into the picture."

The next thing I heard, he was married to some socialite. It was like an April Fool trick or something. I felt crushed. Sort of went into mourning. And the gift that his mother gave him for his wedding present was the home my father was born in. All of a sudden he's married; he's got a home that was the home my father was born in, and he's got the boat I spent the summer working on. . . . I never saw him again. All this generosity and all this luxury — all of a sudden it just vanishes. They have so much, perhaps they don't realize what it's like to suddenly lose something that means so much to you. Once you give somebody something, you can't imagine what's going on in that person's mind. And introducing me to his family and people like Koussevitzky — I felt like sort of a part of it. And all of a sudden I'm thrown out, exiled. To this very day it mystifies me. Like a trick — everything is sort of vanishing. Like a beautiful dream turning into a nightmare. . . .

It still perplexes me. Of course, I've grown out of it now, and so much has happened since. You know, life goes on. I returned to school that fall, and one of my schoolmates introduced me to the man that I married. He liked me instantly and wanted to marry me right away. I don't know whether I was really sure or not, but anyway I accepted the proposal. Jack attended Yale and graduated from Boston University. His mother lived in Westchester — in the Gothwood Apartments. All these names sounded so thrilling!

Before we married, Jack did some work for the *Mid-Ocean News* in Bermuda, and while he was there he got a job as a male nurse for Eugene O'Neill's son. They called him Spooky, and Spooky decided he was gonna swim back to the United States. That ended Jack's job with the O'Neills.... I wonder whatever became of Spooky anyway — whether he was institutionalized. He had an older brother, Shaun, who I met years later down in the Village. Shaun was a heavy drinker. Scrawny. Really a Bowery bum type. Very pleasant fellow, but not responsible for himself at all. I didn't get to know him very well, or I would have inquired about his brother Spooky.

Jack got a job working with the *Daily Mirror,* so after our marriage we lived on Carmine Street. A lovely apartment. Wood-burning fireplace and a patio in the back. My first job was clerical work in a brokerage house — I wasn't doing much painting. Then I was a night manager with Western Union. By this time I had discovered something that I didn't realize before I married — my husband was using marijuana. He said he got started on it in Bermuda. Maybe Spooky smoked it too — maybe that's why he decided to swim back to the States. Our apartment on Carmine Street was filled with people. We were very popular because Jack always made sure there was plenty of wine around and plenty of marijuana, and these beatnik types didn't have the money to buy their own.

Around the time I had my son, Jack started beating me up. I'd have black eyes and things like that. Here I am, pushing little Jay in his baby carriage — two black eyes and people looking at me on the street. It's just plain embarrassing. If his mother stopped by, I would find myself making up excuses, lying to her about how I got these bruises and whatnot. Jack was her pet, and Jack could do no wrong in her eyes. It all had to be me. Couldn't possibly be Jack. All this beautiful upbringing — it just couldn't be him.... I wonder how she feels now?

Really physical beatings — and he was working on my mind too. If I disliked someone or wanted a quiet evening, I'd say, "Let's not have any company tonight." And he would say he'd already invited people over. I'd say, "Well, it's not going to be very quiet, then, is it? What about Jay and his sleep?" He'd tell me, "I'll handle it. I'll keep it under control." And then they'd drink and make noise all night.

By this time he was doing a lot of writing for magazines like *Man to Man* — sordid, sick-minded stuff. It seemed to be a little too much for me to handle, so I went in Bellevue for ten days. It was like a vacation. I didn't even realize it was a crazy house, there was so much erratic behavior in my own home. I thought I'd been rescued.

After Bellevue, I started seeing a psychiatrist. He'd sit in his chair, and I was reading his notes upside down trying to figure out what was wrong with me. The diagnosis was schizophrenia with paranoid tendencies, or something of that nature. Maybe I'd been listening to too many crazy radio programs or reading too many horror tales — Sherlock Holmes and things like that. I'd wake up with the terrible feeling I'd been through these awful experiences — but it was only a dream. I didn't realize that it was getting such a grip on me. I thought I could just shake it off, but it seemed to be taking over. I felt kind of spooked.

Some years later, my mother said, "When you were a little girl you must have had some awful dreams because you used to cry in the middle of the night. You'd cry as if you were really being beaten" I can recall being sort of fascinated when Charles Lindbergh's son was kidnapped; I read everything I could about it. I'd listen on the radio, and then I'd have visions of this happening to me. I'd wake up and realize I'm still in my room. But my dream was so real — it put me in some strange place. It was hard for me to realize whether this was the truth or just a piece of fiction riding through my head. . . .

I'm not even sure just when I started drinking. It tasted good and made me feel rather good, so I just drank. And my husband was beating me so badly — after he got through with me, I was afraid to look in the mirror. I'd be out on the street with a couple of black eyes, and my son reaching up to pat my cheek — "Oh, poor Mommy!" I thought, "Oh, my Lord! What's going on here?" I guess drinking was about the only way I had of feeling good.

At last, I left my husband. I was served with some divorce papers — and of all places he arranged for the divorce to take place — Anniston, Alabama, where my brother had crashed and burned up in the plane. It seemed to me like he was really rubbing it in too deep. By this time, Jay was with his grandmother in Westchester. It seemed to me like it was much more suitable than our life in New York. He was away from all this misery — fumes of marijuana floating through the apartment and me with black eyes. Westchester offered a much more charming atmosphere for him. He was going to nursery school and I thought, "Why should I take this away from him? He's a bright boy, and sensitive. It's just better for him. I'm not going to be selfish and take this away from him." I couldn't wish for anything better.

Later on, Jack remarried. A nurse from Copenhagen — he called and told me that. And then he called; he said she was leaving him, going back to Denmark and taking Jay with her. This would be a good fifteen or sixteen years ago. I remember it was September fifth, and I can't remember the year. That's the last I heard of my son. . . . It wasn't too long after that that I got another call from Jack. "I want you to try and do something for Jay," he says.

"Over in Copenhagen! How do you expect me to do anything for him there?"

He said, "Oh, I don't know . . . " And then the gun went off. Blew his brains out. Somebody picked up the receiver and told me Jack was dead.

How did I find myself homeless? . . . Sleeping in the park? . . . Just trying to stay awake all night because you didn't know who was going to come along and what they might do to you. . . . I'm trying to think what time of year it was, what season. I guess it was summer, going into fall. "Well, I can't live like this," I decided.

Everything was so clear and vivid to me — realizing what a sad situation I was in and how embarrassed I felt. My parents were still alive at the time, but I guess I must have felt too ashamed to have let them know the condition I was in. I knew it would be terribly upsetting.

As I recall, I didn't seem to be fully aware of what was happening to me. Those years were filled in with my being in Pilgrim State and Manhattan State. It was sort of like gliding through another dream. I remember one Sunday a man came to visit me from Brooklyn. He had a big lunch basket, wicker basket, and he had barbecued chicken, a bottle of wine, cake, and hot biscuits wrapped in foil. . . . It wasn't really nightmarish, but it was strange. My enthusiasms would be like the elevator. I would be real enthused about something for a while and then get bored with it — bored and disgusted with myself for being bored. These mental hospitals got to feel like prison. So much confinement and regimentation. You've got to stand in line for this, stand in line for that. And these living wards — no privacy at all!

The first one of these hotels that I recall being sent to was 55 West Eighty-fourth Street. I remember being terrified in that place. I'd never lived around Puerto Rican people. I couldn't carry on any conversation with them because they didn't speak English. They'd have their radios blaring away with all this gibberish talk and wild music. . . . It's just that whoever sent me there — I don't think they knew me very well. It seemed to me they didn't take time to really understand what was disturbing me.

I was very nervous. I'd mostly stay in my room. I didn't know whether I could trust myself out there. I was afraid something was going to happen. So I lived on my own. And I was so ashamed of the condition I was in — to be living in such a flea-bag type of setup — that I wouldn't ask for anything. . . . It got to be too overbearing. Just too much. I couldn't cope with it any longer, so I just — I sort of flipped, I guess.

I've been here approximately five and a half years. I'm not too certain about that myself. I know I was placed here from the

Women's Shelter down on East Fifth Street and ... I'm trying to think how I happened to be in the Women's Shelter now. . . .

Usually I get up when I hear them come pick up the garbage. That's sort of like my clock. I can hear them out in the hallway swinging the cans around. So I sort of come out of my sleep and kind of doze a bit and listen for sounds upstairs which will indicate the lounge is open. If I decide that it must be open, I'll go up for coffee. I like a cup of coffee when I wake up in the morning. Almost everybody goes up for that first cup of coffee. Occasionally, you'll see a new face or someone from some other hotel. The regular people seem to get very haughty and upset — "What are you doing in this hotel?" You'd almost think they were taking the coffee right out of that person's hand and drinking it.

They bring out a TV and we sit around and watch soap operas. That's about the caliber of the interest of the people here. These soap-opera serials bore the blazes out of me and I don't usually pay any attention to them. Ordinarily, I'm waiting to speak to someone, or waiting for the van to take me to the clinic, or I'm waiting for my medication. I'm not just sitting there killing time looking at these sudsy things. Some people just sit there and talk to themselves, or they try and carry on a conversation with you about something that you haven't the vaguest idea about. They're sort of living in an imaginary world — how things might have been for them once, or how they wish things could be for them — how there could be an improvement made. If they had a suggestion box it would be jammed full, and I imagine some of the suggestions would be really out of this world! Plans to turn this into the Waldorf-Astoria or something.

I can narrow down what these people's problems are. There is a drug problem in this hotel. And there's always somebody saying, "Have you got a bottle?" They seem to thrive on this sort of thing. It's an escape, I presume, from reality. A make-believe world. I've been very cautious. I don't get too close to any of them. I don't want to appear antisocial — Miss Who-do-you-think-I-am, you know. I have heard remarks made about me. They think I'm a bit of a snob. "Oh, she's from Boston!" Or, "She's from Cape Cod where the Kennedys have their summer place!"

They give you lunch on weekdays — if people aren't too tired to prepare it. Some days the cook is just fed up with the whole scene and decides, "I'm not cooking today." That's that. I feel that if she's not going to be there to provide the service she's paid for, then I really don't know what she's around for. You just have to wait and see each day. If there's no lunch prepared, usually somebody will volunteer to slice off some cheese and bring out a basket of crackers or something. Or you can go out and get something. With my bad hip that's not easy — and there are a number of people who have difficulty getting around. I've sent people out for things like to McDonald's for a hamburger, or something like that. You gotta have the exact change, or else you're in for a surprise. Say if you give them a five-dollar bill to get a hamburger and cup of coffee for you. Well, they'll come back with your order — but in the meantime they've decided that they need a pack of cigarettes, and they'd like to have a hamburger and cup of coffee themselves — so they take it out of your money. And what can you say? They've done you the favor, so you just — that's their tip. They'll come back with your bag of food in their hand and, "Well, where's my tip?" And I'll say, "You just had it, didn't you? Isn't it in your stomach?" It can get to be a pretty expensive hamburger. More like a piece of filet mignon!

Some of the behavior and the conversations and remarks make me think I'm back in a mental institution again. There's this tenant, Buffalo, who comes up to the lounge — he always has a deck of cards. He deals two poker hands and plays them out. I guesss he's playing for himself and playing for somebody else. . . . A lady comes through the lounge and hands out medication to quite a number of tenants. I think the majority have been institutionalized. It strikes me as odd that they have to have somebody hand them their medication. They're like children. They don't seem to realize what's happening. I know I get very upset if I've run out of medicine, or if I'm running low. I know if I don't have it I'm going to be in trouble — have a seizure or something. Someone said to me, "Oh, my Lord! You have so many pills! You're a pillhead, aren't you?" I said, "A lot of them are vitamins, but the rest is to prevent my going into seizure and hurting myself. You think it's amusing to fall down and break a hip, or almost get hit by an automobile and have the daylights scared out of you?"

This Benny who lives over in the corner of my unit here — I think he's retarded. He doesn't seem to be able to carry on an intelligent conversation. He seems to be kind of lost, and I don't think he has anybody. . . . "Oh, get away from me! You annoy me!" — that's the way people treat him. Like he's in everybody's way. Well, I've had people be patient with me when I've been difficult, so I think the least I can do is remember what a big help it was when somebody showed some interest, some understanding and caring. Someone made the remark to me, "I got a surprise for you — Benny's in love with you! He wants to marry you!" And I said, "Well, that's news to me!" He asked me how I felt about it, and I said, "Well, sort of brotherly love. No more than that, certainly. I feel a little sorry for him. He's been unfortunate. I don't think he's had any sort of family life, and I don't think anybody is really sincerely interested in him — so when somebody does show a bit of honest interest it probably is overwhelming to him. You know, he just can't believe it. It's just a little too much for him."

I tried to find out how Benny takes care of himself. It's obvious that he eats. He must eat. I said, "Benny, what do you do for meals?" He said, "Oh, I go out and eat." I asked him if he had three meals a day. "Oh, yes!" But he's always broke. He's a mystery to me. Well, I'll never forget when I was really down and out and didn't know what end was up — sitting on a park bench and sitting in a women's shelter — and how rejected and disappointed in myself I was. I know how it feels to be working and taking care of myself and then, all of a sudden, being reliant on other people. I may not be in the best of health now, and I'm certainly no spring chicken, but there are little things I can do to help Benny — like going to the bathroom and flushing it. Little things that Benny forgets.

The other guy on my unit is Mr. Winslow. He's a big guy physically. He's black and he's always telling me, "You may think I'm Negro, but I'm not. I'm West Indian!" He's very proud of that. I get along all right. I just don't get too close to him. I say, "Good morning!" to him, or if it's Friday night I'll say, "Have a pleasant weekend, Mr. Winslow!" or something like that. That's as far as I go . . . and he doesn't make any overtures to me either.

They close the TV lounge at four o'clock and lock up the TV. Unless you invite somebody to your room or somebody has invited you to their room, that's the end of people for the day. As I said, I don't consider myself antisocial, but when I'm uncomfortable around a person I'm afraid it's going to show. I don't want to hurt anyone's feelings, so I'll excuse myself and go to my room.

In my room I like to listen to WPAT on the radio, and I like to read. I'm trying to get myself into the . . . I don't know how it is I lost my . . . I'm still interested in painting, but I can't seem to push myself into attempting it again. I don't know whether I'm going to feel disappointed to discover that I can't paint anymore or. . . . That was the big thing — when I lost my portfolio. All my watercolors! I gave quite a number of them away as birthday gifts or Christmas gifts. And I can remember people looking at them and saying, "You didn't do that!" I'd have to argue that I really did it. It was something I was proud of — work that pleased me to do and pleased other people to look at. . . . Now I don't have one piece of my artwork. I don't know, I lost everything I had.

When I need to feed myself, I'll go to the Red Apple and get something to prepare. Nothing too elaborate. I have a hotplate here and a frying pan and tea kettle. I'll get a package of Rice a Roni with spices or something and a couple of chops. One-dish meals. I know I must eat to stay alive, to feel better and to keep my head fairly clear so I can think with some intelligence. But food's not all that important to me.

At night it very often becomes rather noisy. Things get out of hand. People have arguments that they've been saving all day. They seem to use nighttime for . . . you hear some strange noises at night. The night before last I heard a woman screaming. I thought, "Lord, what in the world? What's happening to her? Sounds like she's being molested, robbed, raped, or something." Didn't last long. I never heard anything more about it. It's nothing unusual. You hear a lot of bottles being thrown outside — a lot of crashing of glass. I don't feel too nervous about it, but I wouldn't go outside my room at night. I'm really concentrating on getting a lot of rest. Some woman made the remark earlier this morning when I was getting a cup of coffee — she said, "There really should be a guard in this building, particularly a night watchman." I agree with her.

You know, some of these people just spin off. You wonder what in the world you might have said. You think they're daydreaming or something — then wheeeeeee! and they've thrown something at you. Every once in a while, not too often, somebody will jump out a window. Either last week or the week before last somebody jumped out a sixth-floor window. Laying out in the yard. Bones all broken. All bloody. People shied away. None of the tenants wanted to call for any help. They didn't seem to want to get involved. The person died. I don't know who it was. . . .

I get so disgusted sometimes. I get my cards and play some solitaire. This hotel gets so closed in, you know. They're always talking about, "Well, we're gonna paint your room." It doesn't do any good to complain. My radiator is ice cold. "If you don't like it, go someplace else!" — that's the attitude. If there's no hot water and you want to take a bath, they say, "Well, get some pots and heat the water up yourself!" They don't give a damn as long as they get their rent out of my SSI. I used to take a bath or shower every day, but this bathroom doesn't lock. The sort of thing you expect to have privacy for — we have people just barging in. About all I can do is take sponge baths. And this hole in the wall — this is from one of my seizures. There was blood, quite a bit, and I had to have

stitches — but this road map covers the hole up nicely, I think. . . .
I must get one of Boston.

I just glide along from day to day. Sometimes I say, "What good
does it do to keep thinking about all this stuff? I can't do anything
about it. It's already been done." I don't think I've done very much
living for quite some time. I don't know why I don't get myself together and get another job. Other people do that — get in some
kind of trouble, recuperate for awhile, and then go out and start
life again. It's like learning to walk all over again. I don't mean because of this hip injury — I mean it figuratively. . . . I'm trying to
think. . . . I don't know, I'd like to do something more in the line
of — I'm tired of office work; it gets to be a drag to me — I'd like to
do something a little more imaginative and creative. I always
thought I'd like to study architecture, but I don't do anything
about it.

You can't envision anything better ever happening. This is the
end of the line for you. You feel like that — very much so. I've
heard people brag about how they're seventy-five years old or
something like that, and I think, "God, don't tell me I'm gonna
have to live in this closet another twenty years! Is this the best I can
do? Might as well jump off the bridge right now as to drag around
for another twenty years like this." But if I do let despair take over,
where am I gonna be? I'm certainly not gonna be better off. I've
got to make the best of what I have. The only really good thing
that's happened to me since I've been here is when I was put on
SSI. At least I'd done something with my life to afford me to live
independently. But how independently am I living really? I still
don't have any control over my income. Somebody said to me, "If I
were you I certainly would receive my check and pay my own rent.
I wouldn't let anybody handle my money and deal it out to me —
let me know how much I can have, and when. It's your money."
Back to the almighty dollar again! I tried to reason with the person
that was talking to me. "Well," I said, "if I didn't have someone
that was interested in what happens to my money, I probably

wouldn't have any at all. I'd be back on that old park bench again."

It's a little better than in the psychiatric hospital. I can go to bed when I want to. I can get up when I want to. I can . . . if I don't want to answer the door, I don't have to answer the door. I'm not obligated to really do anything. Days when I'm feeling depressed, I just drag myself out of this room — see if the lounge is open, see familiar faces and try to get interested in somebody's problem. Watch TV and try to review myself and how I can snap out of this — hope to realize that I'm better off than a lot of other people. But who am I really better off than? I'm just living the same humdrum existence that most everybody else around here is living.

It's no good — a collection of sick souls in one building, all bunched together like a lot of bees in a hive, all ready to sting each other. God, I hope this won't be permanent! Oh, Lord no! I'm trying to figure some way to get out but . . . this place just gets smaller and smaller and smaller. It's closing in on me. That's why whenever I have an opportunity to go anywhere, I take it, because it opens up a new window. One window — that's all I've got here. One little window.

DO I HAVE A STORY!

Youngblood hands me a note scribbled in red ink on a scrap of crumpled paper:

> Your friend wants a story! BOY!
> Do I have a story for him! Pimps,
> *Killers*, Drugs, AA
>
> /Secret/   Doug Rm 303

"Two whiteys," Youngblood says. "Sounds like Doug and his brother is ready to talk."

S P R I N G

A NICE DAY

On the street someone is selling a brand-new color television for $150. Two men offer him forty dollars; he says sixty and the sale is settled. Balmy Monday morning. Crap game on the sidewalk. Fistfulls of bills pass from hand to hand. On the Broadway islands the benches are filled. People passing bottles, bumming cigarettes — everyone talking, laughing.

Across from Hotel Walden, at the west end of the block, mommies and daddies are wheeling carriages, pushing tricycles and children to the Montessori school. Above the doorway is an ornate inscription for the Elias A. Cohen Institute for Jewish Education. The Hebrew school is now defunct, and the tired old synagogue of which it was a part struggles along with an aging congregation.

Beside Temple Beth Ansched is a row of five attached townhouses that have been chopped up into tiny dark apartments. Dull grey fronts that look damp and gloomy all hours of the day, in all seasons.

Freya's Beauty Salon is next. It seems to do a thriving business with Hispanic customers. Lively activity inside. Bright fingernails. High heels. Women emerging with sharp, tinted hair. In the window are photos of assorted hair styles — faded, dusty images like stills from old B movies.

The Novelty Shop has a sign promising TV, radio, and stereo equipment — but it has no display, no visible stock — and rarely does it have many customers. The front window is blocked by a curtain that stops just above eye level. There are lots of numbers parlors in the neighborhood. Somehow Novelty Shop is paying the rent.

Jonas Stern and Sons: Kosher Butcher. The sign is hand-painted. A tiny, old-fashioned shop where everyone is busy. There are two other Jewish butchers in the neighborhood, both with Broadway entrances, both of them far busier than Jonas Stern and Sons. A third butcher, Stern's only kosher competitor, was bought out by

Koreans and closed down last year. I've never known anyone who's set foot in Jonas Stern's shop, but like the synagogue on the corner he apparently has a small and loyal following.

The small bodega next to Jonas Stern and Sons has no name. The front window is dirty and cluttered. Its door is open half the year — a haven for flies. Prices on everything here are higher than anywhere else. Fresh foods look miserable. Candy bars are melted and come stuck to their wrappers, potato chips crushed, beer and soda cans covered with grime. But this little bodega gives credit. Probably half the residents of Hotel Walden do some business here, especially toward the end of the month. There're always three or four guys hanging around inside or sitting on plastic milk crates out on the street. Every week or so they huddle with the bodega's owner before crossing the street to pay some visits at Hotel Walden. There are not many bad debts.

At the corner of Broadway is the Tacita D'Oro, one of the many Cuban-Chinese restaurants in this area. The Chinese fare is consistently mediocre, but the white bean soup, sweet plantains, yellow rice and black beans, oxtail, and thick cafe con leche are fine. In spring and summer the doors are thrown open and it's almost like an outdoor cafe in the front room. Beggars, drunks, junkies, hookers, and raving crazies wander in with various pleas, demands, and offers. But nothing startles the Tacita D'Oro staff. Even the meekest looking waiter can rush a drunk twice his size and hustle him back onto Broadway. On more difficult occasions the counterman will raise a hidden cleaver with a martial arts flourish calculated to convince even the most obstinate psychopath that he is up against a rival who is crazier and more violent than himself. So it is a peaceful place. People come to eat — hunkering over the counter, stacking plates and bowls as they are emptied, raising little monuments to satisfied hunger.

Perched on the roof of the Tacita D'Oro is a square, two-story wood house. Squat and funky and unadorned, it would go unnoticed in some tired old town like Troy or Norwalk or Camden. At the turn of the century, and for some years after, such houses were common enough right here in Manhattan, but already this little wood house has some of the strangeness and antiquity of a ruined civilization. The residents of this house have a hammock, a collection of hand-blown bottles, and a powerful stereo system on which they play a good bit of heavy-metal and new-wave music. They also have two German shepherds, which they let run on the roof above the bodega, the Novelty Shop, Jonas Stern and Sons, and Freya's Beauty Salon. The two dogs spend a lot of time staring down at the street. Sometimes they'll strike statuesque Rin-tin-tin poses and bark fiercely at some passing dog, but more often they look trapped and fed up. Today they've crept to the roof's edge to droop their heads over the sidewalk. They look like hand puppets with nothing inside. Lazy day. First day of spring.

BROTHERS

"Excuse me," a man about my age asks, "but could I trouble you for some change?" I give him a quarter. A second guy joins him, haggard and silent — I realize I'm with Doug and Bobby, the two brothers Youngblood told me about. I introduce myself.

"Yeah," Doug says, "we got a lotta stuff for your book. His face is round and unshaven. Eyeglasses held together with wads of scotch tape.

"What about Wednesday?" I ask. "Will you be around at three?"

"Sure, we're always around, but we can't talk then. That's our show — 'The Guiding Light.' "

"Is that the one with Roger?" I ask. "The guy with the beard?" This much I know from my visits to the TV room, a place the two of them refuse to set foot in.

"They're closin in on old Roger," Bobby says to his brother, "but, hey! — he ain't got his beard no more. Cops went down to

Santa Domingo yesterday and told David to carry a piece — but they ain't got no idea how old Roger looks with his beard shaved off." He seems amused at his own enthusiasm.

"Drugs, killing, robbery," Doug says. "We got it all here. I got stories for you like you don't get on television."

"We'll talk about it," I say. "And, you know, we don't have to use your name. We can make sure nobody knows it's you."

"Why hide it?" Bobby says immediately. "It's all true. We could fill a book with everything that's happened. . . ."

They are from a privileged economic background, but they're down and out — room 302 at Hotel Walden, which they share with Frisbee their cat and six kittens, two beds aimed at the failing TV, a hot plate, greasy Toast-R-Oven, tattered green window-shade, some posters, plastic cup where they save their Pall Mall butts, door hanging perilously on a single hinge — not much to show for two lives.

Bad luck at home — their invalid mother and hard-drinking father. And then the bad trips of overlapping decades. Bobby, a ragged stanza from *Howl* — drifting from the East Village drug scene of the early sixties to mellow days in Tangiers; racing head on into a brick wall; and back again to East Fourth Street, to meaner, hungrier times — pure crystal Methedrine, cocaine, and heroin. Mainlining, going for broke. Energy and madness, chemical happiness bought and sold each day. Unrelenting need. And Doug, off to Vietnam too young — too early in the war to know better. Living through horrors that still haunt him. Coming home stoned and shaken, kissing American soil with tears of relief, then crawling in terror on Fifth Avenue at the pop of a backfiring truck.

They are not burnt out, either of them, but full consciousness hurts — so there is usually the strong stale smell of beer on their breath. And sometimes, when money turns up, I see them swaying and dishevelled, fumbling along Broadway, wasted on stronger stuff.

B O B B Y   C A R M A N ' S   S T O R Y

I can tell you how I got here, but h-e-e-e-e-y, it's not simple, man. People see you here — "Oh, you're just a neurotic!" or something like that. But it's not that simple. Like I've been a juvenile delinquent, a dope dealer, a beatnik, an expatriate, and a hippy. Jesus, we *were* the love generation. Reefer, hashish, LSD, Timothy Leary, speed, every fuckin pill you can name! Yeah, and I've been a convict, a wino — I've done it from start to finish. Huntington, the Upper East Side, fuckin Camp Mamaweeda, Hackley School, Trinity, the Lower East Side, Algeciras, Tangiers, Rome, Central Islip — Jesus H. Christ, it's been one helluva trip! And I gotta tell you about Morocco, man, and runnin around the East Village getting fucked up on speed. Yeah, and Mother's death, Daddy's place down by Indian River. And the accident — me, the Vespa, and the wall — a fuckin sandwich. And Doug's gotta tell you about Vietnam cause, man, he still talks about it and we both sit here cryin. Hey — and Uncle James and Aunt Irene, Pineapple and all the old winos — drinkin our Swiss-Up, Mad Dog, Night Train, and Wild Irish Rose by the quart. . . . It's not simple, man. It ain't been no straight line to get here.

I don't wanna talk too much about us bein kids. We're both very high IQs, but we had hell in school. Bad conduct, bad grades, sneakin smokes, actin crazy — but we had some crazy shit to live with. Our mother had some kinda arthritis — wasting away, man, and nothing anyone could do. Dying, but it took a long time . . . our whole childhood. Our bedroom used to be on the other side of the house, and we could hear her crying all night long. Her hands and feet were twisted like claws — just tightened up like this. When she died she weighed about forty-eight pounds. She was only about four foot eleven to begin with. But before she was really really super ill, where her feet just couldn't hold her any more, she would have Christmas parties — sit in a chair drinkin her booze and takin her pain killers. My father asked her doctor, "Should I

stop her from drinking and smoking?" And the doctor said, "Forget it! Just let her enjoy herself." So she'd sit back and drink a
quart of Scotch a day, and in the middle of the party she'd start
feelin her oats. Monsignor Carey — he's a close friend of the family — he'd come over an say, "Come on, Rachel! Let's dance!"
And she'd get up on her little knobby feet and dance. Dance! Oh,
she was wonderful! Such a beautiful girl! Even as she aged and her
body started falling apart, she was still so beautiful. . . .

In our teens, when things got worse, the old man must've asked
himself, "Now, should I keep the kids home, or should I get them
out of here so they don't see all the pain and suffering?" So he sent
us up to Hackley School in Tarrytown. I think maybe if we'd
stayed home it would have turned out a little differently. When I
came home on the weekends, there was that lonely feeling. And
now Daddy was drinkin with Mother. Next thing I knew, I started
takin nips off the bar, doin speed and lookin for kicks. School
wasn't doin me any good, so I started living half at home and half
on the Lower East Side — hangin out at the Old Reliable Cafe
down on C and D about East Seventh Street. A wonderful neighborhood. You could still get a forty-to-sixty-dollar-a-month apartment down there, you know, in those six-flight walkups, cold-water
flats and stuff. I met a guy there who seemed to think — which was
true—that I knew just about everybody — all the teenagers and
young college drop-outs and runaways who were starting to fill the
neighborhood. So he moved me into an apartment with a goddamn suitcase of thirty thousand pills. Dexedrine, Dexamil, Ben-
zedrine, phenobarbital, Tuenol, Nembutal, Seconal — every
damn kind of upper or downer that there was. Ten dollars for a
hundred pills.

Somebody really screwed me — the guy that used to make deliv-
eries every once in awhile. One morning the phone rang and it was
him — "They're on the way up! Get out!" I just opened the door
and the cops were standing right there.

Daddy got me a good lawyer. We couldn't pull illegal search

and seizure because thirty thousand was a bunch of pills. I pleaded guilty to a misdemeanor for possession — like I'd been caught with a couple of pills or a joint. And since I hadn't any narcotics busts on my record — didn't even have drunk and disorderly — they gave me a six-month suspended sentence.

After that was over, I certainly wasn't gonna get a crew cut and move home. I had a lot on my mind. Like when I was about fifteen, a guy laid on me a copy of the *Communist Manifesto* and I read it from cover to cover. That was chilling, man. It was beautiful, kind of pure — very beautiful and inspiring when you're younger like that. But then, like I started getting into Hinduism, things about Buddha, and Yoga. So like I mighta laid off it for a couple of years — goin out, hittin the street and carryin on, just bein a cowboy, or maybe reading comic books and newspapers and looking at the television — but it stuck with me. And I got into the Beat Generation and stuff back to the Lost Generation — expatriates. Man, I was nineteen and ready to travel.

I told Daddy it was time for me to get away from the city. So there I am — tourist class on the SS *United States,* on my way to France! Listen, that was a five-day trip! I met a guy there about twenty-one years old who had an ounce of grass with him. We used to go up on the deck at night — oh, goodness gracious! It was beautiful, really beautiful out at sea. I know what these romantic sea writers are talking about. Good grief!

In Paris I just wandered around by myself — moved from one sleazy hotel to another. A buck a night or something. Then I hitchhiked to Spain — sixty pesetas to an American dollar. And baby, you got your money's worth! Oh, Christmas! Sixty to a dollar! Fifteen pesetas, you got a whole damn meal — go to where the Spanish working man takes care of himself and has his good time. Oh, Christmas! And from there I got a boat from Algecrias across to Morocco. I got a house in the medina of Tangiers. It was made of clay, man, and it was sorta weird. I lived there with two other American guys. We each lived on our own floor, and the main room was on top where we'd all get together. We had this Arab buddy, Mustafa — he got us about a quarter of a pound chunk of hashish for around twelve dollars. Twelve American dollars! But Jesus, God — we sat around smoking those tiny little pieces of hash — that thing lasted forever, for God's sake! And we'd have our kif in these little clay bowls. And mint tea, oh, that mint tea! Jesus Christ!

One of the American guys, Tom T., had just gotten out of the Navy, and we decided to do a little traveling. So we took off on his motorcycle — went to Fez, Rabat, Casablanca, down to Marrakesh. Casablanca was ninety percent Arab, but it had a good garnish of European corruption on top. Gambling and night clubs — it still had some of its old stuff going on. But Marrakesh, Marrakesh is beautiful! Right on the front steps of the Sahara Desert. The sunset was a fanstastic thing. I mean, it went on for hours. Started like four o'clock in the afternoon and didn't end until eight. Layers of hills and different ways for the sun to reflect this way and that. Oh, my God — talk about psychedelic!

Algeria and Tunisia came next. And hey — at that time they hadn't turned the oases into tourist shops. I mean, they were *real* — donkeys, sheep, maybe a camel or something. We'd come in with our motorcycle and sleep there — and oh, God, it would get freezing at night! We spent maybe a week or two just fooling around in Tunisia. But we wanted to see places, man — we weren't just looking for honky-tonk parties.

In Tunis we sold Tom T.'s Honda and took the ferry across to Piraeus. Met this black dude — had a real entertaining name, like a jazz musician or something — a real jivey name, but I can't remember it. He was a cab driver in New York and he used to save up for a year, then come to Greece till his money ran out. He was very sensible about it. I mean, he didn't gamble or high-life or any of that bullshit, man. He just stuck to his hash. Simple, basic living. So he was hanging out with this chick. She had a name too — I swear to God it was Maria Deheuvereau van-something-or-other.

Some kind of European aristocrat stuff that had been in her family forever. Ancient, ancient, you know. And she was twenty-nine, thirty at the time — and oh, she was something! She was — hey, I finally remembered that black guy's name. Dixie Nemo! Captain fuckin Nemo! Just livin over in the Greek isles, for Christ sake! All of us smokin hash on Skyros — the Northern Sporades. . . . Oh, God!

Hung out there all summer till I got news that my father was gonna be in Europe on business. He sent me extra bread and a ticket so I could meet him in Rome. We met at the Hotel Excelsior. Daddy always stayed in those kind of hotels. I mean, you gotta figure, he was a businessman and that was his thing. Daddy was doing a lotta business in Rome, so I didn't see much of him. I didn't know anybody myself. I didn't have any phone numbers; I didn't even know where the whorehouse section was or anything — I mean, I didn't know where to start, man. I just started walkin around from bar to bar — drinking and drinking and drinking. . . . How I found the Vespa, I don't know. I think I just got on it, started it up and started ridin around. Car cut me off. No helmet and I'm going headfirst at a brick wall. Everything smashed. It took the old man three days to find me. What happened, the blood destroyed the name on my passport, and when they picked me up I had no money, no ID or anything. I was still in my clothes from the accident when the old man found me — still had blood caked in my hair and on my face.

After they took care of me in Italy, I was feeling all right. Some broken bones, and I had to have an eye operation because the crash had knocked my eye out of kilter — but everything was fine except for this constantly running nose. And this is a weird story — Daddy took me back to New York to see some big-shot neurologist. I remember his pants — grey, very light grey — but not wool, not flannel — light, like a summer material. So I was sitting in his office telling him about the accident. I was dabbing my nose and I bent to pick something up. And a drop, just like a raindrop, dripped out of my right nostril and sort of splashed on my knee. "What was that drop?" he said.

"Oh, I've been having a runny nose for a few days."

The man was very much on the ball. I think I owe my life to him. He handed me a test tube. "Will you just sit there for about five minutes and collect some of that stuff for me?" He found out it was cerebral spinal fluid. My brain sac had been punctured by a bone splinter from my skull, and it was leaking out through the sinus cavities.

They had me on the operating table fifteen hours. Opened up the whole top of my head. You can see the dent here on the side of my head. They made an incision right along my hairline, all across the top of my skull to the other side, and down my ear here. Just peeled it off like this because they had to fix that sac. And the shock — not only of the operation, but from the original bang-up in Rome — I went into seizures right on the operating table. They call it posttraumatic epilepsy — the shock of doctors invading your system, of all that chemistry and nonsense. Right in the middle of the operation. Right on the operating table. I'm unconscious, they got my head wide open, and I'm going through seizures. Man, that was the end of my grand tour!

D O U G 'S   A N D   B O B B Y ' S   R O O M

The door hangs on a single hinge. You have to hold the doorknob, lift it, and ease it back gently in order to enter.

A square room, surprisingly tidy, with two single beds facing each other from opposite walls.

Television between the two beds. On the floor, a turquoise utility bucket — their "vomit pail" for late night emergencies.

Hotplate and Toast-R-Oven on a small table. Doug makes per-

fect fried pork chops and a good pot roast. He enjoys cooking;
Bobby loves eating — they're both happy with the arrangement.

Their seven cats scramble across the floor, hissing and nipping
and ricocheting off the furniture. At other times Frisbee and her
offspring settle under the beds or behind Bobby's cartons of books;
except for the pungent smell of Kitty Litter you'd never know they
were there. Doug says it's profitable to sell Frisbee's frequent lit-
ters. People in the hotel are lonely, he says; they like pets. Bobby
tells me cats are good at catching roaches. But neither brother tells
me what is most obvious — that the two of them love looking after
their pets, taking care of dependent creatures, having some living
thing to support in spite of their own meager circumstances.

Doug and Bobby have their own gloomy bathroom. The toilet
seat is cracked, the sink leaks, and the bathtub is black — not completely black, but smeared and charred like some malevolent
Rorschach. But whatever the condition of the furnishings and appliances, it is clear that Doug and Bobby have made some effort to
create a home for themselves. They still hold on to domestic order
and the powerful bond of brotherly love. These are their links to
early childhood, remembered comfort, to dreamlike images of the
family — together, prosperous, healthy, invulnerable to pain.

D O U G   C A R M A N ' S   S T O R Y

I'll never forget one time in Huntington. Bobby and me were having a race or something like that, and he pulled some kinda older-
brother number on me — tricked me outa an ice cream cone.
Fuckin ice cream! I dug up a brick and threw it at him. Hit him
upside the head. I still wonder if maybe — see, Bobby had that
first seizure in '63, but I still wonder if maybe that brick. . . . I just
wanted to put that in before I start, cause I still think about it. I
seen Bobby go through fifty seizures — sometimes two, three, one
after the other. I cook for him. I pull him off the street when he gets

too high. We watch TV together. We share that fuckin puke bucket together. And — well, I just wonder if maybe that brick coulda been the start of his epilepsy.

I'm gonna do like Bobby and not get into a whole thing about growin up. Mother was sick and nothin ever seemed right. We were brought up in a drinkin family. I'm not blamin anyone, but we were brought up around drinks. I can remember when I'm five years old — everybody drinkin at the Christmas party. Me and Bobby used to sneak cases of beer down to the basement — chug-a-lug three cans, puke, chug-a-lug another three, and puke again. We was always doin somethin like that — managed to fuck up just about everything. I don't know, we had some fun. . . . Camp Mamaweeda — they used to call me Turtle cause I was fat and slow. Used to have to hit a home run twice as far as anybody else if I was gonna make it around the bases. . . . But mostly it was gettin kicked outa schools and Daddy findin some new place to send me.

I remember when Bobby went off to Europe. Mother was gettin worse and worse — and I was findin new ways to get in trouble. I'd already been in and out of Trinity, Hackley, and the New York Tutoring School, so now Daddy put me in this little school, Croyden Hall — all boys, out in Atlantic Highlands, New Jersey. Nothin to do but fight with the townies. They used to beat the shit out of us because they were rough and tough and we were just a bunch of spoiled brats. It was a stupid school — make your bed with hospital corners — just like being in the fuckin Army. So I ran away. I had a few bucks — five, six dollars would go a long way — and I was just hangin around town, sleepin wherever I could sleep.

That was it for Croyden Hall. They kicked me out. But my father, he understood — "All right, you don't want to go back to school — fine. I'll send you down to Nassau for a little while." So I went down there and stayed with my aunt and uncle. I'm spoiled, right? In Nassau I used to come home at night pukin on the fuckin bed from bein drunk and shit. And one night I took all the money the old man gave me and went over the hill — into the native quarters. Disappeared for about four days. Here I was, a white guy with money in my pocket. I moved right in with this one girl. She had a little grass hut, and it was just drinkin and funnin and dancin and goin crazy and everything. It was great! And then when the money ran out, I had my first real bad hangover — pigs and flyin elephants comin outa the wall. "Uh-oh — it's time to find Aunt Minna," I said. So I snuck back over the hill to Bay Street.

After my aunt kicked me out of Nassau, my father said, "Hey, you're my kid. You're a man. You're doin your thing." And when I got back to New York he put me to work in his office. It was fun — lunch with my father every day, a fuckin steak. But finally I got sick of it. There was an Army recruiting station across from where I worked and — it came to me. . . . I just found myself goin in there and takin the test.

Macho, macho, macho — that's what I wanted to be. I didn't wanna be a spoiled little brat — fat little Doug. I wanted to go and fight, get the shit outa my system. I didn't know any Vietnam or anything. I just wanted to go and fight. Gung-ho. And it turned me into — not necessarily what I am now — but when I got out, I'd gone through some changes.

I got assigned to Germany — radio school. Oh, it was fun! You sit there at the telegraph goin dee-dee-dee-dee-dee. I graduated thirty-thirty — very high speed — so they give me the assignment that nobody wanted. I was the NCS, Net Control Station, for the whole division. A general sittin on my back everyday. Starched fatigues, spit-shined shoes — the whole bit. Gave me top-secret clearance. Here I am, still seventeen years old, carrying a loaded forty-five and a shoulder bag with secret documents. If there was a war, I was responsible for contacting the battalions of the division — I had the code to get them on the alert so they would let loose their missiles.

I couldn't put up with it — workin under this fuckin general. Spit polish every day. Haircut every day. Finally, I got sick of it. I just slowly started letting myself deteriorate. I wouldn't get a hair-cut no more. I wouldn't spit on them boots no more. I wouldn't wear starched fatigues no more. And they got madder and madder and madder at me — started punishin me with KP and guard duty. I'm growin a beard, my hair's down to here, and they're talkin about a court martial. I said, "To hell with everything!" I asked the company clerk, "What's the fastest way outa here?"

He said, "There's a place called Vietnam. We're fightin over there now."

"Oh yeah?"

"You can go with mud on your boots and everything."

"Oh, that's good!" I said. "I wanna get outa this spit-polish bullshit. I'm sick of gettin up every mornin and havin to spit polish my boots. Or before you go to bed at night, havin to sit there and Glowax your boots. It's stupid! It's such stupid shit!"

And he said, "Sign this 1049, and you'll be outa here in thirty days."

I didn't know I was goin to a jungle. I volunteered for Vietnam. I didn't know nothin.

So, I'm goin to Vietnam. I didn't know where Bobby was. He'd had his accident; he was back in the Village shootin speed, that's all. And I was completely against drugs — a gung-ho American. June of '66, and I didn't know nothin about Vietnam. It was start-ing to get bigger, but there was nothing in the paper. A guy gets killed — they was still callin em "advisors" then — or maybe a flag gets shot down. And that's about it.

Training camp in California, right? We come in outside of San Francisco, and they said, "Okay, tomorrow morning you get up at five o'clock, have breakfast, get cleaned up — we're gonna take you into the jungle. Here we are, out in the suburbs — and they had a special jungle training base, a mock jungle in California. I swear, it was only four blocks square. A little jungle. I think it was made by a TV studio, grown especially for films. They'd put packs on our shoulders with twenty or thirty pounds of rocks on our backs, and give us rifles — "Okay, boys, there's the jungle! There's the trail!" And all along the trail there were booby traps and hand grenades. You'd trip a wire, and a fucking hand grenade would go off overhead — an empty hand grenade with a blasting cap inside. And you gotta learn how to walk in the jungle. You gotta watch every step you take cause of the plunger stakes — sharpened bamboo that goes right through the boot, the foot, everything. All this for Vietnam. I said, "What the hell did I get my shit into?"

Training's over. We get on a World Airways charter in Class A uniform — no ties, just the short-sleeved shirts, nice khaki pants, and your spit-shine shoes. Fly to Hawaii, Guam, and then into Saigon. We didn't know where we were goin. I mean, we knew we were goin to Vietnam, but we didn't realize it was a war. Not really. Not yet. . . .

So here we are. It's dark. We're comin in. And you know how a plane lands — it floats down and comes in level, right? Well, here we are, pullin into Saigon — the plane banks — SCHWIIT! SCHWIIT! Fuckin tracers comin up at us. Tracers shootin up in the dark while we're watchin out the window. Vietcong right outside the airport, shootin little popguns and stuff at this big 747. Five hundred of us on the plane. And here we go — divin straight down at the runway. And we're sittin there in our Class A uniform — "What the fuck is goin on?" We didn't know. We were so young — all of us were so young. Soon as we got off the plane — whew! Heat and humidity hits you right in the face, puts you right into shock. And jeeps and all these guys with machine guns and everything surround the plane in a circle — like in the movies — yellin, "Run! Run to the bunkers!" Fuckin tracers goin up in the air. Vietcongs mortaring the fuckin airfield. What the fuck is this shit, right? Two hours we're sittin in bulldozer pits — four-by-fours laid across and sandbags on top — while the Vietcong mortared the air field. That's the welcome to the country we got.

When we came out of the bunkers, they loaded us up on school buses. Now dig these buses — the whole floor was reinforced and covered with layers of sandbags, so if the truck ran over a mine the shrapnel wouldn't come through and hit you. And on the windows it was all screening, like chicken wire, so if they threw a grenade it would bounce off. And it was the weirdest thing — driving through Saigon and everybody wavin at us — "Hey, number one G.I.! How you doin?" I said, "What the fuck is goin on? One minute we're getting shot at, then everybody's wavin." They liked our money — that's what they wanted.

Next day they put us on more buses again, and we went out to a place called the Ninetieth Replacement Center about thirteen miles outside of Saigon on Route 1 — just tents and cots in the mud. Here we are, laying in these cots, and I'm scared to death. I wanted a gun. I wanted to go out in the jungle and shoot. Ten days I sat around in the mud, then — "Carman, Douglas — RA12726418 — assigned to the Seventy-ninth Engineering Group."

"What the hell is that? Where'm I going? Into the middle of the jungle?"

"No, boy — you're goin right up the road. You got a top-secret clearance, man — you're goin to be a colonel's radio operator."

And here I was again — in the middle of Vietnam, 110-degree heat, and I gotta have spit-shine boots and starched fatigues! Same bullshit I had in Germany, only now I'm in the goddamn jungle. So I started sneakin into town at night — take the colonel's jeep, come back four o'clock in the morning. I had a girl in town, and I was takin care of her and her family. I was still a kid — eighteen years old, and to me gettin laid was an adventure. I was giving money to Diap's mother for the rent and food and stuff, and she — "Here, here's my daughter!" What am I gonna do — say no and go back to camp?

This went on for awhile, and the drinkin got heavier and I started smoking grass — very good grass. I was drivin back from town one night, smashed outa my mind, and here comes this minibus. I ended up in one of these drainage ditches with a case of beer and a girl layin in my lap — four MPs around me. I didn't get punished because this Vietnam was supposed to be a fun thing. . . . But Vietnam was crazy. All along the main road were little tiny grass huts — whorehouses, beer joints, and stuff — and right behind, it was still jungle. It was really crazy. I mean, if you went a hundred yards off the road you'd probably get your throat cut, but ten yards off the road — "Man, have a beer. . . . I've got my thirteen-year-old sister over here!" Shit went on like that every day — stuff I'll never forget. . . . We got mortared one night from very close by. You could hear the Vietcong across the road, droppin mortars in the tubes. First sergeant comes around — "I want a squad to go out there and do a search and destroy." Sixteen of us. We split into two squads — everybody carrying shotguns with double-O buckshot. They're like ball bearings — fifty in each shell, you know, and they spread out when you hit someone. Anyway, we didn't know what we were doin. None of us had been in combat. We're trudgin down this trail, dark as hell — all of a sudden, I hear this click. I'm staring into the darkness and this girl steps out from behind a tree with a forty-five in her hand. Young girl. Very young girl. And she points this forty-five at my head. . . . I froze. I just stood there — and I guess she kind of froze. I don't know, maybe she was freaked out on opium. The guy behind me yelled, "Duck! Duck!" I just fell on my ass and he pumped her twice with the shotgun. . . . Her whole . . . she was torn completely in half. I took my shirt and we made a stretcher out of it — that's how small she was. And she was still alive. I was all full of blood.

To this day I'm still in shock. I mean, I killed a lot more after that, but to this day I can see her. The next day — this is what really blew it — I think this is what might have put me over the edge into . . . I don't know — it's not an excuse, but this is what. . . . It hurts. . . . This is what might have put me over into drugs and drinkin and not havin any responsibility. The next day — you know what they did? To inaugurate me on my first kill, the guy who had killed her brought her sandals to me as a prize.

"This is a reward. Here's her sandals. They're nice and worked in. You can wear them yourself." That really blew it. I just kind of put them down and left.

See, at this point . . . I mean, look, I believed in the war. I ain't got nothin against the Communists. It just seems that when communism arrives into a country — like Russia and China — there's so much killing, massacring, and this kinda thing. And that's what was happening over there. The Vietnamese I knew, they wanted us to kick out the communists but they didn't want the war the way it was goin on. We used to go into a village and build buildings and schools and churches — just wood buildings, you know, nothing spectacular — leave em a generator for electricity, leave em bathrooms and gasoline and stuff. And we'd come back three weeks later, and the chief and his wife and his daughters would be hangin by their thumbs, hangin from trees with their skin stripped off. . . . Oh, God! I'm gettin sick. . . . I'll . . . I'll be all right in just a second. . . . Look, I went to Vietnam because I couldn't put up with the spit and polish anymore. So I was combat engineer in the Outer Triangle. Middle of the jungle. Little old rubber plantation. A big mansion where the general lived. Olympic-sized swimming pool. Every couple of weeks we would go out and do a sweep. Search and destroy. Surround a village, and we'd have Vietnamese with us speaking through bullhorns — "Everybody leave the village! It's gonna be destroyed!" And if you were in there when we went through — tough luck. Napalm. Artillery. Just wipe it right off the map. . . . I never got involved in anything like My Lai. I've seen civilians killed, but no massacre. . . . Look, the Vietcong used to kill innocent people. Nurses, doctors, civilians — they carried no guns. Just murdered them. Cut em up. . . . Here I am, makin excuses for what we did over there. It cuts very deep.

It's gonna take awhile to go through this thing about Vietnam. Bobby knows — I've been talking to him for twelve years about it. . . . You run into a guy that's been dead for four or five days in the jungle. Vietcong may have cut off his head, or his ears, or some fingers — wear them for necklaces. Running into a guy that's been dead a few days out in that heat — you remember Jonestown? Twenty-four hours and the body starts to bloat. Worms start comin. The first couple of times — just like you see in the movies — I got sick. You get used to it eventually. But then there were guys that — "Hey, there's a dead guy! Ha, ha ha!" Guys like that. . . . New Year's Eve we got attacked by a whole bunch of Vietcong — runnin straight into our machine-gun fire. We killed a whole lotta them. Three or four hundred piled up around the barbed wire. Next day we bring a tractor up to dig a trench — and this guy got a kick out of runnin over bodies and watchin the heads pop off. We had one guy, even after the battle was over he kept firing and firing and firing and firing. Shooting dead bodies. Frozen to the gun. He just sat there — tatta-tatta-tatta-tatta. It's a weird, weird thing.

Things started getting worse. Go out on an operation for a month — twenty, thirty, forty guys would get killed out of the whole company. Things just started gettin bad. That's when all the men started comin over — half a million that finally ended up over there. I got very involved with the medics — ups to stay awake, downs to go to sleep, and morphine to take on patrols. The medics were supplying us with the works, teaching us how to shoot it. Pure morphine — three days of pure and you'd be hooked. But Vietnam was drivin us crazy — wasn't no drug we didn't try. In fact, that's where I took my first LSD trip. Somebody sent it from the States in a package. From California, so we knew it was good. We split one tab, four of us, and we sat in a circle in the dust watchin a firefight goin on — tracers goin and flares that light up the skyline. We're sittin there — "Wow, look at that! Ooooh!" And over there, guys are gettin killed. And all these new guys were divin head first into the mortar bunkers and stuff, jumpin in and tramplin each other. But the four of us just sat there in the dust — passing a joint around, watching the fireworks. Tripped all night long.

What finally drove me over the hill — me and my demolition
squad were out on a mission clearing mines. We went out there —
three guys in front, one on each side of the road and one in the
middle — with mine detectors, just like you see in the movies. We
had this gung-ho convoy commander — all he had to do was have
the tank spray machine-gun bullets down the road to explode the
mines, but he decided he wanted to put us to work. We're goin
along, goin along. No mines. Nothin. Not even a footprint....
Give me a chance to catch my breath, because what I've got to tell
you next is what put me over the hill. I've said it before to a lot of
people — over and over.... There's this one kind of mine — you
can run a wire off into the jungle and set it off electrically. And
what they have in em — I told you before about double-O buckshot — well, what come out of them is 5,000 double-O buckshot
backed by explosive. So we're comin down the road. I was the boss,
the sergeant. I had three guys with mine sweepers and three guys
as probers, and I was behind them with a radio and my Thompson
submachine gun in case anything happened. And we're walkin up
this road — two of these mines go off at the same time. Ten thousand double-O pellets! And after the dust clears, I'm standing
there. I'd gotten a piece in my foot — didn't even feel it. Holes in
my sleeve. Dents in my helmet. But no serious injury. And here's
the whole squad, six guys, stretched out bleeding, torn up, blasted
away like they'd gotten hit point-blank by a double-gauge shotgun. Five of them died. One of them lived. To this day I don't
know in what kind of shape he's in, but I know he's a cripple. My
instructions had been, "You stay here with the radio; if there's any
action, open up with your Thompson submachine gun." What am
I gonna do against ten thousand pellets? I flipped out....

They were my buddies. A bunch of blacks and Spanish. If I
needed somebody behind me on patrol they were the only ones I'd
choose. The rest of em were rednecks that hated everybody. Hated
New Yorkers. Hated blacks. They hated Spanish. And Vietnamese — gook here, gook there — "Let's go fuck that gook to death!

Let's rape that gook!" Beer-bellies.... But my buddies ... my buddies were all wiped out.... They patched me up in the hospital and said, "You're gonna be all right. You're fine. Don't worry about it." But I was goin through some changes — I was in shock because these were my friends, good friends.

To this day I don't remember their names. It erased everything. Just the shock of seein em dead. I didn't do anything wrong. I didn't blow it. It was the war. All right, the convoy commander maybe could have done something about it beforehand, but it wasn't his fault either. I mean, it was such a miserable war. A stupid, ridiculous war. I don't wanna sound like a warmonger, but the way we did it was no good. We should have just gone in there and did what we wanted to do and then gotten out. A million men and just gotten it over with. We drug it out over all those years, and then we lost it anyway.

So I went into shock. Really feelin bad. Takin a lotta pills. Finally, I requested to see the base psychiatrist. Knocked on his door and — "Oh, it's time for me to go home," he tells me.

I said, "What do you mean? I just come off the truck. I'm all full of red dust from the convoy. My buddies are dead. What do you mean you're goin home? I need to see you. I gotta talk to you. I got a bad experience. Help me! Please, help me!"

"Well, come back tomorrrow morning."

I had my checkbook and $100 cash in my pocket. I walked out the hospital compound and down to the main road where they line up the convoy to go to Saigon. I got on this truck and just sat there. This guy sees me and says, "Where do you think you're goin?"

"I'm ridin with you down to Saigon." Here I am with a rifle, full ammunition, and hand grenades hangin off of me. "What're you gonna do about it?"

"Nothin man."

I went down to Saigon and stayed there for over a month. Just partying. Forgetting. Thirty-eight days AWOL. Became a real junkie-smokin-drinkin fiend. Bouncin fifty-dollar checks in every

PX within twenty miles of Saigon. But we partied — oh, did we party!

I hid in the Chinese district of Saigon, living with the family that I was already supporting. Just the girl, Diap, spoke English. But Mama San was fun — she'd talk to me in sign language. They separated everything in the apartment with screens and curtains, and they had beds on the floor like woven mats. Every day, Mama San would fold back the screens — me sittin there smokin opium and her daughter laying next to me. Papa San just sat with his pipe all day. He was just kind of like in a cloud all the time. He and Mama San had fought the Japanese during World War II — so they were just layin back through this one. Another war. Mama San chewin her betel nut, Papa San smokin his pipe and takin in the money, as little as it was. These ladies used to come by each week and sit around with Mama San. Old ladies — well, fifty years old in Vietnam looked like eighty years over here. All their teeth would be red from betel nut, and they'd sit in a circle and yak while me and Diap was smokin our opium and grass and watchin. One time, one of the ladies looked sadder than the others. I thought maybe her husband got killed in a shelling — or a son. So all these ladies sat this one lady in the middle of their circle — all of em chewin betel nut and spittin — and they started swayin back and forth, all of em in unison. And this one lady in the middle starts screamin, "Aaaaagh! Aaaaaaaaagh!" — like she was communicating with the dead. . . . I was so smashed on opium. It was a weird thing to see. A weird war.

I didn't tell the family about bein AWOL, but Diap figured it out. "You're in trouble, ain't you?" she said. She didn't say "ain't you," but in her own little sweet way — she was only fifteen years old — she said, "There's something wrong."

"Yeah," I said, "I'm in big trouble." She knew. Instead of just being a girlfriend, she was almost like a wife. She followed me everywhere around the house. Followed me even when I went to the bathroom. I'd love to see what she looks like today, cause she's a grown beautiful woman now. Back then she was just a kid. All right, I was just a kid too, but she was much younger than me. I used to have pictures. Oh, I wish I still had that album! Pictures of me and her and Nam.

One day I'm lookin outside. Here comes this motorbike — little Vespa motorbike — with a girl driving and a guy on the back. And there were some GIs walkin down the street — three guys. Machine gun goes off and mows em down. Five seconds and the little Vespa's speeding away — Vietcong. I said, "That's it!" I went and turned myself in.

I just walked in to the MP station with my rifle, hand grenades, my suitcase and everything. They locked me up. Big deal. I could understand giving me a little punishment, but it went on for days. Criminal Investigation Division sent their people in, and they showed me volumes and volumes of photographs — askin me where are the other guys that are AWOL and deserters. Finally, I got mad at all this spit-and-polish bullshit interrogation. We used to call anybody who worked in Saigon — who wasn't out fighting — Saigon warriors. Do their job durin the day, and then at night they'd go out whorin around while we were out in the jungle gettin shot up. So I started yellin, "Ah, you freakin Saigon warriors! Why don't you go out in the jungle and do a little fightin like I been doin?" They got mad — three burly MPs — grrrrrrrrrr, like the Hulk. Handcuffed my hands and feet together and chained me up. I was in fairly good shape, but I was gettin withdrawal sickness from all the opium — pukin on myself, shitting and pissing on myself — and the mosquitos were eatin me alive.

Finally, somebody from my company showed up to take me back for my court martial. Next thing I know, my father's in Saigon — spent three, four thousand dollars to come see me. The company commander took me down to Saigon and left me with my father alone. When I first saw Daddy, it was just hugging and kissing and how are you and everything. That night in the hotel I got up and snuck into the toilet to smoke a joint, and he came bustin in on me. Maybe he thought I was committing suicide or somethin — he didn't really know what it was at first, but he was mad. I told him, "Dad, you were a forward observer in World War II. You killed people and people tried to kill you. You went through it thirty years ago, but I'm living it right now. You gotta understand — this is the only way I can live with it." Scotch and soda was his thing, but he understood. Right away, he realized.

I begged my father to get me a civilian lawyer, but he made me stick with my Army lawyer — "Do it the Army way. You've got a clean record. Just sit back and take your punishment." And he was right — I got a suspended sentence. By this time I only had about two months of service left, and since I was a short-timer they couldn't send me out in the field anymore. All I did was drink and smoke and stay high and just sit back and wait for my orders to go home. . . . So here we are, we're all in Class A uniforms on a truck goin through Saigon to get on a plane to home — and the Tet offensive started. MPs stop our truck — "They're attackin Saigon! We need replacements!" Blah, blah, blah. Our duffle bags, suitcases — everything ready to go home. We're all dressed up nice. Got all our medals on and everything — and they hand us rifles and say, "Get out on the street!"

"Wait a minute!" I said. "I'm goin home!"

"You can't. The airport's overrun." Vietcong were all over the place. These guys had infiltrated the whole town. House-to-house fightin is miserable. We're throwin grenades everywhere. Take an automatic rifle — brrrrrt, brrrrrt — empty a whole clip. If you hit somebody, you hit somebody; if you don't, you don't. Put in another clip and go brrrrrrrt again. You never see who you're shootin.

Three days we're fightin house to house, sleepin in the streets — and finally they come through the street with one of these loudspeaker trucks — "Everybody that was supposed to report to the airfield, there's a convoy forming." Here we are — rolling in the

streets with smoke and grit, same clothes for three days — convoy
took us right to the airport. And this officer comes out — "Well,
you guys are goin home. You did a good job. Thank you very
much. I hope you reenlist." Real Army BS. And then — oh, what
a trip back! Two hundred guys drinkin and smokin — stewardesses
gettin high with us — knowin we're alive and gettin discharged as
soon as we touch ground. Oh, it was so great! And then we
landed — California! Shuffled off the plane. Tired. Sleepy. Jet lag.
All of us drunk — and *alive*. A lot of guys got down on their knees
and kissed the tarmac.

That was the end. I was outa Vietnam. But I guess Vietnam's
never gonna be outa me. When I got home to New York, I bought
a stereo — went in the store — "Give me all the Beatles albums, all
the Rolling Stones." Sat around gettin high in my father's suite,
playin my music twenty-four hours a day. Finally, my father told
me, "Go down and get yourself some suits and pants and stuff, and
I'll pay for them." So here I am walking down Fifth Avenue —
and a car backfired. "Mortars!" I screamed. "Mortars!" Hit the
pavement and started scramblin around on all fours. Cut my
hands up, my knees. And everybody lookin at me — "Where the
fuck this guy come from?" Me still screamin, "Mortars! Mortars!"
What the fuck did they know about Vietnam?

M R .   W I N S L O W

"He got an eatin jones." Youngblood cackles at his own insight.
"An outrageous eatin jones. Bad as a dope fiend. He got a hole to
fill up, he got a heavy need. Full-time business."

Where and how the need started is hard to know. Mr. Winslow's
memory pulls up short at Rockford State Hospital, where he spent
more than half his forty-five years. He's massive but not really
fat — beefy, like a retired heavyweight gone to seed. His face is
dark and huge — an Easter Island monument with eager eyes, des-

perate to fix and hold his listener. He'd be completely overbearing were it not for the Keds and baseball cap that have become his daily uniform. It is as if all that bulk and intensity is there to conceal a secret he is too afraid to utter: *I am just a puffed up little boy. I eat and eat to make myself big — so big they'll be afraid and won't hurt me.*

"R-r-r-rockford! I ain't never goin there again." He stands too close when he talks; his fierce stare, his intense need trap listeners within his field of gravity. "R-r-r-rockford's got showers an a swimmin pool. But at night, at night, at night — they close two doors on you at night, an they never let you go out. This man in the park, he told me he'd die before they put him back in R-r-r-rockford. Well, I told him, I told him, see, I told him I ain't never gonna set foot in there." He stares down at his feet, as if a good stern warning will keep them in line.

"I wasn't more than a boy, a boy when they put me in R-r-r-rockford, and I didn't see nothing but R-r-r-rockford till I was growed. Well, they ain't never puttin me there again. Never, never puttin me in R-r-r-rockford. Here you got your own key, and you can open your door an go on the street. But the showers was better at R-r-r-rockford, an here they don't feed you enough. That was one good thing — that was the only good thing — R-r-r-rockford gave you second helpings an you could fill up your plate. I can't get enough to eat here. I can't ever get enough." He picks up a tiny white suitcase by his feet. It smells like rotten garbage. "I have to keep my food in here, in here for an emergency. But see, see, but see if I eat it I won't have nothin left to eat. I got my key to leave my room, but they don't feed me. I'm hungry. I'm always, always hungry!"

IRONSIDES

Ironsides is squat and tough as nails. When he cruises down 100th Street in his electric wheelchair, it's like a little tank charging off to war. He may be crippled, but he takes good care of himself. Whatever drink or drugs he consumes, he's in control. In fact, control is the name of the game for Ironsides. Now that the winter bite is past, he'll roll down to Broadway and sit there for hours with his weimaraner curled at his feet — rapping with the guys, keenly alert to the passing flow, always looking for a piece of the action.

When I drop by there's a pot of stew bubbling on the small stove just inside the doorway. Kids squeal on the rooftop playground of Temple Beth Ansched across the street. The "Six O'Clock Report" is blaring. "Fuck that shit!" Ironsides says and cuts the sound.

Thick volume of criminal law on the couch. "I'm always reading something," he says. "I can't stand these people that sits around all day and never use their mind. You gotta use your head cause someone's always gonna be out there usin what he know to get some of what you got. Now that's what I like about Francine. You got lotsa women here, think they know all there is to know, see. No use talkin to a bitch thinks she's too smart to listen to nothin. But Francine, see, she's what you call a late developer. She's young and she's good, but people talk to her and tell her things and she'll go off an do somethin to get herself in trouble. I told her, when she gets outa Riker's Island she's gotta stop listenin to all that bullshit and let me straighten her out on a few things."

On the silent TV screen a weatherman is laughing. "We got our sex thing together," he says, "but that don't interest me like really rappin, gettin inside someone's head, you know, gettin together on that level. I'll tell you, she's crazy about me. We're buildin up a trust so when she gets out on April fifth there ain't gonna be no bullshit. She said she's gonna call at six today. You wait and see. . . .

The phone rings at 6:30. "Baby, baby, you savin all that love for me?" Ironsides's voice is soft, low-pitched. Words roll forth, smooth and confident. Give him a violin section, backup vocals, and a good recording engineer, and Barry White can pack up and go home. "Oh, baby! I gotta *speak* to you! I gotta *teach* you some heavy things, honey. Soon as you get out, baby, we're startin a new life soon as you get out." Reggie Jackson is smiling in front of a palm tree. George Steinbrenner scowls behind a desk. "You love me? . . . Yeah, yeah, we gotta look into that. . . . Baby, I'm askin do you *love* me?" He leans forward in his wheelchair, staring into the perforated mouthpiece of the receiver. "More and more each day? That's fine, baby, *fine.* . . . You know how I feel, don't you baby? . . . Right, baby, right on. Soon as you come back home. . . ."

PRIMARY DAY

When I hand Muriel the flowers, her face lights up. "Oh, Bob! How nice! Shall we go to my room?"

I don't have much time. I really just wanted to drop off the flowers and leave, but I can't refuse her invitation. She hops to the elevator and we head down to the third floor. "You bumped your head," I say. Both temples are bruised. Freshly dried blood above her eyebrows and more blood smeared on her woolen turtleneck.

"Oh, yes!" she says as if remembering some old event. "I had a seizure today."

"What about your medication?"

"Unfortunately, I've misplaced the keys to my room. My medication is inside."

We reach the door to her living unit and it's locked. She'll have to wait for Frankie, the desk clerk, to let her in. Back she hops to the elevator, and we return to the TV lounge. "They're so lovely," she says sniffing at her unopened gift. "I'll have to put them in water."

A block away, I stop in the neighborhood high school to vote. "You're the ninety-second person today," a woman tells me. Close to 2,000 SRO tenants live within a few blocks — I wonder if five of them have voted. Yesterday, a wag on public radio suggested that the South Bronx should follow Afghanistan's lead and have Soviet Russia invade them. That way, he reasoned, the federal government would pay attention to the blighted area. The President would declare a crisis and rush millions of dollars of emergency aid to them. Voting today, I feel part of that implied absurdity. America is choosing a leader. And one block away, Muriel Berry sits patiently, blood on her collar, treasured unopened flowers in her hands.

A R T H U R   M O O R E

I've thought about Arthur Moore many times over these past weeks, but I haven't been able to gear myself up for another visit to his room. His monstrous lower body. That awful smell. . . . Today I'm ready. I knock on his door. No answer. I can hear the televison inside. I knock again and call out my name, reminding him who I am. Even here in the hallway the stench from his room is nauseating. "Are you there? Can we talk awhile?" Where could he possibly go with his tired and swollen body? "Arthur, Arthur, are you there?"

"Yes!" His voice rumbles. The televison clicks off and there is only silence.

L O N E R

David Torres talks. Talk is his medium. He's a talk junkie. Not conversation. Not rapping. There's no urgent news to tell. It's just cheap talk — jiving and joking with scarcely a pause. "Hey, you know why they call this French toast? It's because. . . . Hey Abbot, you live on the sixth floor — you know why the elevator don't stop there? . . . They say cigarette smoking is hazardous to the health, but how come they don't. . . ." I can't ever remember a joke, and David's are the least memorable.

You can see his ribcage right through his tee-shirt. Sometimes when he's talking, his mouth slides way over to the left; not just slanting, but a true leer, mouth seemingly changing location, abandoning its familiar position, alighting on his lower left cheek like that of a cubist portrait. I think of some borscht belt comic working up his act. . . . "You know, they say the food here's not fresh, but that's not true. In fact, some of it's still living. Why yesterday, my frankfurter rolled over and barked. Actually, I'm a vegetarian. I ate a piece of lettuce today — nice and green and crisp — and then they told me it was baloney!"

On and on he goes. "How do you tell a male hormone from a female hormone? . . . Easy, pull down their genes! Speaking of females, what do you call 500 Indian women without nipples? . . . The Indian-nippleless-five hundred! But getting serious for a minute — I got a Polish joke. Now that we got this hostage crisis, all these countries are drawing up special plans in case it happens to them. You know what the Polish plan is? . . . Do it just like the Americans! Alright, I guess my timing was off. Everything's been going wrong lately. Take my bicycle — it just isn't working the way it used to. Everytime I want to ride it, it's two tired."

Some people say hi to him; others walk by shaking their heads. Nobody stops for long. He hangs out a lot around the outreach office, and every now and then I try to speak with him, but his incessant talk gives him a momentum that rushes him right past me. Eyes sparkling, bony arms bouncing, mouth sliding across his face — he's bright and attractive, but this manic behavior is infuriating. He's like an impossible kid brother. I feel like picking him up and shaking him, suspending him by his feet: something, anything to stop this flow of silly talk. . . .

David Torres is a loner and talk is his shield against the world. He spent his childhood under almost constant assault — physical beatings and verbal abuse from earliest infancy. People hurt him. Love, dependence, friendship — all those sustaining forms of contact in which words play so important a part, all this is risky territory for David. So he uses talk defensively, as a means of reducing all around him to silence. His enormous nappy Afro gives him the look of a small cat with a lion's mane. The fusillade of jokes continues, but I see a wily old man looking out from behind the boy's eyes. I wish there was some way to get through, some way to reach him without violating his precious defenses — like telephoning a friend in jeopardy across closely watched borders.

"I saw your book on maids in the clinic office," he says one day. "I read it." The first straight words he's spoken to me.

On his first visit to my apartment I loan him a copy of *Palante*, a photodocumentary about the Young Lords Party. "You know, that guy they picked up in Illinois," he says, ". . . Carlos Torres, the head of FALN — that's my brother!"

I ask him how close they were. "We were real close, but I didn't believe in violence or blowing things up. We were separated a lot cause of the family situation, but we got to know each other again five years ago. When he went underground, I could still get letters to him — it'd have to go through three people to get to him."

I don't really believe him. David is poor and powerless; he's dependent on social welfare and its attendant institutions, yet he feels abused by it, outraged at it. It would be easy for him to identify with the FALN leader — a revolutionary, avenger of the Puerto Rican people, America's most wanted man for the past few years — to take him on as his brother. I think of twelve years ago when ghetto youths dressed and strutted in the manner of their revolutionary idols — the dreams and fury of tens of thousands of kids given life in the exploits of these new leaders. And here is David, sharing a surname with this baddest of young countrymen. They *are* brothers, especially now, at the very moment when authorities have caught Carlos, confined him, institutionalized him, begun a process designed to end these dangerous expressions of righteous anger.

But all this is speculation. I have no way of knowing if David is telling me the truth until I check it out. I like David; I'm pleased, flattered even, that he dropped his jiving to speak with me. The skepticism I feel troubles me — I don't want to doubt him at a time of growing trust — but what can I do?

A few days later, I see a photo in the *New York Times* of Reverend Torres, Carlos's father, speaking at a rally in his son's behalf. David told me he'd never seen his father, yet I truly doubt that this minister has left a string of illegitimate children across Manhattan. I tear the photo out and next time I see David I ask him once again to run through his family history. His mother had children by three different men, but he reiterates that both he and Carlos came from the same unknown father. I hand him the *Times* clipping and leave him alone to study it. I suppose it's a moment when I should be there, watching his every response. But I don't want to.

He's still staring at the photo when I return, frowning, looking very serious. "I don't understand," he says. "Maybe my grandmother knows. I wanna show this to her."

I have the strong feeling of being an intruder now, as though I've picked him up and shaken him the way I'd imagined doing on our first meeting. All of us create necessary fictions to bind our lives together — little changes, adjustments of truth, that justify us where we once felt guilt, fictions that shield us from pain, console us for our failures. To call what David has told me a *lie* is almost beside the point. By sharing this fiction with me, by trying to render it true in speech, he's led me to a guarded space where need, imagination, and language converge with the outer world of suffering and struggle. It is an immensely important act, an attempt to seize control of his past by recreating it. We are talking at last.

DAVID TORRES'S STORY

I could never get a single night's sleep. I'd wake up screaming all through my childhood. Nightmares. I would wake up in the middle of the night and sit there staring at the window. And some sort of power I had — I would stare at the window so hard, it would move along the wall and go into the next room. Now comes some sort of spirit, some sort of being that was standing right there in the window. I wouldn't move a muscle. If I had to sneeze I'd do something to stop it cause I knew this thing would jump me. It was this white robot about four feet high — one minute he's here; one minute he's over there. It was just weird. I could never get a good night's sleep. . . .

I was born in 1960. April thirteenth at exactly 7:54 A.M. A poor family. My father I never even knew. He's not even on my birth certificate. My mother and her mother were all born in Puerto Rico — came over in the late fifties. It was basically a rough time. They've been struggling, still struggling up to today.

There's nine of us. The tenth one died at birth. First one is Ilma — we call her Pepsi. Then comes Carlos. The third one is Baby Torres, which is Juan. Then comes Julito, which is Julio. And see, there's three different fathers. The first three were from Torres. The second three, which is from my father — Julio Molina. And then comes another father and Aidida, Cecilita, and Pedrito Morales. So like there's three different names, but we all use Torres. I didn't know none of the fathers — my mother separated from all of them. I don't know why, but, you know, there was never a man in the house.

My mother sort of flipped out when I was eighteen months old. I was getting a lot of child abuse — being thrown everywhere, hit in bad ways. She kept saying stuff about witchcraft, so they sent her to Bellevue for psychiatric care. And every time she would come back, she'd beat on me — make a different scar on my face, my body, whatever. No one else in the family has ever gotten that treatment. So after all the psychiatric tests and everything, the Bureau of Child Welfare took me and my sister and put us in foster homes.

Every foster home was the same. Beatin me left and right. I remember the first one in Bayshore, Long Island. Every time I was beaten I had to kneel down on one of those things they grate cheese with — forced to stay there for some kinda punishment. I never had no friends because I never could go outside to see anyone. I was always either coming home in the car and going in the house, or going in the backyard and playing with my Tonka trucks. That was my best thing — Tonka trucks. I would mix the parts — take the crane and put it on back of the fire truck. That was the only thing I ever had to play with. And if you're stuck with the same trucks for two years, I wanted to see something different. Just like the new car models — they change once in awhile.

Child Welfare moved me to Brooklyn in the early seventies, but I got struck by a car and they moved me to Queens. A group home this time — Speedwell Services for Children, for people that had problems in other foster homes. The first day I was there, the lady that runs the group took me to Key Food. Wow! Never been to a supermarket. And she bought me some Jimmy Pop popcorn. A few weeks later comes two brothers — Sammy and Michael Williams. I greeted them at the door — "Hello!" you know — and they looked at me like I was gonna hold em up or something. At that time I wasn't racially minded — what was black, what was white. You know, if you've got two legs and you got two hands, and you walk and you're able to speak — you're human, that's it. So they started getting into arguments with me, sayin that I was white, and all of this. More people moved in — I noticed everybody was black and I was the only white person in the house. They started calling me Whitey — always looking at me as something different. I would tell the couple in charge that so-and-so is calling me names, but nothing would be done about it. I was just being left out of everything that happened. And every time I would go outside — boom! I would get beat up by one of the brothers and sisters. I was being abused again. It's like the same circle over and over, and it's still there — no parents to protect me.

At the age of twelve, I was the first one in the group home to start working. I walked into this place — "Listen, do you need any help? I'm good with electrical work." And the guy said, "Yeah,

come around. I'll see what we've got to do for you." I started getting paid fifteen dollars, which back then was a lotta money. When
I was fourteen years old, I signed up with the Neighborhood Youth
Corps and got a job at the Storefront Museum and Paul Robeson
Theater on Liberty Avenue. Basic wiring, set up the PA system,
mopping the floor, cleaning up — things like that. They began to
like me — more money, more raises. They took me out to lunch at
International House of Pancakes. Gave me birthday parties. Took
me to Great Adventure. They were like parents — someone to do
all these things for me.

Every time I would get the slightest little amount of money, it
would always go into something that deals with electricity. CBs,
stereos, cassette recorders — you name it. Anything that works or
ticks I would always go for it. Then at the age of fifteen it became
very, very heavy. The circle was still there and it was getting worse.
I was getting hit by bats and other things. The kids at my foster
home were breaking my radios. The problem really got out of
hand. I was starting to fight back, calling the cops whenever I
needed protection.

Around that time, a couple of weeks before my birthday, the
agency reunited me with my mother and we had a one-to-one talk
at the agency in front of a counselor to make sure things went all
right. I was hoping for someone to say, "Oh, my baby!" It didn't
happen like that. The social worker brung me down, and I walked
in the room and she was sitting there — a lady claiming to be my
mother. Wow! She looked all right. I kissed her, said hello. The
bad part about it, the whole conversation she was talking to me in
Spanish and I wasn't understanding nothing. Something was telling me to say yes when I was supposed to and no when I wasn't.
Something was telling me to go ahead and say these things — and
everything fell into place. The day went well, so we scheduled for
me to go over to her place for my birthday.

I just wanted things to start off smoothly. When I rung the
doorbell, I heard all this running around. "David's coming!

David's coming!" The door opened. . . . A nice apartment. Beautiful! Everything was all of a sudden so quiet, and here I was, sitting
there and wondering who all these kids were. Over to my left sat
one of my sisters, sketching some sort of Bugs Bunny rabbit that
they advertise in magazines — you know, "Learn to Be an Artist:
Sketch This!" My brother was sitting next to her, and all these
other people are sitting there. "Are you my brother?" I made the
first question. And he said, "Yeah!" So then I went around the
room and asked for everyone's name. Two hours later, one of my
older brothers and his wife walked in with a baby. He grabbed
me — "David! My brother! My little brother!" Patted me on the
head, and all that stuff. We started talking, and I'm actually —
what do you call it? — an uncle to the daughter he has. Then, here
comes Carlos — the so-called black sheep of the family. He came
in and grabbed me and kissed me on my forehead. And when he
took off his shirt, I saw all these muscles and everything. He sort of
play-punched me on my shoulder, and it hurt! This guy was tre-
mendously built.

We sat down and ate dinner, and I was the slowest person to eat
something because I wanted to enjoy it. They was all — wow, can-
nibals! I'd never seen this before. "Hurry up! Hurry up! You're
slow." Then here come my sister walking in with this big white
box — big ribbon on top and everything. Soon as she opened it,
they laid it on the table and sung "Happy Birthday" and everything. My mother kept arguing with my sister about how she
turned the cake upside down in the box so that all the icing came
off. And you could see on the inside of the box it says, "Happy
Birthday David Torres!" I said, "Don't worry about it. I'm having
the best birthday of my life."

Me and my sister — I don't know, we sort of felt attached to one
another. She was having problems with my mother, and she understood what happened to me and everything. She started pulling
me away from my mother and the crowd. She took me to meet her
friends that night and we hung out on Fourteenth Street. Wow!
Fourteenth Street!

Then the night was over. Back to the foster home. It hurt. I was saying to myself, "*This* is my home. Why do I gotta go?" So that's when things started happening. After a couple of weeks visiting and sleeping over at my mother's — getting to know them more — I started feeling attached. You know, this is my *family*. The people back at the group home in Queens was still abusing me, beating me up and everything, so I picked up my things and went over to my mother's. There was a lot of pressure with her, and one night I slept in the park cause we had a fight. After spending the night away I called home and she said, "David, come home!" I told her, "No! Y'all going to surround me with all these cops and everyone looking for me." I walked in her door and everything was all right. Then, here comes all these police cars — I'm running through a plate glass window out the backyard. These cops chased me and grabbed me and put me in the car and took me to a psychiatric doctor at Elmhurst. The doctor told them, "This boy does not need psychiatric care. He's just having family problems." Three times of running back to my mother. Then came the night of me actually getting locked up, which was July 19, 1976.

See, I've always been involved helping people. Any crime — if I see something, I'll tell the cops. Help ladies cross the street. Carry packages. . . . I had a radio scanner that picks up police calls. Got a call there's a lady down on 169th Street and Hillside Avenue. I got there before the cops, before the ambulance. The lady was drunk — cut up on her face like she had got into a fist fight, but she refused medical treatment. She was thirty-four, about the same age as my mother. The police left, and then she asked me to help her cross the street and show her the way to a bathroom. I tried walking her into different places and they wouldn't accept her. I was ready to leave her, but something came into my mind that I needed money. I had a job and everything — I knew I had money — but I told myself I needed extra cash. I hit her on the neck, very quickly, and before you know it I had one dead corpse on my hands. It happened in minutes. Felt her pulse and there was nothing.

I never had a criminal record in my life. Never stole a candy bar. Nothing.... I dumped her bags all over the place. Took my Boy Scout belt, put it around her neck and just slightly tightened it and left it there so the police would think that it was strangulation. Then I went home. Left my scanner on, so I heard all the detectives going to the scene. They were all there — DOA. I took a shower, changed my clothes, combed my hair, brushed my teeth, went out the door, went back to the scene. My plan was to mess with the cops' brains.

"We just left this lady a few minutes ago at 169th Street," I tell them.

"How do you know it's that lady?"

"Oh, isn't this the one?" And that's when I gave myself away, because how am I supposed to know that's the same lady that was at 169th Street without even looking at the corpse?

Sitting in the detective car at the scene of the crime, one detective came in and questioned me. "What did this lady do last that you remember?"

"Okay. I saw her walking up Hillside Avenue with her thumb out, and this car came over and picked her up and the license plate number was...." I kept giving them the same number all the time.

"What kind of car?"

"I don't know." The same thing over and over.

Then he said, "You don't mind if we take you to the precinct, do you?"

"No, I don't care. My parents won't mind."

"Do you want us to call them?"

"Yeah, sure."

When I got to the precinct — wow! The supervisor from the group home was already there. He said, "How you doing, David?"

"I'm okay." It was so cool and cold outside. Some sort of breeze was blowing. Twelve o'clock when I got there, and I was questioned all night.

The cop offered me a glass of soda. I drunk it and ate a bagel, and he took me downstairs to another room. Just the detective, the group parent supervisor, and me. So then he said, "David, now I'm going to get serious with you. Enough of all this playing now. Did you or did you not kill that woman?"

I said, "No, I didn't!"

"David, get serious! I took your fingerprints off the cup upstairs." And right there I bursted out into tears and everything. He said, "Your fingerprints were all over the car that the body was found next to, and the fingerprints matched the ones on that cup upstairs."

I bursted into tears. Right there I said yes I had killed her. I didn't want to be punished. I just wanted a way out of all the bad treatment I was getting. In my Bureau of Child Welfare record it described me as loveable, kind, and obedient — all those things that people weren't to me. I wanted out totally, so I wouldn't have to come back to beatings or go through the same circle again. It's like asking the community or society, "Just take me! Do whatever you want, but take me away from these people!"

The papers were processed, and by 5:30 in the morning, I was walking through the gates of Spofford Prison. They put me in a single room about eight feet wide and ten feet long. A bed. Little table next to you. That's it. No bars on the window — just this tough screen. When I came in, everybody was just getting up for a shower, getting cleaned up for breakfast. I was so hungry — I wanted more, but there was so little on that plate. Then some lady said, "All right, let's go to recreation!" I was so tired.

We got on line, went to the gym, stayed there for hours. I kept asking them, "Can I get some sleep? I'm so tired." I didn't want to play basketball or nothing. I was zonked. Killed someone twelve hours ago. Been up all night. I was just — I wasn't really awake.... Lunchtime. Then, "Line up! Let's go outside!" I sat around looking at the sun. Finally, night came. I went straight to bed. I cried for mercy. I prayed....

The court hearing was just words — passing papers back and

forth. They showed Exhibit A — the belt. That was it. I was no killer. I could have gone back into society and be changed already, but I didn't want to go back where I came from. I begged my lawyer, "No jail setting!" He told me he was gonna try to get me into a psychiatric facility, and on November twentieth I got placed at Creedmore Psychiatric Center.

The first day I got to Creedmore, I had three visitors — my boss from the Storefront Museum, his girlfriend, and the guy that was training me to be his assistant in electronics. They brung me a certificate, a citation from the Mayor: "On behalf of all New Yorkers, we want to thank you for your cooperation with the New York Fire Department for helping to reduce false alarms in your community and others. On behalf of all New Yorkers — Abraham D. Beame." I cried. I felt a kind of joy because they said, "You were supposed to go down to City Hall and appear in front of television and receive this from the Mayor. Luckily, he doesn't know you're in here, or you wouldn't be getting it."

Creedmore was nice. I kept the murder quiet. That was a secrecy done better than Watergate. I felt safe there. My nightmares went away. It was luxurious compared to the group home. Better food. A swimming pool. I felt more open. Got along better — less fighting. It was all right. I learnt a great deal of my childhood Spanish back. All the foster homes had made me speak English, and when I would speak Spanish I wouldn't say the right things. The words would be jumbled and not understandable. Up to today I'm still learning. My grandmother does not speak English, and I made a promise to her — "Before you pass away, I'm gonna have a perfect conversation in Spanish."

In Creedmore they gave me a great birthday party — oooh-oooh! I didn't know how to dance before I went there. I didn't know the Hustle or anything, but now I'm a superstar. They gave me a disco party — live DJ and everything. At that time the new dance was the Freak. So I was out there doin the Freak, and here comes — oh, my God! — all these girls just circled me and nearly smothered me, man, doin the Freak around me. And everybody clapping. I'd never had a girlfriend in my life, and here were all these girls leadin me to the bathroom. I figured I got a long time ahead of me — I'd better go get it while I've got the chance.

I was elected chairman of the TC — Therapy Community Meeting. The unit chief, head doctor, everyone said I was a leader. I got really interested in new skills — carpentry — I made a tremendous improvement. I know my tools. I know how to use them. I know safety. I became shop foreman. I built one of the most biggest projects that was ever built in any of them shops — a four-door cabinet.

The day I finished at Creedmore — oh, wow! They released me and sent me to the welfare center. Gave me an emergency check to pay the rent and food. Welfare had a room reserved for me — sent me to an SRO at 222 Riverside Drive between Ninety-fifth and Ninety-fourth. I looked at the place — I don't know, I got disgusted. Right away I got depressed. I didn't have no friends. I had a check which could not be cashed because I didn't have no ID card. No food. Nothin. It was an experience that can't be explained. Roaches! I saw mice go by. I hear all this glass breaking. People fighting. I couldn't go to sleep. There was a bathroom, but they were all inoperative. I went to McDonald's to take a shit — lucky they were open all night — and once I got outside I went down to the subway. Didn't even have money for a token. Told the cop, "Let me on the train! I'm going to the hospital!" And before you know it, I was walking through the doors of Creedmore.

This time they sent someone with me and took me here. I slept on the floor the first two days because the springs didn't have no mattress, but everything looked nice. It was a new floor, new linoleum and dresser. The locks don't count — had to install one myself. It was a cold, cold winter. I remember that. I stayed in my room a lot and did a lot of thinking. I said to myself that I've got to look at things differently — got to look for my mother or grandmother or something. I was sitting there in bed one night, just sitting there daydreaming, and I remembered a foggish night, a light rotating, and I remembered a bridge. So then one day — just by curiosity, coming home from somewhere — I stayed on the train and went all the way up to see if I remembered any of the stops. The train came out into the light — I saw these big projects — and then the train went back into the tunnel. This was in my dreams, even in some of my nightmares — getting out of the tunnel and the train falling over. It was Harlem, the 125th Street area, and I was actually following my dream. I took it all the way to 181st Street. I got off the subway, and what did I see? The bridge with the light on top — it was the George Washington Bridge. So then I remembered another thing — these big red letters — 804. So I walked up the block and rang the doorbell. . . . There was my grandmother!

Staying in the hotel began to be a little easier once I knew I had family uptown. A lot better, as a matter of fact. My money came from SSI. They tried to find me work, but I refused. I mean, no one's going to want to work right away after being confined for so long. "I want time to relax," I said. "Time to enjoy what freedom I got!"

I didn't know what summer was like. When the weather changed, it was nice, you know — my first summer on my own. I woke up as soon as the sun came through the window. I would sit there and smoke what little cigarettes I had, and then wait for the meal downstairs so I could eat a good breakfast. Then I would go walking. I wouldn't say nothing, because I didn't know nobody — plus I'm the type of person that before I get involved in a crowd, I have to really see what that crowd is like because I don't want to get involved in a bad mess or whatever. So I would go out — just go walking on Broadway. Walk more mileage than a car runs on a can of gasoline. Go to the park, sit there looking at the squirrels, checking out the birds, you know. One time there was a whole swarm of birds around me, eating. And people were looking at me — this kid's in the middle of the bird field and they're not bothering him. I was just sitting there, checking them out. A nice summer.

Every weekend I'd go to my grandmother's house and take a bath. I'd never take a bath at the hotel. Never. Would you like to take a bath or shower in a rusted tub that doesn't have no water? There were a couple on some of the floors that worked, but I really didn't feel safe cause there were no locks on the doors. I tried to spend as little time in the hotel as I could. Everyone was doin drugs and wine. A bad crowd. Everyone was involved in every little mischief that they can. And I was the youngest one in the building. I was only nineteen.

I did my best to make friends. I can walk in a crowd of people and crack jokes all day. No one knows me in that crowd, but I make myself known. . . . A funny thing happened to me the other day — I was walking with my friend and he said, "Hey, watch out for that hole!" I said, "What h-o-o-o-o-o-le?" You get it? I had this other good one — people have been telling me, "You don't stop until you're asleep at night." I said, "Funny thing you should mention that. I walked upstairs last night, turned off the light switch, took off my clothes, and jumped into bed before the room could get dark. . . ."

Wasn't long before everything that I spent my money on was stolen. CB, my stereo system — they broke in over the top of the door and walked off with the little I have. This is the kinda place — during my first summer this guy had just got out of a mental institution. Really bugged out. They didn't want him in the hotel, so what they did was they threw him out a window — out a seventh-floor window — and he died. I know who the people who threw him out was, but it's just a dumb thing to do. I mean, what did it prove? If it's against the law, then you know not to do it. I'm a law person. I've stayed very attached to the law, but that don't make life any easier here. This place is an animal house. Unpredictable. There's really nothing that you can say good about this or any SRO because the same stuff goes on in all of them. Drinking. Money dealing. Drug dealing. Maybe ninety-nine percent take drugs. I'm the only one in the building don't want any of this. It's just a whole — it's one community, and I don't want any part of it.

You should see it on Check Day. Mailman gets here about

eleven, and everybody is down on line at ten thirty so they can be
first to get it. That's the biggest drug weekend. Heaviest wine
drinking weekend. Weekend where a lot of fights happen because
people owe people money and don't pay them. Then comes the
beating up and everything. That's why I have a radio. I just zero
that out. But sometimes when the radio's not on — late, late at
night — I hear the first wine bottle fall. BANG! That's the first
one. After that you hear a whole lot of them. DING! DING! Every
so often. They're all crazy.

To tell you the truth, it comes to my mind sometime, death, you
know. People ask me, "How come you're thinking about death at
such an early age?" Hey! Anything could happen here. Anytime.
So I sit here thinking. I want to live to be 150. No, make it 200.
And I want to stay young. Never grow old. And if I could turn the
clock back, I would go all the way back to . . . which was the best
years of my life? . . . To sixteen years old — my first year at Creedmore.

The money situation is pretty tough now that prices is goin up.
SSI gives me $270 a month. A hundred forty goes for rent, so I
gotta live on four dollars a day. Every little bit of money I get goes
towards food and cigarettes. I take a dollar, go to the pizzeria —
one slice and a small soda. Or go to the store, buy me three Devil
dogs and a Sunkist soda. Stuff myself whenever I can. I always run
out of money, and no one wants to lend. Everything is for yourself.
I go along with what little I have. I've tried to move outa here —
looked in the *Village Voice* under apartment sharing. But so far,
they're asking too much. I've gotta keep within reasonable money
range. Also, the landlord looks at me — "How many brothers and
sisters are going to move in with you?" I look too young, so he'll
say, "How come your mother can't be here with you?" That's
rough. If I could get outa here — if I could find a decent place
where I could put an antenna on the roof — I would fix it up, I
would guard it like pride, I would do everything just to keep it.

If they're gonna keep putting kids in these hotels, I'd make a

lotta changes. Before he gets out of jail or the hospital, I would
have a decent SRO room waitin for him. Completely secured. Not
a cheap door, cheap locks. Everything waitin for him. If he's gettin
out of a psychiatric institution, his SSI should already be at the
bank waitin for him. If he's getting outa jail, have welfare papers
already processed — photo ID already made — so there won't be
no hassles, no lines to go through. And the social work place
downstairs — I think that should be a little safer and nicer. Instead
of a cramped office, have a whole unit. Having a dining room, not
one of these small off-the-stove-onto-the-plate set-ups. Get a full-
time TV room. You know, get something worthwhile and have the
staff to monitor it. Utilize the schools if you have to. There's a
school right up the block, and it's empty on weekends when a lot of
people here go hungry. Have all these things waitin to help people
when they move into the hotel. And from there I would assign one
counselor or one probation officer to try to gradually bring him
back into the outer world. That's what we call it when you're
locked up, you know — "Oh, check out what happened in the *outer
world!*" It's always the outer world — everything that people don't
know about, don't see. You gotta get a person gradually involved.
If he has a goal to reach, don't let him try and do it on his own because it's just a whole lotta frustration.

But you can't let things get you down. I live in this corroded
building. People are rotten. I can't let that get me down. I mean,
I'm young; here I am with twenty, thirty more years ahead of me.
It's like the man who jumped off the Empire State Building, you
know. A guy saw him falling past the fortieth floor and asked him
how he was doin. The guy looks back and yells up to him — cause
he's fallin pretty fast, see — "So far so g-o-o-o-o-o-o-o-d!" he says.
That's sorta what it's like. I wonder sometimes how things woulda
turned out if I was rich. Like with my parents around and a nice
house and a decent school and stuff. But that kinda thinking don't
really getchya nowhere except maybe more unhappy. So what can
I say . . . So far, so good. So far, so good. . . .

STREET SCENE

Mattress, charred and smoldering, out on the sidewalk beside the hotel entrance. Black and ashy, broken open to burnt springs and bits of singed fluff. Penetrating noxious smoke spills down the block in thick billows. People pause and stare as if it were something else — a corpse or ruined building, a devastated city seen from some great height.

SHIT

Benny smells awful. He's unshaven, filthy, in total disarray. Retarded, with a speech impediment to boot. "Yuh wanna talk tuh duh lady?" he says when I knock on the door to Muriel's living unit. Yes, I tell him, and he leads me to Muriel's door, hunched and shuffling like a horror-movie servant.

"I try to be nice to him," Muriel tells me. "He's hard to understand, so most people won't bother with him. He'll come and knock on my door to say hello, and I'll try to make him feel good. You know, say something friendly, be pleasant for a minute or two. He appreciates it so. He's like a little boy really. He doesn't take very good care of himself. I don't know what he does about food, but he always seems well fed. I don't think he could get much further than McDonald's without getting lost. There's so little he's able to do, and still, he looks in on me. I think he's happy someone smiles at him and gives him a little attention."

We're about twenty minutes into my visit when the hotel handyman comes by to fix the lock on Muriel's door. "I don't understand," she muses. "I bought this new lock myself, and now none of my keys seem to fit." The handyman goes about his task, jiggling each key unsuccessfully.

"None of these work, lady. You musta done somethin with the key."

"Now what could I have done?" Muriel's voice wafts her into that peculiar space she inhabits — an eccentric aunt retiring to the attic.

The repairman seems peeved by her wistfulness. "It smells awful here," he says. "Someone's been messing." He stares at her, expecting some reply. Muriel has nothing to say. He abandons the lock and follows the smell to the kitchen unit Muriel shares with Benny and Mr. Winslow. There's a decent sink, a large plastic trash basket, and a greasy second-hand stove with a few knobs missing. "Look at that! Disgusting!" He raises the lid of the trash basket. "Shit all over! Disgusting!"

He returns to Muriel's room. "Shit in the kitchen!" he declares. "You can't breathe in there, an I gotta clean it up. You know who's been doin it?"

"I'm afraid I can't help you."

Benny shuffles past on one of his frequent patrols of Muriel's door. "Is it Benny?" the repairman asks. He's already made up his mind. Mr. Winslow is fastidious. Muriel, in spite of her periodic fuzziness, is a lady. Benny it is.

"Benny! Benny!" the guy barks. "You shit in the kitchen?"

Benny shakes his head. "Uh-uh," he mumbles. "Uhy dinnint do nothin."

"Benny, look at this!" He leads him into the kitchen and lifts the garbage lid. "Shit all over!" The smell is wretched, but Benny sticks his head up close to examine it. Shit smeared and stinking all over the container. "Benny, you can't shit in here! It's disgusting, and I gotta clean it up."

"Uhy dinnint do nothin."

"Come on over here." He strides to the other end of the corridor. Benny follows doggedly, pleased by the unexpected attention. "This is where you shit!" He points to the bathroom. "Benny, you gotta use the toilet like everyone else. I'm not gonna come in here every day and — uuuuuuggh!" Shit, splattered diarrhea, all over the toilet seat, toilet bowl, smeared inside the toilet lid.

Benny stands by the bathroom door staring at the handyman, staring at the toilet, waiting for an explanation, a scolding, or threat—waiting to hear his name again so he can smile and listen and make what he can of the precious, puzzling words. But this time the handyman just shakes his head and walks away. Shit is overtaking him, engulfing him. He can remove Benny and it will still be there. Muriel and Mr. Winslow can leave, and there will still be shit to clean up. Piss in the elevators, vomit in wastebaskets, dead pets, a fetus once, mess of blood and brains to swab when people hurl themselves down into the courtyard — but it is shit, everyday shit, that is most a part of this place: loose shit of alcoholics; shit from days on end of canned soup; shit from undigested dog food — desperate old people, hungry and poor, spooning it cold from the can; shit of junkies; bloody smelly shit; shit of suffering, of humiliation, and despair. Stink and mess of life — but life still. Still life.

CHECK DAY

> Oh Lord!
> Oh Lord!
> Take me to Paradise
>
> Got my mm-mm-mm
> Got my mm-mm-mm
> Be some dancin in the street
>
> Oh Lord!
> Oh Lord!
> Gonna jump this window and fly

BOOKS

Fine Spring day. Around the corner on Broadway, Bobby Carman has set up shop. Two large plastic trash bags torn apart and spread in front of the hardware store; thirty paperbacks laid out in neat rows. *The Group, Summer of '42, The Crash of '79, Bullet Park, Nightwork,* Hammond Inness, Robert Ludlum, a few World War II histories, and a bunch of lurid titles like *Fast Friends, Newcomer,* and *Daphne Goes Wild!* "Hey, Bobby! Bobby!" a man calls. Braided hair; Indian headband across his forehead.

Bobby waves. "I can't leave my books! Come on over here!"

Candy, his name is; a sweet, attractive man in his forties. "That looks nice," he says, inspecting the display. He pronounces *nice* with breathy emphasis, the way a male impersonator might do Marilyn Monroe.

"Five for a dollar," Bobby says. "Twenty-five cents if you buy em single."

"Fine me a love story, Bobby. I want a love story that'll make me cry."

"*Summer of '42,* now where'd that go? . . ."

"Ah'll tell you somethin," Candy confides, "Ah go to *pieces* over a good love story. Ah read this one book, an ah jus cried my eyes out. Ah'll tell you the truth, honey, ah'm half Indian an ah'm gay. Ah've been married twelve years now — ain't that right, Bobby? — an when ah read this one love story ah started cryin; got up on mah man an we made it together. It was beautiful! Beautiful! Cryin about that love story and makin it with mah man. Fine me a good love story, Bobby. Ah wanna cry my eyes out."

"Comin up." Bobby rubs his chin as he peruses his stock. Old maroon blazer, threadbare at the elbows; he looks very bookish, very professional. "You want sex or love?"

"You jus fine me a book that makes me cry. Ah'll be honest with you. Ah'm forty-eight; ah'm not pretty the way I used to be. Ah gotta read about all the things ah wanna do."

"How about *The Group?*"

Candy rejects the plain cover, reaching instead for *Party-Girl.* On its stained cover a slutty young woman in a torn nightie cringes at the feet of a tee-shirted man who hovers over her with a liquor bottle and a knotted fist. "Now this one turns me on!" Candy says laughing. "Tell him, Bobby, tell him how ah been married twelve years."

"I been in this shithole nine years," Bobby testifies, "and you were here when I started."

"An tell him, Bobby, tell him jus cause ah'm black an gay don't mean ah been in any trouble. Ah got Indian pride."

Bobby nods.

"Ah used to work; ah used to go out an fine me somethin to do — but now there's no jobs, an ah'm black besides. Ah got nothin to do, an a lotta time to do it in. Come on, Bobby honey, you fine me a nice love story...."

FAMILY

David and I are walking down West End Avenue. "See that?" he says on the corner of Ninety-eighth Street. "I think that's the woman with the black Corvette." I look down the familiar street and have no idea what he's talking about. "I seen her car parked here a couple of times, so I think it must be her." He's pointing to a ten-foot antenna on top of the building. "Her name is Shorty. I been tryin to figure out where her antenna is. She says she's divorced, lives alone in the neighborhood. Twenty-two years old and she rides a black Corvette. And I've been lookin . . . I seen a black Corvette one time — had a CB antenna and everything on it, and the license said SHORTY — but I couldn't get her to stop."

"That's En Conica," he says after another block. "We jaw over the Spanish-speaking station. And down there's Leprechaun." I've never noticed CB antennas before, but now the rooftops seem filled with them. "There's my man," he continues, "Space Cherokee. That's a coupla thousand dollars he's put in that. Spins 360 degrees like radar." The apparatus is four blocks away on Columbus, mounted on a twenty-story building. It looks big and expensive. "If I had that, I could hit Europe with no trouble. You know, I was once called the Power House in this area. I mean, when I would talk, if you had a CB and didn't hear me you was deaf. I was doin all kinds of illegal stuff — linear amplifiers, illegal microphones, illegal wiring — if the FCC would have caught me, you would have seen me in the front headlines. . . .

"When I build my next transmitter — if I could, if I would be accepted — I'd live with my mother. I offered her money to live with her, but she doesn't like radios at all. She only watches the boob tube. If I could live with her, I'd be home twenty-four hours a day, since she lives right there on Coney Island. I'd set up a station strong enough to shoot across the water to Europe. I'm serious. It's been done from Montauk Point, which is the closest point to Europe. Get an infrared beam and put it on a 700-foot tower and point it towards Europe. Sit around talking to France and England and Spain. If I could live with her, I'd get my antenna set up and no one can tell me you won't talk to Europe. But she's still getting on my case. If she didn't know better, she would still try and hit me.

"One reason I gotta get outa here and get a place of my own is here I can't even put up a CB. All my life I've been talking to a CB, but management claims I'm interfering with television reception, so they cut my cable. I used to sit here talking DX all day — that means distance. One late night in my room I spoke to central Oklahoma. We started talking back and forth, started giving each other's address, before all this interference got in the way.

"All my friends, everyone that I know now, I met them on CB radio. Check out the rooftops," David says. "It's a city within a city. Thousands of em — rich and poor, men and women; they got blacks, Puerto Ricans, Jews, guys down in Chinatown — you name it. I know their brothers and sisters, wives and cousins — all of em. Check it out — it's a city within a city — a family."

MOTHER'S DAY

Benny slouches before Muriel's door, grey tongue spread out on his lower lip like a fat slug come out to sun. "Get away! I don't need you!" Muriel scolds. "Stop following me, Benny! I don't want you all over me!"

"He's so damn stupid!" She tugs a purple topcoat over her nightgown. Scowling. Perplexed. Bad day. Her purse is missing; she can't imagine what's become of it. She crawls over her bed, digging in crumpled covers and heaps of clothes. "I always try to keep it out of sight, but it appears I put it out of my sight too. Well, you know — out of sight out of mind." She smiles at her little joke. "It's my ID cards I'm worried about. It takes so long to replace them. I recall all the information — AD, that means 'disabled,' 2016498-1. The one is because it's only myself. I know my number, but that's not the same as having my card."

Her clock radio clicks on with Perez Prado's rendition of "Harbor Lights." Rinky-tink cha-cha organ music, perfect for an ice-skating rink. Muriel limps about the room, continuing her search. "Why, there's my dinner!" Two small steaks and a packet of Bird's Eye Oriental Rice on the window sill. "That must mean I went right to sleep," she reasons. "Yes, yes, of course that's right! I went to the Red Apple yesterday afternoon. Doc saw me on the street and helped me with my bags. I gave him a beer and I was so knocked out I crawled into bed and went to sleep." She nods thoughtfully. "So I must have had my purse yesterday. In view of the fact that I keep my keys in my purse, in view of the fact that I needed my keys to let myself in, I must have had my purse. . . . Why of course!" she exclaims with mounting excitement, "My shopping is here, my medicine is here, *I'm* here. I must have let myself in! I'll ask Mr. Winslow. Maybe he can tell me something."

Mr. Winslow is right outside the door, padding about bare-
footed. Leather cap, black turtleneck, and ragged underwear with
his testicles poking through. "How, I say, howya doin?" he asks.
Muriel slams her door.

"I told the handyman two weeks ago," Muriel says. "My door
doesn't lock; we have to fix it, I told him. And he goes, 'Uh, uh, uh,
uh, don't worry about it; nobody's gonna bother you.' And all
these people creeping around here! ... I'm sure I had my purse
when I came home from the Red Apple. The only time I left the
room after that was to use the toilet. It wouldn't flush and I filled
my red kettle with water — back and forth 100 times to clear it
out. There wasn't time for anyone to slip into my room then. It
must've happened when I was sleeping. Yes, that's it! They waited
till I was fast asleep and entered my room very quietly. . . ."

Her voice trails off. She stares at the map of New York on her
wall, shaking her head in a brown study. Beside her window a
shopping bag hangs from a nail. Muriel snaps from her trance and
reaches up to investigate it. "Hmmmmm — needlework." She ex-
amines the unfinished crocheting as though she's never seen it before. "This could be important. Now let me see. . . . Saturday; it
was Saturday. . . ." She limps to the dresser, studies her face in the
mirror, and runs a comb through her hair. "Saturday!" she
exclaims in a spirit of luminous discovery. She tosses the comb
aside and finds her calendar. "Yes! Yes! Saturday, and — oh,
my! — today is Mother's Day! Isn't that nice! And it's only been
a day since Saturday. Do you think I might have misplaced my
bag?"

Muriel steps into the corridor to check the kitchen trash barrel.
Benny shuffles past, cradling his cock in both hands. He marches
to the toilet where he pees with the door wide open, child's smile
breaking across his face as he sprays on the toilet seat and against
the wall. In the kitchen Mr. Winslow is frying a huge piece of
meat. "I'm gonna, I'm gonna eat it all," he declares. When Muriel
opens the trash barrel the stink of shit is overwhelming, but Mr.
Winslow whistles a tune. He doesn't seem to notice.

Muriel limps back to her room. "If someone took my bag, they wouldn't want the IDs," she says. "They'd keep the money, but they might just throw my bag out the window. Why, of course! I should have thought of that before!" Each new possibility delights her, yet the purpose of her search seems to recede as her enthusiasm increases. She leans out the window and peers into the littered courtyard. Soggy newspapers, smashed bottles, an "I Love New York" sweatshirt, a baby carriage, and — "Why look at that! A purse! No, two purses. There's another on the fire escape! Isn't that something!" Neither one is Muriel's. "Theme from *The Sting*" concludes, followed by "See You in September." The volume shoots up suddenly, though Muriel has not gone near her radio. "I'll try Doc," she decides. "He may remember something."

"'Everyone here is missing something," she says in the elevator. A few floors up, a young black guy pops in, orange comb poking from his Afro, fresh red rose in his lapel. "Happy Mother's Day!" Muriel says.

"I'm blessed," he replies. "My Momma's still livin."

On the seventh floor Muriel knocks on the door to Doc's unit. "Yeah?" a woman's voice croaks from the other side.

"Is Doc there?"

"Dot? We ain't got no Dot on this floor."

"DOC! Is Doc there?"

"We ain't go no one by that name either."

"Wait a minute," a muffled voice calls from the background. "That's what some people call me."

"He's comin," the woman says.

"Thank you," Muriel answers. "Happy Mother's Day!"

"God bless you, darlin!"

Doc opens the door in new loafers, wool socks, and a soiled Boy Scout shirt. Nappy hair, grey beard, and metal-frame glasses. Tired, serious face — like a doctor's. "Happy Mother's Day!" Muriel says.

"Why thank you, Muriel. I meant to look in on you this morning."

"I can't find my purse. Do you remember seeing it yesterday?"

"I think so. It was in your grocery bag. You took it out to fetch your keys. Then you set it on your bed when we had our beer."

"I wonder where it went." Her voice floats off, bemused, as though pondering the disappearance from our planet of elves and druids.

"And I wonder where my food stamps went," Doc says. "They disappeared last week. I'll tell you, there's too much of this goin on here. I'm sorry I can't do more to help."

"Well, you've been most generous with your time." She sounds like some Park Avenue matron making door-to-door calls for charity. "Happy Mother's Day!"

The elevator descends one floor where Muriel is joined by a young woman and Ralph, the man who thinks he shot Frank Sinatra. "Hiya, Muriel!" Ralph's eyes are weird and bulging beneath his thick glasses. "Howya doin?"

"More or less," she replies.

"Well, I'd like to give you more," he quips, "but you say you want less." He's greatly pleased with his joke.

"That's a good one," his companion says. "I heard it on 'Sanford and Son.'"

He cracks a big smile. "It's dirty, you know. No offense, Muriel."

"Oh, I appreciate a good laugh. There's so much sorrow in the world. My, my, we're here on my floor already. Happy Mother's Day! Happy Mother's Day to all of you!"

ARGUMENTS

"DAVID! HEY, DAVID! DAVID, LET US IN!" Frankie, the desk clerk, pounds on David's door, smashes with his fist. Music blares inside, but no sign of any activity. Three good locks keep David safe, plus a small sticker: THIS ROOM PROTECTED BY POLICE ALARM. "Could be out; could be dead," Frankie tells me. "They die so often it don't bother me no more."

Summery weather today. Flower pots out on sloping window sills: spider plants, rubber plants — the ordinary Woolworth's selection. Mop poking from a fifth-floor window. Woman in a turquoise work uniform peering down at the street. Ironsides cruising the block in his electric wheelchair, walking his lanky weimaraner. The dog relieves itself on the sidewalk.

David and I were supposed to meet this morning. I go back upstairs for a second try. Same loud music, same silence when I knock.

"I heard you," he says that evening, "but I thought they might be foolin me to open the door." David's room is small and tidy — new linoleum floor, day bed with leopard-skin fabric and bolsters, Muppet Movie poster, magazine rack in the center of the floor filled with *Hi-Fi* and *Gentleman's Quarterly,* all in their designated places. David's at a small desk. Six packs of Newport lined on a narrow shelf like little books. Young doberman curled in a corner.

"I didn't know you had a dog," I say.

"Yeah. She was parta the problem. This woman said Lady attacked her. They was bangin on my door till four in the morning, sayin they'd kill me and everything. I heard you this morning — I'm sorry, but I didn't wanna open the door." He tells me how it happened. It was warm last night — the first burst of summer — and Hotel Walden residents spilled onto the street to drink and bullshit and be free of their stuffy rooms. "I was standin out there watchin," David says, "and this woman tells me I'm in her way. She was completely stoned. She didn't know what she was doin. I kinda backed off, but she kept pressin me, yellin an sayin what she's gonna do to me. You know, I try to stay outa trouble, but this lady was so stoned, she wouldn't leave me alone. I don't know, somethin snaps when someone treats me like that. I'm little, right? Well, I just picked her up and pinned her against the wall. I don't even know how I did it — I mean, I didn't know I was doin it. It's like she's yellin at me, then BANG! I'm holdin her arms against the wall. An my dog — Lady's barkin, all excited, showin her teeth an stuff.

"After that's when it got bad. I came back here an lay down, an she got some of her friends and tried to break down the door. Bangin an yellin an tellin me what they're gonna do to me. I called the cops at four an they warned her an took her name, but I wasn't gonna answer the door for nobody this mornin."

He sips Coke and picks at a plate of fried chicken as he talks. He takes a bite or two and chucks a piece to Lady. "That's another thing," he says while the dog pulverizes the chicken bone. "I hadda get someone to take my meal ticket an bring this up to me. They won't let me in the clinic no more." The outreach clinic office, with its crowded alcove and food service area, is one of the few places where David feels relatively secure. "It was stupid," he says. "I was standin there talkin to Marsha, my social worker, an another social worker came in an pushed the door. It hit me an I pushed it back a little; so this worker pushed it back on me. We did this — pushin the door back an forth — an then Marsha tells me to stop. She saw who started it, but now she's yellin at me like she's my parents or somethin. Nobody's got the right to do that. I got my own parents. I've had enough of them — I don't need no more."

"So you argued with her."

"You can't let nobody push you around here. You don't stand up to em, they gonna walk all over you. I'm small. I wanna stay outa that stuff, but you push me hard enough an somethin snaps."

"Marsha is your friend. You told me how much you like her."

"Yeah." He shakes his head slowly, "but she says I can't come in there again. Anyhow, that lady from last night, she says she's gonna bring friends tonight — knives an guns to get me. I got my cousin in there speakin to her now, tryin to tell her we ain't got no reason to fight. She was so stoned, she don't know what she said to me. I'm gonna stay right in this room tonight, keep my door locked till mornin.

DOOR SIGNS

```
Daddy
Daddy
        Tony
        Funky #3
```

```
RALPH       Love
-N-         Always
ROBIN       by
            Robin
```

```
You Are
Parked Here
Illegally
```

```
Nail Em All
```

```
Please Do Not
Kill This Tree
```

SNAPSHOTS

"You shoulda seen it," Doug says. "Twelve quarts of Old English — fucked ourselves up pretty good last night." "As the World Turns" is droning. Pot roast cooking in the Toast-R-Oven. Kittens scratching for attention. Doug and Bobby — shaky, pale; washed-out faces soft with exhaustion.

"H-e-e-e-y," Bobby says, "you gonna r-o-o-o-a-s-t some potatoes with that meat?"

"We got some Rice-a-Roni I'll throw in."

"Rice-a-Roni! R-i-i-i-ce-a-Roni!" He slaps five with his brother.

Strung out like this, Bobby passes through a kind of time warp, sinking further into his stoned slouch, pulling his mellow croaking voice from deeper and deeper in his throat. "H-e-e-e-y, you know Rice-a-Roni is g-o-o-o-o-d shit. You dig? I m-e-e-e-a-n, I seen the ads on television — 'the San Francisco treat!' They got h-e-r-r-r-b-s and sp-i-i-i-c-e-s an shit. Hey, I mean they got their fuckin Rice-a-Roni act together." Bobby digs into a plastic cup, looking for a good butt.

"Did I ever show you our snapshots?" Doug takes out a small cardboard box. "Here you go." He hands me the first photo: himself out on 100th Street, seated on a car fender near the bodega. Blue hat on his head, a joint poking from the worn band. Frisbee perched on top of the hat. Doug's head tilted back, eyes rolled upward, trying to catch a glimpse of his pet.

Next, a series of shots from Indian River. Palm trees. Orange groves. The two brothers sprawled out on lounge chairs by their father's pool. Lazy, well fed — Junior Chamber of Commerce Republicans. Bobby a good forty pounds heavier. Doug, too, carrying extra weight from easy days in Florida. Their father sits with them for a few group portraits. Bearded robust man, face relaxed, comfortably retired.

Black and white 8 x10 glossy from Vietnam. "CAM BINH 1966 — 115 °" written on the back. Army camp emptiness. Two young black guys sitting on crates, catching the scant shade of a ramshackle bunkhouse. Drinking beer. Faces glazed with boredom. A deep trench in the foreground; Doug standing in it, shoulder deep, clean white tee-shirt and crisp chinos. Fourteen years ago — just a pudgy eighteen-year-old boy, crewcut and grinning. "M-a-a-a-n!" Bobby croaks, "all these guys got blown away." He spreads his arms and shrugs. "Standin in the wrong spot, dig, wrong spot at the wrong fuckin time." Into his rhythm, words simply come. "Soldiers, man, poor fuckin soldiers. . . . Hup, hup, hup — BLOOOM! . . . One second an there ain't no one left but Dougie. Ain't that right, Doug?" Doug stares at "As the World Turns." Cocktail party. Someone spills a drink. Tipsy nurse making a pass at a shy intern. Everyone looks quite well. "Vietnam was one big casino," Bobby says. "One big casino, yeah. Lose, and you ain't never gonna play again. No IOUs, baby. And Dougie here walked right through it. Hup, hup, hup — BLOOOM! Gets up an walks away. But the others, man — all them dudes are gone. Blown away cause they were in the wrong fuckin spot. Put their chips on the wrong number. O-U-T. An Doug here was the only — "

"Okay! Okay!" Bobby stops instantly, and when his rap ceases, a certain glow disappears from his eyes. He slumps back on his bed and turns to watch the TV.

The last photo is a polaroid shot of Bobby, stoned and junky thin, cobalt-blue love beads, can of Colt 45 in hand, partying in a room down the hall. Cadaverous white skin. *Motorboat* magazine by his side. Five-thirty on an alarm clock on a small table. This is their world, their home now — yet these snapshots of Indian River, Vietnam, pudgy Bobby, and eighteen-year-old Doug have their own peculiar presence, like household gods that have lost their power.

The snapshots go back in their box. The box goes back on its shelf. "Doug, Doug," Bobby says, "throw some water and onions into that pan so we can have some gr-a-a-a-v-y. Gr-a-a-a-v-y, baby, gravy. Tomorrow we'll get some good bread an slice up the cold roast and make us some open-faced sandwiches. Pour gravy all over it." His eyes dance as a new rap begins. "Slice the meat real thin, toast the bread, an heat up the gravy. Now you've got a sandwich! Hey, you got a whole fuckin meal! I can't get enough of Doug's gravy."

BOBBY CARMAN'S STORY

These doctors were telling me that I couldn't do anything cause of them fucking seizures. So — hey, I moved way the hell down to

East Fourth Street and — Jesus H. Christ, there was some Methe-drine freaks down there! Listen, Methedrine crystal was sixty dol-lars an ounce. Put a coupla drops of water on it and it'd cook up by itself. Pop it in your arm — BAM! Top of your head blows off. You'll be rushin — aaaaaaaaaah! It's beautiful. I used to do a shot and rush for two hours. Hey, I was travellin, let me tell you. Jesus H. Christ, I used to be out in the fourth dimension. Spaced out for hours. Then I'd get hyper as hell — runnin around the house, cleanin, defrostin the refrigerator, moppin the kitchen. Shootin two, three times a day. You'd be up for a motherfuckin two weeks at a fuckin time, man. Just wanted to get high and stay high.

Then I got busted and they gave me a choice — seven and a half to fifteen years in jail, or six months in the state hospital at Central Islip for temporary insanity. I was pretty freaky behind all that speed, so they locked me up. No straitjacket, but they locked you in your room. Then you graduate to where you got the run of the building, and then where they give you a pass and you can go out-side. I saw a motherfuckin psychiatrist about once a week. But lis-ten, hey, there was a fuckin hole in the hospital fence. Go through that hole and right over there, man, fifty feet from the fence was a fuckin bootlegger's house. Used to buy muscatel, fuckin muscatel wine, and booze away my time.

I came out of Central Islip and they put me on SSI — moved me into a hotel somewhere down on Bowery. Had a front desk set up like Sing Sing with all them bars. I had a seizure on the elevator, and they threw me out. Just like that — "You ain't wanted here no more!" No questions asked. There I am, flopping around on the floor, and they're trying to push me out on the street. H-e-e-e-y, I was tired of gettin pushed around. Since I was sixteen I've been diagnosed as a psychopath. Actually, those Park Avenue psychs, they don't call you psychopath — it's sociopath. I love that. So I walked up from the Bowery to motherfuckin Fourteenth Street. It's wide open there. Beautiful. A brightass day. I was standin there and I said to myself, "Bobby, you ain't gonna do no more of this shit. Every time you turn around there's a cop on your tail. No more drugs. First of all, it's too expensive. Second, you end up in the fuckin can. I'm gonna fuckin drink liquor because it's legal." Can you dig it? Oh, shit. I went to a fuckin liquor store and chug-a-lugged a fuckin pint of muscatel.

Next place welfare sent me was the Hotel Walden. That's ten years ago now and — hey, this place was one of the best! Laundry room and everything. It looked so good when I moved in here, man, and now it looks like shit. I moved in on the fuckin ninth floor, baby. I was in nine oh fuckin nine, right opposite the elevator. I didn't know anybody, but then I started gettin around. James and Irene on the fuckin seventh — oh, man, they were some couple! Hey, that guy must have been seventy-nine, eighty years old, and she must have been like eighty-three. And — oh, Christ, but they were old winos! And motherfuckin Pineapple! Pineapple was from Hawaii — fought in the fuckin Korean war. He was beautiful. Beautiful! And Dottie, fuckin Dottie Crawford! Pineapple was huge, and Dottie's about this big. Almost albino, but she didn't have no pink eyes. . . . Everybody drank. Like that's *all* we did, man. One night Pineapple was so drunk he started a fire in his room. That's when they moved him up to the penthouse floor. The penthouse — but we called it the poorhouse. Little rooms and no bathroom. Just us winos.

Oh, Christ, when you're a wino, man — hey, I used to have my bed here and I used to have a bucket there, so I could just turn over and piss in the fuckin bucket and puke in it. I used to get up in the morning and go to the fuckin refrigerator, get out a cold bottle of fuckin wine and, oh, guzzle it, man. First thing in the morning. Quart by quart of Swiss-up. And Mad Dog — Mogen David — all chemicals and sugar. Next day you'd be comin off the hangover — you could feel sugar comin outa your skin. Scratchin, oh! Seein things around your room on your wall. Oh, God, that stuff is bad! Me and Pineapple, Charlie and Walter, and all these other guys — Jesus H. Christ, man, we used to drink six thousand quarts of fuckin wine a night! I mean we boozed it — all of us gettin high, sittin around and shakin hands — "Hey, what's happenin, man? Gimme a drink!" We didn't talk about shit.

Drinkin would have killed me if it weren't for Uncle James and Aunt Irene. Christ, they were wonderful! He was never clean-shaven. Always had gray stubble on his face and long sideburns. He had a flat nose, fat lips — but he wasn't a typical looking nigger. He had his own kind of beauty. And Irene — they treated me like fuckin family. They used to share food and everything. Make a big pot out of pig tails and lima beans. We all contributed. Used to go up there and eat and play cards, and — oh, man — they were fantastic down and out drinkers! That's how we got along, how we lived. . . . James died first — right in bed, with a swollen gut. Cirrhosis of the liver. Yeah, and Pineapple died in bed one night. For Christ's sake, he was young, baby — only forty-six or forty-seven years old.

Those were good old times, my first years here. My wino days, before Doug moved in and got me to switch to beer. Sometimes it seems like that's the only real past I got. I mean, the rest was like — Huntington, man, Huntington, Long Island, on the North Shore. Half an acre and a nice house. Four bedrooms and maybe three baths. And goddamn birds used to fall out of the trees. A goddamn middle-class community and — oh, baby — everything was just. . . . Hey, we went to the best schools — beautiful grounds, and they give you hot lunches and stuff like that. Baby, we had the best, all the way through kindergarten, first, second, third, and on to private school. The best, all the way up.

DOUG CARMAN'S STORY

After Vietnam I moved around for a couple of years. Daddy would get me jobs in hotels — the Biltmore, the Commodore — joints like that. I went from place to place and ended up in Atlantic City at the Shelbourne. Steward. In charge of the kitchen. Workin fifteen, twenty hours a day. Every payday I was goin out gettin high — smokin reefers, shootin dope. But when winter come everything got closed and I got laid off. I had no money, no place to go — and I had me a pretty bad habit. I didn't want to call up the old man and tell him I fucked up again, so I got on the bus — fifteen dollars in my pocket — and came up here.

Bobby was livin in the penthouse at the time. I'm knockin on the door. "Who is it?" he says.

"It's Doug!"

"Who's Doug?" He hadn't seen me for a couple of years.

"It's your brother. Open the goddamn door!" Tiny little room. He had a little bed, a dresser, and a puke bucket — and that's it. Oh yeah, and John Henry — that West Indian son of a gun. Him and Bobby had the two beds, so I took the cushions off the chair and slept on them. I stayed in there for two weeks, layin there pukin on the wine, pukin on bein sick from the dope. Cold turkey. Two weeks I was fucked up, and Bobby would come home each day with Hamburger Helper and make sure I got a little somethin to eat. When I got better, I hung out on the corner and started panhandlin. I felt embarrassed, but I was makin fifteen dollars a day out there, especially when it snowed. Some guys, they follow you down the street — "Gimme, gimme, gimme." Right? See what I do, I just stand — "Can you spare a little change? Thank you very much." I don't follow — I'm a real gentleman. I even know how to do it in Spanish — *"Poquito dinero, para mio?"*

A few months after I got there, Daddy called up. "Don't get excited," he said. "Your mother died tonight." I was okay. I didn't feel nothin till I went to find Bobby. "We gotta go to Florida," I told him. "Gotta go down and see the people. . . ." I broke up. And we flew down to bury her. Since then, me and Bobby have stuck together.

He won't mind my sayin this — when I moved in here, he was drunk all the time. His clothes were dirty and everything was on the floor. James and Irene — those people who used to cook for him — they were dead, so he wasn't eatin good. He was havin seizures, gettin in fights. He didn't care. He was happy as long as he was gettin high every day. All he remembers is gettin high. You gotta understand — Bobby don't know if he was standin or sittin. He needed someone looking after him. See, and for me, I couldn't seem to stick with any one thing after Vietnam. It was kinda the spit-and-polish thing all over again. Anytime someone starts tellin me what to do, I walk away from it. And each time I'd feel a little worse, cause Daddy was usin his name to help me get these hotel jobs. I'd tell myself I was gonna work extra hard and make up for all the old times. I'd work overtime — eighteen hours a day — work all I could, so I wouldn't have to be alone and thinkin about Nam and everyone gettin killed and Mother dyin at home. And then I'd start gettin nervous, so I'd be shootin dope. And soon I'd be borrowin money and lyin to people and gettin in arguments. . . .

So, bein here with Bobby — after Mother died, Daddy remarried and moved to Florida — we was all the family either of us had. I was cookin for him and gettin the laundry done and makin sure he cleaned up. And later, we moved to this room and got us a TV and some cats. Livin here, I can keep an eye on him, keep him from gettin hurt and put him on his bed when he has a seizure. He needs someone cause on his own he don't know how to stop himself. . . . And, I don't know, it gives me somethin I can do. It just seems like every time I get a job I start thinkin about Vietnam and . . . I just . . . some kinda pressure builds up, and I get in a fight or somethin. I don't know if you can understand this — I can't take care of myself, but I can take care of him.

I'm talkin about Bobby and how crazy he can be, but he oughta tell you about four years ago when SSI made some kinda mistake and sent him a check for $3,400. I spent it all in about four weeks — just sittin up there eatin manicotti, shootin dope and pure speed. And one day, all of a sudden it hit me — there's no more money. "What am I gonna do?" I said. "I conned Bobby out of all his money." So I almost jumped off the roof of the hotel. I went up on top of the building, out on the penthouse ledge, and sat there lookin down. I was gonna do it. If I had had another shot, I might have done it — been Superman, you know, and just flew down. My buddy Broadway, he seen me from the street. He came up and just stood about ten feet away from me — "Doug, don't do it! Come on!" I'm stoned. Two or three hundred dollars worth of dope I did that day — cocaine and dope. "Come on, Doug! Get off the ledge!" I got off. In the elevator he says, "What do you wanna do?" I just looked at him glass-eyed — "I don't know, man. I wanna die."

I went down to the Veteran's Hospital, and they took one look at me. One look! "Oh, I'm sorry. We ain't got no beds." I freaked out. Jumpin up and down and cursin at everybody. Here I was, stoned on $300 worth of dope. Strung out. I was sick — gettin sicker. "All right," the doctor said, "take this guy upstairs." Took me to a locked ward. I'm sitting there smokin a cigarette, noddin on my high. Nurse comes up to me and says, "Here, this will help you sleep." I told her I'm already high, I don't need no more of that shit. "Oh, don't worry. It'll help you." Thorazine. Ten minutes after I took that sucker, man, my head was down here. Next mornin I woke up in the same chair — and here goes the nurse — "Medication time! Medication time!" Fuckin Thorazine! People sittin there all day going, "Uhhhhhhhhh." That ain't my idea of a cure. And it ain't my idea of how to treat someone after he's been riskin his ass over there in Vietnam. I don't think we're heroes or nothin, but we did what they told us — we went over there and fought the goddamn war. Thorazine! You ain't gonna make Vietnam go away with Thorazine.

Yeah, so I spent all Bobby's money. But he forgave me. We gotta forgive each other, cause when you're drinkin you can get into some pretty mean shit. Like ... this is very hard. See, we don't drink wine no more cause ... he almost killed me twice. The first time, we were living on the sixteenth floor — in the poorhouse. We were drinkin wine and we had an argument. He pulled a knife and stabbed me right here in the leg. I sat down and dropped my pants — blood was squirtin out. I'm screamin at him, "Bobby, go down and get an ambulance! Quick!" We didn't have no phone. I was scared to death, man. Drunk and freakin out. Bobby took a shirt and tied it around my leg to make a tourniquet, and then he ran all the way downstairs — sixteen fuckin floors.

The cops come, of course. When you call the ambulance, the cops come. Here I am, sittin in the chair. Tryin to hold the cut closed and blood squirtin across the floor. Cops come in — "Who did it? Who did it?" I told them I went down the hallway to throw my garbage away and somebody tried to rob me. You know, to get the blame off him. But he'd already told them he did it. "Don't touch my brother! Leave my brother alone!" I didn't care about my wound. "Don't arrest my brother! He didn't do nothin!" Because I'm worried about his seizures and the plate in his head — afraid someone's gonna beat him upside the head. They tied me down because I was crazy.

That was the first time. But in 302, where we are now, we had another fight. He was out on the street gettin drunk, and I was gettin dinner together. I opened up the window and said, "Bobby, come home, man! Get off the street and come up here! I'm makin pork chops, potatoes and onions." So he comes in and I fixed our plates — two pork chops each. He's drunk and he starts pickin at my plate, so I gave him a little push — "Get away from my plate! I gave you the same as mine." And he picked up the carvin knife and stuck it in my belly. No blood. Just a hole in the fat. I didn't even know he hit me until I walked over to the mirror. Then I seen this hole. Oh, God! And I was burnin in my side, like heartburn. "Bobby!" I said, "there's a hole in my side!"

"Oh, there's nothin," he says, "it's just a little slice, man. Put a Band-Aid on it."

And I'm looking in the mirror. "Shit, I gotta go downstairs!" I threw on some clothes and hurried down to the lobby.

"You're gonna die! You're gonna die!" Everybody in the lobby goin wild. They called an ambulance, and they're all sayin, "Bobby did it! Bobby did it!"

"Bobby didn't do it," I said. I didn't want him to go to jail. Hey, someday I might hurt him — and I hope he don't put me in jail. Ambulance came. Cops came. I said, "No, my brother didn't do it. I got it in the hallway."

I knew Bobby felt bad. He don't have to say nothin. He ain't got nothin to apologize for — cause we're brothers. Everybody in the hotel says, "You and Bobby stick together, don't you?" And we do. We're always together, because if anything happens they're not gonna jump on two guys as easy as they're gonna bust on one. In fact, when I go to the store by myself, or he goes to the store by hisself, we be lookin out the window watchin. Some people see two brothers like us, they be jealous because we got each other. You know what I mean? See, they don't have nothin. If we don't have shit in the morning, we got each fuckin other. And see, a lot of people don't even have that much.

PARIS

The tree outside Muriel's window is about to blossom. Fat green buds. Garbage and glass sprinkled around its trunk. Ugly tree, even in spring. Muriel's hip is improving. She limps now, instead of that aggravating birdlike hop of early March. A street map of New York still hides the gaping hole from one of her epileptic falls, and now there is a map of Boston taped low on the wall beside her window. It covers another large hole. "I've got quite a hard head," she says with bemused pride. "I think I'd like a map of San Francisco for my next seizure."

Just before I leave, we return to an earlier conversation when she told me how depressed she felt after city agencies sent her here directly from a mental hospital. "What would you do," I ask Muriel, "if someone was coming out of the hospital and they weren't ready to work, if they didn't hold up well to pressure, if they didn't have friends or family to help them adjust? What would you do? Where could they have sent you to make you feel better?"

She flops back on her bed like a bobby-soxer who's just received her first valentine. White light from the ceiling fixture shines full in her face now, smoothing her skin, sparkling in her eyes. She smiles and sighs, more like a purr, really. You'd think she lay on thick summer grass, dreaming up at a full moon. "Paris," she says. "I think I'd like to go to Paris."

A DEATH

When the home assistance worker came to clean Arthur Moore's room on Monday, she found him propped in his wheelchair, swollen feet set on the floor like some grotesque anchor. The room smelled worse than usual. Arthur Moore had been dead three days.

After his body was discovered, Arthur Moore remained in his chair a while longer. Phone calls — police, ambulance, and social services — brief interviews, forms to be signed, before the body could be moved. Then they rolled Arthur Moore out of room 402 in his wheelchair. It seemed the easiest way to move his 300-pound bulk down to the waiting ambulance. They heaved him inside, folded up the chair, and drove off. A few people stood around watching, but they were not the ones who knew him best. His friends stayed away, keeping to their rooms, gathering outside later in the day to talk about the man they all seemed to like.

"I couldn't believe it," Doug says. "I didn't know there was anything wrong with him. I mean, there was the wheelchair and his leg and everything, but I didn't think he was gonna die."

"He was beautiful," Bobby says, nodding. "Righteous dude. No hustlin, none of that shit, you dig. You talk with Arthur, an like — well, he was beautiful, man, beautiful! He used to work on one of those, uh, you know, makin beds, an fixin meals, an travelin around — "

"A porter," Doug adds. "He started as a porter for the railroad and worked his way to chef."

"Yeah. It was beautiful to hear him talk about it. Tell him, Doug. Drinkin his way from Kansas to Delaware. Card games all night, an women grabbin him into their rooms. He lived, man, he lived."

"I couldn't believe it. I went kind of numb. Then a few hours later I cried like a baby. Didn't know what was happening."

"I gotta explain somethin, see, cause we knew the man, we knew him. We'd push his wheelchair outside an talk with him while he had a look around. And it was a privilege — a privilege, can you dig? Listen, Arthur Moore did the same shit we do, got fucked up on wine, alcohol, an dope. He did it all. But like when he hadda use that wheelchair, it turned his head around. He didn't wanta be fucked up no more. He wanted to think, an talk, an look at things straight. It was beautiful to be with the man. He never copped a goddamn quarter. It was a privilege. . . ."

"I told the woman at the A&P on Amsterdam. We used to take him up there to do some shopping an he'd roll right through the check-out line in his wheelchair. This woman — he'd get in her line every time — and she cried, right in the middle of the A&P, when I told her. We gave money for flowers so they could bury him right. Didn't want them just takin him away like they do with the others. He wasn't like them."

Yvonne Smith is outside with Ironsides, sharing a beer, checking out the passers-by between West End and Broadway. "He was a *nice* man," Yvonne says. "He always had something to say when I'd see him. You know, there was this way he had about him."

"Yeah," Ironsides says, "but somethin happened to his mind. I'd tell him he hadda get outa his room more. I wasn't seein him on the street like I used to. He'd sit up in that room all the time. I'd tell him there wasn't nothin in that room of his for him to be stayin there all the time, but he didn't listen. He changed. Shit, we used to run all over town. Hitch him up with some rope an haul him in back of me cause he didn't have the money for an electric rig. Go over to the park, head downtown on Broadway. Get out. Look aroun — that's what you gotta do. But he lost interest. Wouldn't listen. I'd go up there and he'd just sit. Didn't wanna come out."

"Like he wanted to die."

"Didn't wanna live. Lost interest. Listen, you die when you close yourself up in your room. Three days in that chair before they took him out. That ain't gonna happen to me — sittin aroun dead waitin for someone to find you. Shit, once we went all the way to Harlem together. I'd come by an ask where he wanted to go — have the rope an everything ready — an he'd say how he wanted to stay in his room. His voice changed. Everything. He lost interest."

K I N D   O F   A   L E T D O W N

"I remember," Muriel says, "when I was told, 'we're sending you to Hotel Walden.' I said, 'Oh, that sounds exciting!' I had an entirely different picture of the place — something more Continental. I don't know whether I expected a villa on the banks of the Riviera, or what. Maybe breakfast in bed. Hotel Walden sounded just great to me. It was kind of a letdown when I arrived. I guess I expressed how I felt about it to one of the social workers. He said, 'I note a tone of dismay in your voice.' "

SUMMER

SUMMER SONG

We don't need no education
We don't need no thought control
No dark sarcasm in the classroom
Teachers leave the kids alone.
Hey, teacher leave us kids alone,
All in all it's just another brick in the wall
All in all you're just another brick in the wall.

April, May, and into June — this bratty drone-head chant. *"We don't need no ... We don't need no ... We don't need no ..."* This season's song. For the recession. For the presidential primaries. For Iran. Afghanistan. For Miami in flames. For new high-grade heroin pouring into the city from all the countries we've newly destabilized. CLACK! CLACK! CLACK! *"Hey, teacher leave us kids alone!"* Amps blasting from the crazy wood house atop Tacita D'Oro, windows thrown open to 100th Street. *"All in all you're just another brick in the wall."* This season's song.

"You gotta watch the windows this time of year," Ironsides says. He pulls a lever; his chair reels back a few feet. "Bottle come outa the eighth floor a few weeks ago — missed me by a foot. They gotta crack down on that kinda bullshit."

"That's right!" Yvonne Smith says. "I saw a bottle hit on a car window — glass shootin off in every direction like it was a hand grenade or somethin. Little pieces cuttin this baby carriage, you know — right through the sunshade, little baby sleeping right inside."

"There was this guy last April, hit his number an bought $900 worth of coke. Thought he was supposed to snort it all at once. . . . Blew his mind. Runnin around naked. Screamin about Nazis an God an all kindsa shit. Standin in his window saying how all of us here was trying to eat him. He musta jumped from somethin like the eleventh floor — an all these people standin out here on the sidewalk. Coulda hurt someone."

Teacher leave us kids alone
CLACK! CLACK! CLACK!
Hey, teacher leave us kids alone

A police car stops in front of the hotel. A mustached officer opens the rear door of his vehicle to help a grizzled drunk out of the rear seat. The guy wobbles, shaken by strong morning sun. The officer takes his arm, guiding him up over the curb. "Shit!" Ironsides says. "They know he don't live here!"

The officer reaches out to push open the hotel door. The drunk shrinks back. He tries to shake his head, but it throws him off balance. He spins a few feet, then recovers himself.... *"We don't need no ... We don't need no ... We don't need no...."* The officer stands back, watching alertly, hands ready if the man falters — like someone building a house of cards. The drunk seems nailed to the spot. As the officer returns to his vehicle, Frankie abandons the front desk and comes rushing outside, arms flapping, gesturing at the drunk, calling to the officer to dump his man somewhere else. "You watch," Ironsides says. "You think they're gonna pack this dude up an drive around with him pukin in the back seat?"

Frankie rushes out onto the street, but the patrol car starts up and rolls slowly down the block towards Broadway. "He's not ours!" Frankie yells. "He's not ours!" Behind him, the drunk shrivels, sprawling himself flat out in front of the hotel. "Shift's over," Ironsides says. "They ain't comin back." He presses a lever and rolls away.

Passers-by veer off to get around the drunk. Frankie goes back inside. The drunk's legs tuck up, curling tight in perfect fetal sleep. Another brick in the wall.

BREAKING AWAY

With all the weirdness and sleaze, the punk and funk of summer costumes, Mr. Winslow still stands out as he waits for the Broadway Express at Ninety-sixth Street. He's wearing red Keds, a couple of sweaters, and a tiny John Deere cap emblazoned with a leaping green deer. In one hand he clutches his little white satchel; in the other, a lady's shoulder bag. As the subway approaches, Mr. Winslow's face lights up with rapture as if he willed it to come, its arrival a personal triumph. I sit beside him and ask where he's headed. "They got, I say they got a lunch program," he booms. "You know they give me, give me lunch at Fountain House. Baloney, baloney — they got baloney sandwiches and sometimes chicken. Maybe they'll have hot dogs today . . . Tell me, you tell me, you can die if you don't get enough, get enough to eat. I say you can DIE if they don't feed you!"

Mr. Winslow's fellow passengers shuffle uncomfortably in their seats. "At R-r-r-rockford, at Rockford they wouldn't feed you right. They treated you, they treated you like a prisoner." He pouts like an injured child. "You wouldn't, you wouldn't think of going back to a place you had escaped from, would you?" People stop staring and begin to shift to the other end of the car. "You'd have to be CRAZY" — he bellows the word with enormous gusto — "to go back to R-r-r-rockford. You wouldn't go where they treat you bad, where they don't, where they don't feed you properly. . . . I was, I say I was good. I didn't hurt no one or say nothin. I didn't say nothin bad. And they give me, give me a pass so I could walk the grounds. . . . I took a walk and I walked right through, I say I walked right through the gate and took a bus to my godmother on 125th Street. You wouldn't go back, you wouldn't think of going back to a place you had escaped from, would you?"

Our long bench is empty now. In fact, our whole half of the car is empty except for a fidgety woman who seems to regard herself as a beleaguered outpost. At the other end of the subway car sixteen people sit pressed together, staring at their feet, the unturned pages of paperbacks and newspapers.

SUNDAY AFTERNOON

It's Sunday and there's no AA meeting for Carver Washington to attend. His room is stuffy, so he decides to take a walk. His wallet seems to have disappeared, but then he spots it wedged behind his television. He tried to lift the TV but it's heavier than he expected, so he slides it out a few inches till he's able to wiggle an arm back there and retrieve his wallet. He puts on a canvas hat, throws a windbreaker over his arm, and at the last minute decides he'd better bring his umbrella. Carver Washington is a very cautious man. He locks his door, checks his pants pocket to make sure his wallet is packed securely, then he heads outside.

Carver Washington sits at his favorite bench in Riverside Park. This is what he likes to do now. He cannot really say what it is he really does there — he does not bring anything to read; he rarely speaks with anyone — yet he's never bored. He'll look at things — kids reeling in eels down by the river, joggers, dogs, the way pigeons walk, skaters, all kinds of bikes, a scrap of paper blowing across the pavement — and that seems enough. It's as if he's never seen anything in his life. All those years of concrete highway, empty western skies, two quarts a day of ninety-proof — monotonous blur. Now he can *see*. He can think. It is almost like the slide show at the Seventieth Street church — Jerusalem and Rome, new life rising on ruins of the past. He has seen the show a dozen times. He feels good just thinking about it. A kind of quiet happiness settles over him. A normal life. No excitement, just a normal life is all he asks for now. . . .

A block from the hotel he passes two men lugging a load of stuff down the street. One guy has a hefty carton rattling with appliances and whatnot. The other guy carries a heavy TV console. Carver Washington remembers how much trouble he had just budging his own TV a couple of hours ago, how when he was young and driving his first truck he could lift almost anything. But the thought passes quickly. He knows it does no good to brood over things past.

Carver Washington puts his key in the door. The door swings open before he can turn the lock. No television! No stereo! No clock radio! No hot plate! He hurries to his closet. All his clothes are gone. He feels faint — violence rushing up in him, yet weak and rubbery at the same time. He flops in his armchair. *Those fuckin kids! That was my TV I seen em with on the street, my things rattlin in that one box. Walkin right past me.*

He storms out of his room, yanks an empty Gallo jug from the garbage outside, and hurries down to the Mobil station on Ninety-sixth Street. He asks the attendant to fill the jug with gasoline. "No gas in that jar," the attendant tells him. "We're only allowed to fill metal containers." Carver Washington smashes the bottle in the gutter. He finds the nearest pay phone and calls Geraldine Footé, a friend from AA.

"Don't go and get drunk, now!" she says.

"I'm not thinkin about drinkin. I'm gonna get me some gas and burn that son of a bitch up. It's gotta be somebody on my floor tipped em off."

"No, Carver! Please don't! Let me come and talk to you."

"No one's talkin to me. I'm goin to burn the hotel! They took everything I got and I'm goin to burn the place down!"

But he doesn't. He goes back to the park and sits. It's chilly. He ran out without his jacket, but he just sits. Everything is wrong. The park itself looks cruelly ravaged — ruined benches, scarred tree trunks, mashed dog shit, broken bottles everywhere....

"Carver! Carver! I was so worried. I thought you were gonna do it." He looks up and sees Gerry.

"I'da done it too if I coulda bought the gas."

"You gotta get outa here, Carver. Soon as you can."

"What the hell! All these places are the same."

"You can afford it. Go and get a decent place and be done with this. Settle down for a year, get your life right, get away from the pressure."

"How in hell can I make it another year?"

"Get out! You gotta get yourself out!"

"Yeah, but that ain't no life. I gotta live a better way than this or it just ain't worth the trouble. . . . "

TWO NEW WATCHES

David has two new digital watches with dark faces that light up with square, dotted print-out numerals when you press a button. Forty dollars for the two of them. A magazine offer that caught his eye. A special his/hers offer for sweethearts. "You wanna buy a good watch for twenty bucks?" he asks me. "It's worth seventy," he says. "I got a good deal by getting two of them together." I don't have the heart to scold him. "I had a girlfriend I was going to give it to, but by the time the watches came I wasn't talking to her."

"David, David," I say. "People are going to like you for who you are and for how you respect them. You don't have to bribe people with gifts and money."

"I don't know. It was such a good bargain, and I always wanted a watch that could do all these things. It's got an alarm and a stopwatch and you never have to wind it. I could've had one that does math for you, but then I couldn't have gotten the ladies' watch that came with this."

It strikes me that the last thing anyone needs here in Hotel Walden is a timepiece accurate to a hundredth of a second. Days here are blurred. Time happens in chunks rather than minutes and hours. There is not much to do and nowhere to go. Most residents have shed time — it has no need for them. And here is David with two new watches.

LOST ENERGY

"I don't know if I've lost energy or what," Muriel muses, "but I've kind of lost faith in myself. Like yesterday, my friend Jack Berry called and asked me to come down to the Village for brunch. I told

him I was seeing things blurry. I didn't know if I could stand outside long enough to get a cab. He sort of scolded me, and it was like
he was saying I didn't really want to come. How can I tell him that
I passed out on the street last week, right in front of Sloane's? The
doctors think I may be over-medicated, but they're still testing.
The point is that Jack thought I was acting, putting on some kind
of show. But look, see that toothbrush on the floor? I know that's a
toothbrush. I know it goes in your mouth, that you don't leave it
laying around in the dust. I know better. But see, that's no act. I
didn't put it there. I can't, I can't — I mean, I know what a proper
home should look like. I admire a nicely appointed apartment, the
touches that make a house a home. . . . Some of the homes I've
been in! Upholstery, delicious meals, such taste! And I can't explain to Jack, I can't explain to myself, how that toothbrush got
under the bureau. I've lost a lot of confidence. And see, you run
into somebody who expects too much, who won't believe there's
some simple thing you can't do, and it makes you feel like closing
your door, just staying put in your room."

Muriel sits on her bed like a tomboy at a fishing hole — knees
tucked up, feet turned in to nudge one another. Her walking cane
pokes out from the tangle of rumpled bedding. A few empty Buds
under her bed — I'm afraid she's been drinking again. Her soiled
grey mattress is sprinkled with crumbled soda crackers; there are
huge yellow stains and a brown cigarette burn. Sweet foul smell of
a baby's soiled diaper, heavy in the summer heat.

"At least things are quieting down in our unit," she says. "Benny
is gone. I don't think he was paying. Or maybe he was bothering
people. But he's gone. He was such a pest. And Mr. Winslow. I
know how to handle him. He comes walking by in his underwear
and says, 'Hi, Muriel!' Very subtle. And I say, 'Good afternoon,
Mr. Winslow.' 'You can call me Willie,' he says. And I'll say, 'Have
a good day, *Mister* Winslow!' And I emphasize the *mister*. I make a
special point of that so I won't have difficulty. Nobody bothers me
now. I've been keeping to myself, sleeping a lot. I don't know, I'm
always ready to sleep. I seem to be falling into a pattern. I listen to

WPAT — such relaxing music — and when shadows fall, I say, 'Okay, Muriel, you can put your solitaire away. You can go to sleep now. . . . '

"And my son, I've been thinking about him a lot. I bless him every night. Then I close my eyes and — but what was I saying? — I've lost energy, faith in myself. Oh, I still go upstairs and watch television for a few hours in the afternoon, but I feel like I'm always here, in this room, ready to sleep. The walls, they get so —" Muriel stiffens her hands and holds them in front of her face. She brings them closer and closer till they touch. She keeps pressing, fingers rigid, till there's nothing in between.

GERRY

Like her friend Carver Washington, Geraldine Footé is an alcoholic. Each weekday morning she walks up to Trinity House at 107th Street where she attends a regular group meeting. She speaks with an individual counselor twice a week. The rest of her time at Trinity House is unstructured. People play cards or sit talking or hang around the pool table teasing one another about missed shots. But often Gerry drifts back to Hotel Walden, back to her room to watch the soaps and play with her cats. There's a loose wire or some such problem with her television, so Gerry keeps it running twenty-four hours a day. When she goes to sleep, she shuts off the sound, but the blinking grey screen is alive and there to greet her when she wakes up.

When we speak, she sometimes shakes her head in mid-sentence, falling into a near hush. It's as if she refuses to believe her story has any interest or meaning, as if she does not want to acknowledge that she is here in this room, remembering hard years, repeated mistakes, clinging to receding dreams.

GERALDINE FOOTÉ'S STORY

I'm tired, tired of the whole scene. It isn't any one thing that bothers me — it's the whole hotel. Gettin outa here would be the first move; I'd really like to leave New York. Anywhere but New York City. I know it's not gonna be easy — it has to come one step at a time — but I feel that one day this will happen. The country is what I want. I never lived there, but the few times I have went to the country I enjoyed it.... I certainly am in the wrong place, aren't I?

My father died from diabetes when I was two. My mom was a domestic — used to work in the laundry. She took sick one time and I went in her place. I was about thirteen or fourteen, and I thought it was very hard work. Thirty years, off and on, I've still been doin it. With work and all, I didn't see that much of my mother. Sometimes I'd get mad at her and run away from home and come over from Brooklyn to stay in Manhattan. I guess that was another reason they sent me to reform school.

I stayed in reform school a year. Eight months and I coulda come home, but I had a terrible temper. I tried to tear up a room one time, so I had to stay longer. I calmed down from that and got out at fourteen — ended up getting pregnant.... I was deathly afraid of facing my mother because I didn't know what kind of reaction she would take. And this is part of the tragedy of my life — my mother's people were backward. You know, it wasn't the kind of relationship where you sit down and talk. There were certain things you didn't discuss. What I learned, I learned from the street, and I always felt that if my father had lived, my life would have turned out different. I have plenty of regrets about my childhood, which is why with my son I do so much talking. I'm determined he isn't going to be like I was. When he was young I talked to him very hard, and thank God, I've never had no problems with him.

But I was never told anything. I just always thought my life would have changed, would have been better — there are so many pitfalls I've taken.

Not too long after Monty was born, I moved to my uncle's in Newport News, Virginia. He had a vegetable lot and used to sell vegetables to the shipyard. I worked at a lotta temporary jobs — domestic work in private homes and waitressin for awhile around the shipyard. Helter skelter. It seems like I ended up doing some of everything.

I used to go to a bowlin alley, and a couple of times I went to after-hour joints. I met this fella, and he was tellin me they had a thing in Virginia for new young girls, they had what they call runnin a train — all the guys sleepin with you to break you in. I didn't know about pimpin or anything else, and this man — it seemed like somethin would tell me to listen to him. Well, he had a party and he told me to smell somethin. Made me feel good.

I was sixteen now and got into business sellin whiskey — moonshine and vodka. I'd buy it by the gallon and then charge for the jar. Half a gallon cost you five dollars — out of that five-dollar bottle you can make seventy-five. So it was a nice turnover. I got the soldiers, sailors, the merchant seamen. Taxi drivers — they'd know you sold whiskey, so they'd bring everyone by the house. I had two girls who were turning tricks. Rented the whole house for twenty-five dollars a month — so they took part of the building; I took the other. Young girls. None of us over twenty.

We ran a booming business. I really don't remember what I made. I didn't know what I was doin. I'd go buy a lotta clothes, foolish things, you know — I was just a little kid havin fun. As for havin these girls work for me — I felt about six feet tall. I felt like I was into something. I put a red light in my hall, and I never knew, I didn't know what the red light represented.

Cops finally busted me. I jumped bail and came back to Brooklyn with my son. I got a sleep-in job and had Monty boarded out near where my aunt lived. I went on and tried to work two jobs so I could have my own place. I was overworked and diabetic and didn't know it. One day I passed out. Woke up in Coney Island Hospital and spent two weeks there. When I came out I got work as a nurse's aide. I really enjoyed the nursing, but I was drinkin kinda regular then. Gin and Cutty Sark. Drinkin on the job, and I was goin to bars, too. I was scared bein on my own. It was a terrible feelin. Then I met this fella from Jersey. One day I had a toothache and the dentist was closed. This fella I was with was shootin heroin. "If you take a shotta this, it will kill the pain," he says. Anything to get rid of pain. So here I go. . . . It relaxes you, makes you *very* relaxed. And I found it gave me a lot of drive that I don't have normally. And then after awhile it gets to the stage that you need it. Have to have it. You get dry heaves, chills — and if you go long enough without it, you're throwing up. You're just miserable. People say, "I can handle this like I handle everything else." There's certain things you can't handle. You really can't. I wasn't strung out, but I was on my way. I had the craving.

Then I got busted. I happened to be in the wrong spot at the wrong time, and the weight was put on me. I was down in this area then. Ninety-fourth Street between West End Avenue and Riverside — one of these hotels. In every other room somebody's doin something. People from Jersey, Connecticut, and Brooklyn comin over to get their supply. If they haven't got a shootin gallery, they're sellin dope or doin somethin. What happened, I went upstairs to invite this girl down to my room for dinner, and the police were there. This dope dealer they were lookin for happened to come in at the time, and they snatch him, they snatch her, they snatch me and busted all of us.

I come outa jail — went right back to an SRO. Dismal. Very depressing. I don't know how to put this into words, but the surroundings, the place itself, was just depressing. Like, I walk home this past week, and this man who lives on the fourth floor — they found him in his room dead. And see, I go into comas myself sometimes — diabetes — and this shakes me up. The thought of bein alone by myself, layin dead in this little room and no one even knowin it — that scares me. I have a lady in the building, she lives over me. She's diabetic too, and if we don't see each other for a day or two, we go to check, see how you're doing. A while back there was a fella lived right down the hall. He was already very small — dehydrating — and I knocked on his door to see how he was. I didn't get no answer, so I told my friend, "Well, maybe Sonny went to see his family uptown." But she knew he was sick — been tryin to get him to the hospital and he wouldn't go. "No," she said, "I knocked on his door yesterday. Somethin's wrong." Frankie, from down at the desk, opened the door for us. Sonny was already dead. . . . I'll tell you — this place is no good for me. If I could just get a foothold into some kinda work, I'd crawl back. I'd be determined to get a better place, no matter how sick I am.

Anyway, I come outa jail and they sent me right to 103rd Street. The Marseilles — that big hotel on the corner they're renovating now. Get up to my room — it's filthy. Somebody had threw up on the floor. In the middle of the bed there was ashes. And the door — all you had to do was go and push it and it opens. No clean sheets. Went down and asked the manager to give me another room, and that was all they had. This is the room they give me the first day that I come out of jail. This is my room! My mind is all messed up. I'm trying to get myself together, and I'm surrounded by dope fiends and everything. I was angry — angry at *them,* whoever they are. This is where they put me! This is their idea of where I should be. . . . Step out on the street, the first thing I saw was a girl I had been in jail with and a bunch of junkies getting ready to go upstairs and get off.

Here's the dope and here I go. I got sucked back in again. By now I'd broken parole — just feelin bad, period — so I went downtown to turn myself in. I wanted to go back into rehabilitation and get myself together physically and mentally. I go down to rehab, and they told me I had to have certain papers before I could come in. "What is this?" I said to myself. "I'm a violator. I belong to you." They wouldn't accept me. It didn't make sense. They got people runnin around lookin for parole violators; I'm turnin myself in and can't get in. So I spent another week shootin more dope while they got it straightened out. They kept me in the rehab infirmary about a week, and then they shipped me back to Mattawan. I felt at home again. I could relax. Jail has saved my life more than once. It's a terrible thing to say, but it's true. I have to face reality.

Got out. This time they sent me to an SRO on Eighty-fifth Street. I went into vodka, gin — drinkin wine heavier than I ever had. Then I met a new fella and he was dyin to get married. I wasn't ready to get hooked up with anybody. I'd duck him, but he wouldn't give up. He didn't ask me — he *told* me he was gonna marry me. I looked at him like he was some kinda nut, but it was a good feelin to know he cared so much.

In the beginning it was beautiful, really beautiful. We'd do everything together. We used to get a quart of vodka and walk from Eighty-sixth Street to Roosevelt Hospital — drink our way on over to his methadone program, cause he stopped usin drugs. I'd wait, and then we'd drink our way back home. And all this is nothin to me — I'm not thinkin about no alcohol. I'm livin in a fantasy. And my husband is a very — he walks around — you'd never believe that the man has heart trouble, sclerosis, is a diabetic, and two or three other things. I don't think there's a hospital between the Bronx and downtown he hasn't been in. He was on booze and pills — anything he could get his hands on. His day consisted of goin to the hospital, staying down there, come back home and be sittin on the edge of the bed — fight goin to sleep because he doesn't want to lose the high he has. No conversation unless he wanted to eat or somethin. Bombed all the time. This was my marriage.

Well, one Friday my husband was in the hospital, and I heard some noise in the hall. I opened my door and seen a fella across the hall packin. "You movin?" I asked him. "Everybody's movin," he said. Then I see these two huge giants. They went down the hall harassin people — drawing guns and rushing them out. They cut the lights and gas off, and I started gettin panicky. We had to move like everyone else. The corporation sent these young Haitians to move stuff out — throw it in trash bags, dump it on the truck and move you. A lot of people's stuff got lost, and the Haitians are walkin off with televisions, whatever. This is how the landlords do it. They'll have one corporation hold five or six buildings, and when they make their move they'll change hands and bring in some giants to chase everyone out. It wasn't that this wasn't known. The welfare knew about it, but they don't do nothin. See, the average person lives in these places don't even know who the landlord is. All they know is who's sittin behind the front desk. Nobody sees the corporation — just see their giants when they come to kick you out.

So that's how I come here. When the giants rushed us out of Eighty-fifth Street, they moved us to another corporation building — to Hotel Walden. My marriage ended about four years after we come here. In a way, this place played a part in our breakin up because through the alcohol and everything we were happy before we came here. It's like in this hotel people don't have nothin to do. They stand on the corner — what they think they know, they talk about; what they don't know, they talk about. You know, just keep somethin goin. And my husband tried to tell me, through the alcohol and everything, "Let's get outa here!" At the time I couldn't see it. I liked the apartment — there were possibilities of makin it comfortable. Anything outside of that I didn't pay too much attention to. And I'd never been in an environment where there was a lotta gossipin. I never had too many dealings with the people, but my husband did — out on the bench on Broadway, drinkin with the fellas and whatnot. They would make up things to tell him. One time, he came outa the hospital, and before he got upstairs Ironsides told him I was strung out on dope. All these little things to keep confusion goin. And it still goes on, but now I more or less have put it to the side. I go and I come. Hi and bye. I leave people alone. You get too friendly with them — like they say, "familiarity breeds contempt."

I never really feel safe, secure. It's like an up-and-down trend — for awhile things is pretty quiet, and then you have rooms bein busted into. Twice I lost my stereo, TV. One time, I had just got my check and put my money in the drawer and went downstairs to call my son when the blackout occurred. Since I couldn't get back upstairs in the dark, I sat across the street on the steps goin up to Freya's Beauty Salon. Lights out all over the city, but I could see people comin round the corner with TVs, furniture, this, that, and the other. For a week after, fellas were sittin out on the Broadway benches with watches up their arms, rings on every finger. When I came back up to my room, the door was open, my money gone.

All this goin on, you gotta get high on somethin. You don't wanna deal with your problems, with what's happenin around you. I'd say nine out of ten people drink in here. No moderation. Drink from morning to night. Drink to get bombed — till you can't drink anymore. if you're out early, you'll see a line waiting for the whiskey store to open. And if that's not fast enough, you'll see people with a bottle from a bootleg place — just to get the shakes off. That's breakfast. When you get high, you more or less don't care about the world around you. One woman, when it really gets warm, she sits on one of them benches and gets sloppy. She's over 300 and some pounds. She doesn't eat. Doesn't get up to go to the bathroom. Just drink, drink, drink. Takes about three or four people to take her upstairs. And like I said, my husband was chronic. Used to hallucinate a lot. He would stand in front of the mirror and hold his eyeglass case like he was drinking out of it. Talk out of his head — paranoid things, like somebody was — I don't know how to explain it really. People were tryin to do somethin to him — not physically, but like play his mentality cheap.

And with all the drinkin people do, pills and methadone is almost as big. Valiums and Elavils — you go to a psychiatrist with your Medicaid, tell him your nerves are bad, you can't sleep. They'll just write out the script. And say you've already used your prescription this week — you take somebody else's Medicaid card to the same doctor and get more pills. I had about three doctors I used to go to all at once. Didn't use pills myself. I sold em. Had this doctor on Amsterdam Avenue, everybody was goin there for pills. You'd have thought they were sellin heroin in there, the way we filled the waitin room. I guess in a way she was sellin heroin, cause we were sellin the pills and buyin heroin with it.

With all this pressure on me, I wound up gettin hooked on methadone. I still like it today. If I'm feelin low and I have somethin to do in the house and I don't feel like doin it, it give me that false energy to do what I gotta do. But I'm not hooked on it — I went into de-tox and kicked the methadone-alcohol habit altogether. Actually, de-tox is just the start to get the alcohol out of your system. It takes years, really. Now, I'm in the alcohol program at Trinity House, and I still drink a little. I know I should stop — I feel that eventually I will — but I'm just not ready to cut it loose. In a sense, I'm still foolin myself.

So this is how it is. I get $123 every two weeks from SSI. Eighty-five twenty is rent. Five dollars is phone. That leaves about two-fifty a day to take care of myself. I'm diabetic — supposed to have a special diet, right? Eat a lot of foods with fibers. Okay, I get food stamps, but it's still impossible. For a week and a half, two weeks, I'll follow my diet as much as I can. The other two weeks is whatever comes. The money that I get, there's no way. I can't even buy a pair of socks if I want. This is really the truth. Twice a week we have lunch down at Trinity House, but the rest of the time I eat alone. Each day it seems like it's the same thing — except when it gets warm, starting about July. Last year our AA group went on bus outings to the Central Park Zoo. I love all animals — gorillas, rams, everything. I get a big kick out of it. I know I could get there any time on my own, but see, I have a problem dealing with the East Side. West Side, I'm fine, but when I get across the park I'm lost. . . .

I'd go mad in here without my TV. I'm hung up on soap operas. There's quite a few I like. My TV hasn't been off for about a month. There's a short circuit or somethin, and if my TV is off sometimes I can't bring it back on. So I just don't turn it off, period. If I need someone to talk to, I go see Doug and Bobby. There was Carver Washington — he's nice, but now he's moved away. I have another friend, but usually he's bombed — really left field. There's a girl down the hall I see once in awhile, but I don't like to get hooked to women too much. They keep too much goin — "He say; I say," you know. And then I got my cats to talk to. You'd be surprised — they're a lotta company. I got Tinker, Precious, Bamboo, Sputnick, Badness, Poopsie, and Calico. See, there was a girl bein put outa the hotel, and she came to me cryin with her cats. I didn't wanta see the cats in the street, and she was supposed to come and get them as soon as she got herself together. That was way last June. Every time I see her, she got a brand new lie for me. I saw a fella who knows her, he told me he don't think Monique wants the cats. So now I'm stuck. Those cats are like children. They do little funny — one of em can be doin somethin and I'll know which one it is without even lookin. Each have a personality of their own.

So I got my way of livin here, but I still have this feelin I'm in the wrong place. Gettin outa here — I've been doing a lotta thinkin lately. You know Arthur Moore in 408? He was in a wheelchair when he died. It was on a Monday morning they found him; he'd been dead since Friday. I went in and looked at him — in his room, in his wheelchair. It's true he was a big man, but it looked to me like he swoll up even more. And I'll tell you, it shook me up quite a bit. See, I been in two insulin comas in this hotel, and the thought of bein alone — this might sound silly — I don't know why all of a sudden I started gettin this fear of dyin alone. "What's the difference?" I say to myself. "When you're dead, you're dead." But I don't want to be alone and go like that. Don't want to die in a place like this. There's so many people that I have known since I've been here, have died that way — alone in their room.

A DEATH

[On the Elevator Door]

> Notice
> Mr. Fredrick (Freddie) Leonard
> Funeral will be:
> Thursday 7–3–80 ——— 10 A.M.
> at
> Lance Funeral Home
> 109 W 132 St (Near Lenox Ave)
> Wake Wed 5–9 pm

LLOYD SMITH'S ROOM

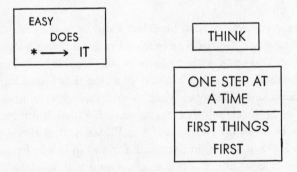

EASY
DOES
* ——→ IT

THINK

ONE STEP AT
A TIME

FIRST THINGS
FIRST

Hand-painted signs tacked on the closet door. Neatly folded towels on a rack beneath the signs. On his bed an unfinished solitaire game along with his day's schedule carefully written on a note pad. Taped pictures above his bed — night panorama of Manhattan, Empire State Building glowing brightly; beneath it a black and white publicity glossy of John Travolta and David Alvarez; beneath that, two *TV Guide* covers. Small bookstand beside his bed. *Compulsion, The White House, Criminal Investigation, Film 69/70, The Octopus, The Betsy, Return to Paradise, Little Murders,* and *The Poems of Emily Dickinson.*

He keeps his insulin in a small refrigerator beside the bookcase. On top of the fridge is an inky looking print of a naked white woman — a "tasteful" pose, like Ingres's bather, yet it reeks of porn-shop yearnings. The black background seems to vibrate, but it's only a few roaches on a short excursion. Lloyd keeps his room tidy, but there are roaches everywhere. He takes his broom to clean up some spilled ashes and a dozen roaches drop from its bristles, scattering in all directions. "I'm a periodic." Lloyd rushes to speak with a mixture of tension and quickness of mind that suggests a stand-up comic. Long hooked nose. Sharp, smart grin that reminds me of Mort Sahl. "I go along fine for awhile. Then every four to six months I get nervous. I worry about everything. The place starts getting to me, I start worrying about money, about finding work — the pressure gets too much for me, so I go off and drink."

LLOYD SMITH'S STORY

Alone. Bein alone. We had three ladies here jumpin out windows from the pressure. If you haven't got a radio or a television you could go bananas. The walls start to close in on you. When I turn out that TV and I can't go to sleep, I lay here and hear all kinds of squeaks, slammin doors, people yellin. It really upsets you. You live in these rooms and you got no friends, no place to go, nobody to talk to. It's weird. It's terrible. And I guess these ladies just chucked it in — "That's it, it's hopeless" — and jumped.

Sometimes when I'm tryin to get to sleep I'll leave the TV on all night, just so I won't hear all these noises. And you know something? I think there's ghosts in this house. I can hear little movements. I've had, I don't know, hallucinations and things. I believe there's some kind of spirit here. One time when I woke up — my eyes was open and the TV was on, and I had a flush of goose pimples. There was a cartoon on TV, and I thought the people would come out of the television and attack me. One time I'm laying down and I see my brother's dead face — Ralph, the one who died of acute fatty liver from alcohol and drugs. I lost seven people in my family. They all died young. So I saw my brother's face, and I started crying. All of a sudden my ear starts to feel like a wind was blowin — and somebody was pullin the covers off my back. I yelled out "God is great!" — and everything stopped. . . .

One time my girlfriend come back to me. Connie Smith — she died in my room. She was six feet one — tall, lean, light-skinned black girl. Used to comb her hair real flat. Pretty girl. Real pretty girl. Connie was a two-quarts-a-day drinker of vodka. The night she died she asked to sleep in my room. I said, "I haven't got any money to spend on booze." I gave her a pack of Salem, and I left for the day. I came back about eight o'clock that night and I see Connie lying there in her panties with her eyes open. I never knew Connie to sleep like that. "Connie! Connie!" I said. She just lay there. "Connie! Connie!" I started movin her, shakin her. I listened for her heart, and all I could hear was my own heart movin fast. I called an ambulance and gave her mouth-to-mouth for twenty minutes. It seemed like she was breathing, but actually I was blowing in the air and feeling my air coming out. I was crying. I never knew how much I loved that girl until she passed on.

A year later, I was just finished drinking and here I see Connie in spirit. "Connie! Hello!" I say. I'm talking to her just like I'm talkin to you. "Connie, what's that?" I say. She's making signs, but she's not talking. She was nude and I said, "Oh, let me hug you!" I tried to hug the spirit, and she puts her mouth on the knob of the closet door. "You want me to open the door?" I say. I open it and she goes in. I see golden steps goin up. I'm seein this, but then there's the Devil, sitting on the steps laughing. He had horns and kind of a horse body. He was short — like those guys that blow them little flutes — not a whole horse body, just the hoofs. . . . A satyr, yeah! And he was smilin. I said, "Oh, shit!" and slammed the door. Then I look in the mirror — and you know the Coney Island mirrors, when you see fat and skinny? — well, my face is split, split in half. "Holy smoke! What's happenin to me?" I was petrified. I hear voices in there, moanin like, and I say, "Connie! What's the matter?" In a tiny voice she says, "He's beatin me! He wants you to come in the closet." "I can't Connie! I can't! Don't let him beat you! You're bigger than he is." She says, "No, he's my master."

I got outa my room, man. Five o'clock in the morning and I ran outa that hotel, stayed out in the street, far away from it till that night ended. . . .

I was born in New York City. East Harlem, Spanish Harlem, they call it now — but then it was mostly Italians and some Jews. They didn't like blacks — they was always chasin us and everything like that. My father, before he got married he was a captain in the Salvation Army. He lived a churchgoing life. Didn't drink. Didn't smoke. My mother, she didn't smoke, but she would drink on the weekends with the girls. Mother wasn't a drunk or nothin — it was just her reward for bein good all week.

I was a very bad kid. Tough. A real bully. One time at elementary school I went on the roof — took rocks and bottles and everything — waited for the teachers to come out and started bombarding them. I was crazy. Then we had our gang wars. The Enchanters, the Turbans — some bad clubs. A lotta guys gettin killed, gettin shot, and everything else. The Comanches — that was the black club — used to hang out at my house, used to put their guns up, and me and my brother used to fool around with them. We could have blew our heads off. Didn't know what we was doin. Eleven, twelve years old — they called us Comanche Tots. Got older and became a Comanche Junior and then a Comanche Senior. A tough guy. I was a good athlete; I had tremendous fights in bars.

After I graduated from the High School of Commerce, I started workin for the city at the East End Welfare Center on Ninety-fourth Street. Special Officer — like a welfare cop. They give you a uniform and badge and you patrol the building, try to keep peace. There's a lotta violence in welfare places, you know. I had master keys and everything — thought I owned the building. We had a real social club. Used to shoot dice at night. And each morning — come in, pour some whiskey in a coffee cup, and drink continuously. That's where I picked up my drinking habit.

Also, I was goin out with a couple of girls in the building even though I was married. It really made me cuckoo after awhile because one would want you to spend more time with them than the other. See, my wife knew there was somebody out there. Alice knew about my wife. Susan knew about Alice and my wife. . . . I used to go from home to the job; see Alice in the afternoon and early evening; shoot down to Susan's house on Thirty-third and First; then shoot back home about one o'clock in the morning. I took my wife for granted and got away with it for sixteen years — living a triple life. . . .

I had quite a family, but I lost them to alcohol. My wife knew I was a flirt, but the thing that bothered her — I was crazy because alcohol was affecting my mind. Dewar's, Johnny Walker Red — used to drink morning, noon, and night. Now I see I was crazy. Your mind becomes distorted. . . . My wife was a very sweet woman, wonderful girl. But the way I was behaving, she changed very much. She's like a drill sergeant today.

See in my early life I never had girls. I was all thumbs. Then I started to hang out with a guy who was an Erroll Flynn. He taught me how to get a girl. And when I learned I could make a conquest, I became superior to the women. I wasn't leaning towards them now — they were leaning towards me. Having all these girls made me feel like the Sheik of Araby. I was gonna have every woman, and it seemed if I drank enough to keep myself goin I could make anything happen. With Susan Bellino — she was pretty, very pretty and classy — we used to go to fine restaurants — Cattle

Baron, Japanese and French restaurants — and crazy movies — French movies and other type movies that's not like the standard thing you go to see. I used to have an Afro and a beard — she loved long hair — and when I got angry with her, I'd cut off my hair and she would hate me. I'd do that to punish her. But that was when we were on the verge of breakin up and she had dominated me and had me goin crazy. Before that, we had some times!

All those years I was drinkin and abusing my body, but it didn't bother me — I was pretty strong. Now is when I'm paying for it. . . . With my drinkin I was becoming outlandish. I'd get hysterical. Scream and curse. Then things got worse. First, Alice had me arrested for harassment. We'd broken up by now, but we used to see each other once in a while and fight. I'll tell you — I had went out with Susan and drank all night. Left her that morning and went out with Alice in the daytime. Here I'm thinking I wanna knock off a piece of ass, and the body didn't let me. I fell asleep on her, and when I woke up I see this note: "You promised to be a good boy, but you're full of shit!" I blew my top. Somethin went crazy. I socked her, slapped her, picked her up and threw her in the tub and ran hot scalding water on her. She looked at me like I was a nut.

Then Susan had me arrested for assault. We had gone to Atlantic City and checked in this hotel — twenty-six dollars for two nights. "This place is dirty!" she says. So we take a fancy room for fifty dollars a night. Now we had to eat and go see the Temptations and go bar hoppin — she wanted to live fancy, so the money wasn't gonna last. We started fightin over that, play fighting — only this time I got pissed off and choked her. Next thing you know, she called the cops on me. I got paranoid — I thought they were Mafia. Hid out in the basement till I found out they were detectives. She had abrasions around her throat. Harassment and assault they charged me with. That was the end for me and Susan. . . . And all these fights and run-ins with the law lost me my job.

So now I didn't have Alice. I didn't have Susan. Didn't have no job. My wife was petrified of me. I was having outbursts all the time. Breaking furniture up. Punch the doors. Knock over garbage. The alcohol, the girlfriends, the fights were gettin to me. I was going crazy. My wife couldn't stand to see me around the house, so I'd go to the bar at eight and drink all day long. Blew $4000 in a short time. Next thing, I had to go on welfare. It was a strain — I was really breakin the house up. "Stop it, Daddy!" the kids would cry and yell. "Stop it!" Finally my wife took me to family court, and they made me move.

So on that note, I moved into one of those SROs on Ninety-fourth Street — the Mount Royal. It was a two by four room, no bigger than a telephone booth. A dozen winos on the front stoop, dirty and shabby looking. I didn't pay any attention because I was stone drunk; you don't see those things till you get sober. The toilets are all broken up. People don't clean nothin up. Terrible.... I'd become useless. Useless and a handicap to my family. I was draggin them down. No one left to drag down but myself....

By now, my health was kinda messed up. See, alcohol affects every part of you except your fingernails and your ears. Ruins your bladder and prostate and all that. And your central nervous system — I started havin seizures. Your liver, blood, and brain — everything all out of proportion. It gives like a short circuit, and you get disoriented. You get the shakes and everything.

And you get lonesome. When I used to drink at the welfare center, I'd have a mob around me; but now I became, not a closet drinker, but a lone drinker.... There's an alarm clock in a wino's stomach. Seven-thirty you wake up. Liquor store opens at eight, and you go down and buy a pint of wine. If the store's not open, you can go to the bootlegger on 103rd Street — open all night long. Just knock on the door and tell them to give you a pint of Wild Irish or Night Train or Thunderbird. And then you'll start walking — long walks, just sipping your bottle. I'd go to Central Park, Riverside Drive, and what happened to me, I would dwell on the past. I would think about good times and bad times. I would cry and wish I had did this or that — tryin to relive my life. You dwell on this, and your day goes by. Sometimes I would go where the guys are hangin out, everybody drinkin, and they become your drinkin partners. But they're not really friends. Goin here, goin there, with all kinds of scum — that's how I would kill my day.

The way I got outa the Mount Royal — my wife put me in jail for three months. See, I'd get intoxicated — go into these blackouts and wind up bangin on her door, tryin to get back in. "Forgive me! Let me in! I wanta live in a nice clean place!" She'd call the cops to come up and get me, escort me back to the hotel. One time I got mad and urinated on her door. I used to do nutty things like that. But with all I done, she still kept in touch with me. So one time we went to the movies, and I got angry because my wife was going up to Hunter Mountain skiing — you know, having a fun life without me. I started harassing her in the show, so she jumps out of her seat and runs outside. I stopped her and she said, "Cut it out! Leave me alone!" I said, "Come on, honey!" "I'm not your honey!" she says and starts hittin me with her big pocketbook. I tried to restrain her, and she's still hittin me — so I started throwin punches. It's icey and snowy — she's backin up, and she went through a window. CRASH! I grab her to pull her out — had to have three stitches in my finger. She didn't get cut. No lacerations, abrasions — nothin. Anyway, I pulled her out and she kept strugglin with me — slipped and fell on the ice. BAM! She bust her nose — fell on her face and got two black eyes and a bump on the head. I ran away. Thirty-five cops come to get me at the hotel, guns out and everything. . . . Took one look at my wife in court, I said, "Oh, shit! It looks like I kicked the shit out of her!" I got three months.

When I got outa prison, my wife took me in for a week — she'd missed me. I had intercourse with her, and hey, wow, she was gettin her hopes up. "Get a job! Get a house! Get out of that hotel!" Then she started gettin nervous again, remembering all these atrocities I'd done. Banging on her door, hitting her with my belt. All this started comin back to her — all the bad times. Nightmares. Diggin up the past made us both nervous, so she locked up the house and disappeared. I roamed the city. Wanted to go back to jail.

These were the years when there was always another poverty project to join. When my little money ran out, my parole officer asks me, "Look, they're gonna have a drama workshop for ex-offenders. Would you like to be in it?" Theater for the Forgotten. I thought it might be fun. Our director, she was tough — oh, she hated me! Called me a male chauvinist pig whenever I'd forget my lines. I was playin a senator — had a cigar and spoke in a raspy voice. Dyed my hair white. I'd say, "What's the holdup? What's the standstill? What's the slow-down there?" Sounded like King-fish. "You said you tired of me gettin all the money and the power and you gettin nothin — well, from now on you get nothin and I get all the money and power. . . . " She didn't like my acting be-cause she figured I was imitating somebody else. The Stanislavski Method — be yourself — that's what she wanted. . . . One day NBC was comin to film us — a documentary about drug rehabili-tation. I came to the theater too early. Nothin to do, so I went to a bar, killing time till they came. Next thing you know I was wasted — fell right asleep on the theater doorstep. They picked me up drunk and drove me home. Blacked out. "He's drunk! he can't perform!" They threw me out of the car. . . . Fear of failure. Fear of success. You don't see the in-between. You just drink.

Back to another SRO. People dying. People stabbed. People thrown out of windows. I had a girlfriend — she shot herself in the head. Laverne always said she was gonna kill herself, askin how was the best way. She tried pills first, and someone saved her. Then we moved from the Carleton House to the Armstrong on Riverside Drive. What a dump! People screamin, hollerin. Shower's broken. Ice box leakin on the floor. Roaches. Smoke in the hallway — you think the house's on fire — somebody's cookin. People screamin murder all night. Shit on the floor for a week cause nobody's there to clean it up. Walls cavin in. No sheets on the bed. Vomit in the bathroom. It was disgusting! Hey, it was hell!

Getting back to Laverne, She'd had everything once — family, husband, living high on the hog. She wanted to get back to a normal type life, but it's really difficult for an alcoholic to recapture their life. It's been seven years and I can't even get started. I mean, I get started and then I fall back again; start over and fall back again. . . . Well, Laverne bought a gun from somebody and just blew her brains out. She lived for a while, in a coma, in intensive care, but she never came out of it. She was always depressed. And living in these hotels sure doesn't help. Definitely not.

Well, now Laverne was dead and I didn't know where to go. I had forty-seven dollars. Got into a work therapy program at Salvation Army. I never knew Salvation Army was so wealthy. I'd always thought of them panhandling on the street, a little storefront church, everybody poor. . . . They got fabulous buildings! They own trucks! Own a whole warehouse. It's a big business! Soon I was doin great. A "good soldier" — manager for four or five stores. But here's the catch-22. They have television, clean rooms, good food — it's hard to leave. It's good for a little while, but then you get institutionalized — incapable of makin a decision. They wanna keep you, and you become dependent. I developed some morals. I wouldn't go out with drunken women. I wouldn't go with prostitutes. I'd lived all my life like a wildcat, and now — it was like somethin was sapped outa me. Bein sober was difficult.

One day I drank on the job. Blacked out in my room. I found myself tearin up my locker, throwin all my stuff on the floor. Goin crazy. Then they tried to throw me out, and I wouldn't let them. I wanted to move out but I was goin crazy because I couldn't make a decision. So finally, in comes the captain. He never talked to me when I wanted his comfort. This time he listened to me for about two seconds. I wanted to express myself, and he turned his head and started talkin to somebody else. "That bastard!" I said, "he always does that!" I kind of shoved him, and that was it for the Salvation Army. . . .

I took to sleepin on rooftops, walkin around Central Park. Piss in a garbage can, shit in the grass. Even now, I look at guys in the street and say, "That's me!" I always feared being that way. Skin peeling, scratching scabs off my legs — I always feared being like that. And here I was, an animal. Wouldn't change my clothes. Underwear stinks. Don't comb your hair. You become sick, very sick. Eyes watering. Nose running. Got the shakes. Nervous system breaking down. You can't eat because you're throwin up. Can't drink water — all that poison in your system. You get seizures. You get the wino's itch. Your hair stands up on end and you scratch. An animal. . . . Ended up in Roosevelt Hospital.

So here I am. And I'm fortunate for the fact that I got Trinity House to go to. Now I'm sober most of the time, but I'm still a periodic drinker. 1977 I drank one time. Seventy-eight I drank twice — every six months. I drink twice a year, that's all — seven to ten days, then I stop. After that, I won't drink, but then pressure piles up on me. I get depressed, and if I can't shake off the depression in two weeks, I start thinking drinking. "I need relief," I tell myself, and then I try to fight it off, think the bad things about drinking, hoping there'll be a change — some joy, some happiness. Mostly, it doesn't come. . . . I don't know, I used to be a tough guy, a pretty strong person mind-wise, but alcohol weights you down where you become weak. They say you can fight it with will and all, but that's bullshit. You get all the alcohol education you can to fight against it, but like, you win some, you lose some. People die from this stuff. This is slow poison.

I wanna get into the mainstream of things. I wanna get a job, work, make some money. I can't do this with depressions on my mind. I was lookin at television the other day, and the guy says there are gonna be less and less jobs — and he was a business expert. I'll tell you simple as possible — welfare makes you lazy. Waking up, looking for a nine-to-five job — you end up saying, "To hell with it! Why spend five dollars a day for transportation? Why take orders? I don't have to do this. I get a government check."

It's been seven years since my wife left me. Downhill, uphill; downhill, uphill — I can't get it on one straight line and continue up. I used to be like — everything's gotta happen quick. Work overtime, get another job — I was hustlin. Now, hey, time has changed. I can't hustle because it's been my downfall on too many occasions. I got an alcoholic type of brain, and the pressure would be too much for me. I have to learn patience . . . time. . . .

DAVID'S ROUGH MONTH

David is sitting with an open appointment book in his lap. I gave it to him six weeks ago and asked him to keep a record of his activities and feelings over a single month. He sees social workers in the outreach office with their folders, memos, and case histories; he sees doctors with their medical records; he sees me with my note pad — people are always keeping files on him, it seems. So he leapt at my suggestion that he keep his own notes, write his own history.

What follows is his spoken commentary on his month's journal:

I'm gonna bring you back as far as May. That's when everything began to go downhill. I sort of trusted Marsha. She was there when I first started on SSI and — I don't know, I sorta felt adopted to her. She helped me budget my money, but by the time May came I started gettin wiser and I wanted to do more things with my money. On May first I had that fight with her in the social work office. I told you how I got angry and blocked the door, how Marsha stepped in and said I was outa line. "Don't come back till you apologize," she says. So that's how it started. She gave me back my SSI money and told me I was on my own.

Second day of the month and I've spent seventy-three dollars. That's half of what I got to live on till June. In my journal I wrote my code letter NTG, which is "not too good." I lent ten dollars to a girl I was gettin ready to be involved with. She needed to do her laundry, so I went and got it done for her. Next day, her boyfriend came upstairs and took her to Queens — so there goes ten dollars. Then I spent twenty-one dollars for a strobe light to make my room like a disco so I could bug out a little bit. I knew the lights would really set it right. Oh yeah, and ten dollars to my cousin Merry. She's not a real cousin — we were raised in the foster home together. See, after Marsha kicked me outa the office area I couldn't go down there and use the food program. I have to use Merry's kitchen to eat, so that's why I gave her ten dollars. And there's no way she'll let me in there unless I give em some of my pork chops, so I bought twelve dollars' worth to make sure there'd be enough.

To get things started off right, I took Merry and her two girlfriends out to dinner. The most expensive restaurant on the upper West Side — Humane Royal. I felt so good! Money in my pocket. "My treat!" I told em. "What do you want, Chinese or American?" Twenty dollars it cost me. They had pork chops, shrimps with rice — all kinds of stuff. They didn't even eat it all. And they don't know how to act. They went in there actin all crazy — arguin across the table and talking loud. Really embarrassed me. I didn't even eat. All I had was a seventy-five-cent cup of soda.

After we got back to the hotel, I got thrown outa their room. They argue a lot, so they told me to leave so they could finish arguing. I snuck out and got me something to eat from McDonald's.

Saturday, May third. Everything went okay. Just laid around the house all day eatin junk food.

Sunday, May fourth. Went uptown to see my grandmother. Everything went okay. Go in there, sit there, talk, run my mouth, she runs her mouth, then I go. Sunday night everything went bad. Merry and the other two were still arguin, so I didn't have a chance to cook my pork chops which I got in her refrigerator. I think that Merry is using me for my money. All she wants is for me to buy her beer and pot. I buy food, but I never get a chance to eat it. I told her, and she got angry — "You can take your pork chops and get outa here!" And then, later on that night she tells me she was just playing. . . .

Monday, May fifth. A new week began. Things didn't go too good because of the office situation downstairs. I had someone with my meal tickets go in there and sneak me a dinner. Things were still not too good.

Evening class — Auxiliary Police Force, Twentieth Precinct. Must be there. Course number seven. I'm in the training program — eyes and ears of the police department. I wanna see justice being done for a change. If I went into McDonald's and saw somebody snatch somebody's purse, I could intervene — night stick and tear gas. And when I catch the person, I'm allowed to place him under arrest — read him his rights, call for a police car, and haul him away to the station house. I think I will be the center of attraction. If I see something wrong, I'm gonna say something about it — like Serpico, you know. He got shot because he was doing that.

My intention is to work away from the hotel. I don't want nothing to do with the people here.

Tuesday, May sixth. East Side to food-stamp office. Went to Metropolitan Hospital to see about a job. West Side High School to hand out fliers for my old teacher, who is running for Community Board elections. "Vote for Mr. Levine. Vote column one on Primary Day."

Wednesday, May seventh. Red Cross meeting seven P.M. Must be there. AFA and CPR — Advanced First Aid and Cardiac Pulmonary Resuscitation — then I'll be eligible to work in the emergency room at Metropolitan Hospital. Take vital signs — blood pressure, respiration, pulse, and heartbeat. I've already worked in

Pediatrics as a messenger. I've had it in me all my life — wanting to be involved. I can't stand to live in a city where things aren't done the way they're supposed to. If I were mayor I would be on the case. You ever watch "Baretta?" That's the kind of instinct I have — get involved with the community. Let the community know you. Talk to them. Know their problems. Know their kids. Know their family structure and what the community is like. What their needs are. And when something happens in the community, at least they know you're their friend, you'll be there. You have your contacts within the community to let you know what's going on. I'm gonna let the people know I'm there and I'm their friend — I'm there to help. I'm not like these BS cops out there just busting anybody. You know, the more you know the community, the better they can work with you.

Marsha was gettin like those cops — being too bossy. Startin to sound like my mother. It's all right to get bossy, but once you get too bossy . . . I don't like nobody bein too aggressive. I don't let nobody control me but myself.

Three and a half weeks ahead. No food stamps and no money. Must do something quick.

Thursday, May 8th: Went to food-stamp office. Got my ID card and cashed check on 119 West Thirty-first Street. Saw my sister-in-law on the street right after I left there — walking with my two little nieces. Haven't seen her for so many years. She says we'll get together. So that was exciting.

Talked with Marsha about problems, and it was solved. It's good to be forward, you know. I went in and sat in the chair and said, "Marsha, I want you to listen to me. Don't say nothin. Let me talk." And we talked. I didn't directly apologize for nothin. I told her just what she was doing — "You're covering up your own staff member's ass, and you know it! And because I'm not dumb like these other weirdos around here, I know what's going on and I can fight back with what you're hittin me against." She knew I was right. I didn't go in there screamin, whoopin, and hollerin. I came there in the right manner. Plus she knew she can't do that to me. She can't. I'm too smart. So things went okay.

Friday, May ninth. Sweetpea, the dog from upstairs, got killed by a car. A mutt.

Saturday, May tenth. Went up to see Mommy, which is my grandmother. Everything went okay.

Sunday, May eleventh. I'm okay.

Monday, May twelfth. Speak with Marsha. Call hospital to see when I start working. Call Mommy. Borrow thirty dollars.

Tuesday, May thirteenth. Auxiliary Police Force course number eight. Call Red Cross to see when I work. Three food stamps came — twenty dollars — a grand total of sixty dollars. Wow!
Marsha isn't in.

Wednesday, May fourteenth. Metropolitan Hospital for job. Orientation went very well. Worked from nine to two.
Marsha wasn't in.

Thursday, May fifteenth. Last and final CPR and AFA Red Cross class. Second day at work went just right.
Marsha wasn't at work today.

Friday, May sixteenth. Marsha still didn't come to work. Third day at hospital was all right. Rest of the day was okay.

Saturday, May seventeenth: Sex with a girl named Cookie. It went very well. Cookie is nice . . . gorgeous!!! Black. Long hair. They just come to me, knocking on my door. It just happens. Can't control it. I met her upstairs — my friend upstairs, it's his girlfriend. He's a good friend of mine. He doesn't know that me and her are engaged in this little.... Where was I? Okay—Red Cross emergency. Three-alarm fire in the Bronx. I went and served coffee and doughnuts.

Went to Mommy's house. She gave me a black-and-white TV. Everything went okay.

Sunday, May eighteenth. I stayed at home all day. Didn't even go out.

Monday, May nineteenth. Merry getting ready to move. Still haven't had one of my pork chops. Running out of money and food stamps. Must think of something quick.

Marsha didn't come into work again.

Fourth day at work. Everything went well.

Tuesday, May twentieth. Auxiliary Police Force—last and final class. Course number nine.

Wednesday, May twenty-first. Ran out of money. I can't wash my clothes. No food for this next week, and Marsha won't help me. Don't know what to do. I'm getting sick of everything. A lot of pressure. I'm scared when I run out of money. I don't have no friends or nothing, and I'm just trying to figure things out enough to pull me together to hold me out till the next check comes at the end of the month. Things are goin hectic because I'm getting into fist fights. I have a job on the line, but no one cares if I get there clean or don't get there at all.

Whatever happens, no one cares.

Thursday, May twenty-second. Lady stolen. I went walking in the park and, I don't know, she went running loose and somebody came up to me with a knife and started telling me that the dog was bothering him. So they started baiting the dog in with chicken and everything and I lost it.

Friday, May twenty-third. I found the dog again. Somebody had her on the street and was getting ready to walk her without the leash. I clapped my hands and Lady responded — came right over. There was no questions asked or nothing. Too bad it happened when it did, because a half-hour earlier someone gave me a puppy Great Dane. Two big dogs and I haven't the money to feed myself.

Saturday, May twenty-fourth. Gave Lady to a man upstairs. Lady knew twenty people and would respond to mostly anyone. She was too friendly. I figure I can train the Great Dane to know only me and not to listen to anyone else.

Sunday, May twenty-fifth. I was working at the Storefront Museum today. It was raining real hard, and Tom told me to go outside and pick up some papers. I said, "It's raining!" And he said, "You scared of water?" So what I did was I went out there and did the job — got two days pay for one, because I'm supposed to come in tomorrow and I won't. Called him and told him when I got back to the hotel. He said, "You sneak! You did a tricky thing on me!" and all this stuff.

I'm not gonna go back there. He's getting too bossy. Starting to act like my father. I don't like that. It's all right to be a boss, but when you get too bossy I'll let you know.

Monday, May twenty-sixth. Last night I think I seen a lady pick up the puppy Great Dane and put it into a car. I feel miserable. I feel terrible. I slept weird. I expected to see a dog sittin there. I can't do nothin — couldn't even kill a fly.

Tuesday, May twenty-seventh. Had sex with a lady thirty years old — and I'm only twenty. Oh, snap!

Wednesday, May twenty-eighth. I just feel cut off. Right now I feel lost because there's no money. I'm losing weight fast. These pants I'm wearing are size twenty-seven, and they're getting too big for me now. I'm trying to get my act together. Trying and trying. I got appointments coming up to go places, but things get in the way. A month ago things were okay. I mean, I had problems but things were okay. I was eatin good. I was enjoying myself. Things were all right. Now I'm hungry. Money is the root of all evil.

Thursday, May twenty-ninth. I don't drink. Don't get high. But I woke up early today like I just got hit by fifteen potato sacks. Felt like a hangover. Last night I slept in Merry's room, cause she stayed out late. I woke up on her floor and crawled back to my room — left my sneakers in there, left everything. Just went to my room and fell back asleep. Strange. Today I remember — I dreamed that I had my little puppy back. I dreamed that I was finally going through Auxiliary Police graduation day in full uniform. Everything I dreamed were things that — wow! haven't even been accomplished, but are so close.

This week I'll be seeing my friend's car. She's gonna ride me home in it from Auxiliary Police training. Oh, wow! And I want to plan a party — something special for me and her after the ceremonies on graduation night. Just me and her. I wanna go to Roseland — seven dollars apiece. And if she drinks, probably an extra four. Me — just a pack of cigarettes and a can of Coke. I'm hoping my SSI would hurry up, or else that's the last time I might see her. If I don't ask her out soon, I'm gonna feel like. . . . I've gotta speak the initial words — stop looking, stop playing, saying jokes — get down to the facts. I'm a very direct person.

Friday, May thirtieth. Had sex with a girl named Stephanie. She wrote me a note — "Today, like all other days, David, you're something special. So keep doing what you're doing and your days will be meaningful. . . . Love, Stephanie."

* * *

Saturday, May thirty-first. Check Day! Everything went beautiful! Oh, whooo! I felt good. Went to the movies by taxi cab — first time in my life, first time using a cab. I saw *The Empire Strikes Back*. That was a serious movie. I mean, I didn't see *Star Wars* because I was doin time, but *The Empire Strikes Back* deals with the true concept of life — how to control the Force, how to do things the right way. Yodo, or whatever the guy's name was — he was smart. He told Luke Skywalker all he knows. And they actually reveal that Darth Vader is Luke Skywalker's father. Luke never knew his father — like me. They said his father was dead — and when he found out his enemy was his dad, that was shocking. They fought against each other — and yeah, Luke Skywalker survived, but he's got an artificial hand. And Darth Vader is roaming around the universe still. But wow! — it was how to control the Force that was really something. The Force is with you at all times but you gotta learn how to control it.

Sunday, June first. I went to see *Fame* in the afternoon. Kids going through Performing Arts. They wanna be discovered. They wanna be someone. At the beginning of the picture you see this girl trying out for the school — and she's trying out with this other guy, but only for her to get in. It happens that they don't accept her and they accept this other guy who doesn't know how to read or write or nothin. But yet he made it through school, and he became a good dancer and everything. That's me. I did try out for some type of film, but it didn't work.

Later on Sunday, someone gave me some roller skates, and I wanted to use them. You know — wow! This whole day's goin nice! Someone give me free skates . . . of course, they were hot, but no one knows. So I went roller skating. Came back, smoked a cigarette in my room, shut the door, and went back outside. Just as I step out front of the building, someone says my room's on fire. A lot of smoke, a lot of flames toward the window area. I tried going in after my money, but it was too hot — some type of toxic fumes.

And the building manager telling me, "Why don't you call the fire department? It's your room!" Everybody hassling me. Then the water sprinkler went off. Everybody running out the building like it was an atom bomb or something.

So I been burnt outa my room, and all my money's gone.... Today started off so nice. The whole weekend like took me to the top of the ladder — two movies, my first taxi ride, new roller skates — right to the top. And then it was like somebody said, "Down!" And down I went. There's some kinda emergency relief, so I'll get food and another room. The point now is picking up the pieces and putting things back together slowly. So far, it don't look too good.

FRIDAY THE THIRTEENTH

Afternoon sun slanting low across Broadway. Clear crisp day. Doug and Bobby are sipping Old English 800 malt liquor out on one of the narrow Broadway islands. "Good week," Doug says. "Worked three days distributin Buy-Rite flyers. I'm losing some of that beer-belly flab. I feel better. Ron, my boss, is okay. I hadda hit him for an advance a coupla times and he just sticks his hand in his pocket and counts off the bills."

"He's okay. H-e-e-e-e-y, he's okay man," Bobby says. "You know what he said yesterday? I was out in front of the hotel looking like — man, you know that checked jacket I got? And I had my ascot on, and Ron drives up and says, 'Professor! Hey professor, how ya doin?' You know what I mean? I mean, can you dig this guy callin me a fuckin professor?"

A fidgety white lady arrives on the island lugging stuffed shopping bags from Alexander's and Zabar's. She sets her bags down carefully and plucks a newspaper page from the wire waste barrel. She rubs the newspaper over the top of the low concrete wall that shields the island from Broadway traffic. City grime, wine, beer, birdshit, and bits of shining glass — she rubs her spot, nods, sits down.

"Nice day," Bobby says.

"Friday the thirteenth!" she answers and pulls a note pad from her bag.

"Friday the thirteenth," Bobby says. "Hey Doug, she says its Friday the thirteenth." Doug is watching a squad car across the street. "Bad luck. B-a-a-a-a-d luck," Bobby croaks. "Hey, we already had our bad luck. Ran outa fuckin food yesterday. Had this piece of fish, but — hey, I mean we'd cooked this thing five days before. I put my plate on the floor and the cat ate it right up. But like I'm glad, man, I'm glad, cause that fish was *funky*."

"Yeah, but Dianne come in from next door an give us a box of macaroni and cheese."

"That's right!" Bobby's eyes light up. "That box! That box! Listen, I mean really listen, cause that box — what she did was really beautiful. Listen, when all you got is maybe two ounces of spaghetti an a piece of funky bluefish, that box of macaroni and cheese is like a fuckin steak."

We got Sloppy Joes today," Doug says. "I worked, an Ron give me an advance for the weekend."

A crazy white-haired Puerto Rican woman inches across Broadway towards the island. She's wearing two or three raggedy sweaters over a soiled red-and-white polka-dotted dress hitched high above her knees. Heavy black shoes with no laces. Turquoise ankle-length stockings. She balances herself on an aluminum cane with a tripod base. The traffic light turns red. Slowly, very slowly, she begins her crossing. She's gone maybe ten feet when the light flashes green, leaving her stranded in northbound traffic. A few cars zip around her, but she continues to inch ahead. Old humorous eyes. Traffic halts. Horns blare. The light turns red again, leaving northbound cars blocking the east-west cross streets. Bobby steps over to help her mount the low curb. "How ya doin today?"

"It's Friday the thirteenth!" she caws.

"I hear yuh," he answers and backs off.

The note-taking woman stares at her bare wrist, as if to check the time; she steals a quick jerky glance at the bizarre new woman, then slips the note pad into her Alexander's bag. She removes four gold ribbons, stuffs them in her pocket, and quickly switches the note pad into her Zabar's bag. A mangy Hispanic guy wobbles into her as she leaves the island. Her eyes stay fixed on the concrete. She hurries on.

"I make my Sloppy Joes with real meat," Doug says. "You get some green peppers and onions. Throw fresh garlic in, tomato sauce and seasoning — you got yourself a sandwich. Ain't that right, Bob?"

"H-e-e-e-y, I musta had three or four of them already. After that fuckin bluefish — "

"I gotta have meat now that I'm workin."

The Hispanic guy wobbles for balance, strutting preposterously, sometimes catching the sound of a blaring radio and moving to it for a few moments before falling back to awkward gesticulations. Dancing to booze, not music.

"They're all out today," Bobby says.

"Bootleggin's goin up," Doug adds. "Last Sunday I turned $200 for Eddie. Gave me fifteen dollars an a pint of vodka."

"He's all right. Like he knows we ain't gonna rip him off or nothin. Doug loses a few pints, an Eddie ain't gonna get on him for the bread."

"See, if the cops catch you bootleggin they don't wanna bring you in an write out all them forms. They'll just take the stuff and break it there on the street. Now most sellers — that happens an they gotta pay the bootlegger for lost stuff, but Eddie knows I ain't gon — "

CRASH!! Splintered glass. "What the fuck!" Bobby's on his feet, tense and hunched over like he's ready to spring.

"Bobby!" Doug's voice is deep and slow. He hasn't moved except to turn his head to look at the tiny cuts along his arm. Thin threads of blood. "Bobby! Get back!"

The Hispanic man saunters towards them, grunting, head thrust forward. "Yuh try, yuh try figh me."

Bobby removes a tiny glass sliver from his lip. "Look what that dumb motherfucker did! I oughta get my blade and stick him!"

"I don't want no cops today. Okay, Bobby?"

The man is four feet away, glowering at them, flapping his arms. Bobby spits in his direction. The guy growls and spits back, but it dribbles down his chin onto his shirt. He stumbles off balance from the exertion. "He's fucked," Doug says dabbing his bleeding arm with a brown bag. "We take him now an those other guys here gonna take us. Listen, he's fucked, mean an fucked up, an someone's gonna slow him down before too long." He rises and nods to his brother. "Let's get outa here an let these motherfuckers have their fun. He ain't gonna make it through the night."

Bobby stands and stares hard at his unsteady enemy. "Yeah baby, you're lookin at Friday the thirteenth!"

IN THE HOLE

Lloyd's rent has gone up to $200. It may well be that the twenty-dollar increase is illegal, but Lloyd's been feeling down lately — he just doesn't feel up to making the phone calls and going through the bureaucratic hassles to find out. "And my girl friend's fucked up," he says. "All that drinking finally caught up with her and they put her in the hospital. And like I've been trying to find work and she's been giving me money for carfare and something so I can get a sandwich and a cup of coffee. So without her I'm a little short."

It's worse than that. Today is the eighth of the month. Check Day was just a week ago, and he's already out of cash. After he paid his rent he had to use the remaining $100 from his SSI payment to pay back debts from the previous month. He got that settled, but now he's in the hole once again. "It's all right," he explains. "I can handle it. It's my third anniversary in this place, and I'm still hanging in there."

True enough, but he sounds tired, discouraged. Lloyd will have to hustle and worry through a second bad month. A periodic drinker in the hole — I'm not sure he'll make it.

MOURNING

There are some people I cannot approach. I have intimations of craziness, violence, or fragility — fears I can't explain. Whatever the reason, when I feel these stirrings I keep my distance and watch from afar. One man I remember was huge and young and seemingly indestructable. He wore the same clothing year round — knee-length bermudas, a tee-shirt, and old sneakers that he slipped on like sandals. He never stayed on sidewalks, and he always seemed to have a bag of groceries as he shuffled down the street. He walked like he had some intricate route to follow, a fixed plan that could be abandoned only at the greatest peril. One day I saw him stop by a trash basket. He unpacked his groceries on the sidewalk, fumbling through the produce till he found the check-out slip. He tore it to pieces, violently and thoroughly, then kicked and stamped the scraps — the way a horse might trample a snake. On even the bitterest winter days, I'd see him shuffling about in his flimsy shorts and tee-shirt. He seemed impervious to cold. I don't know what he felt.

Another man always wore dresses. There are a number of queens around, of course, but this man never made the least effort to act feminine. He was lean, in his mid-fifties maybe, with gentle intelligent features that reminded me of Roy Wilkins. Sometimes he wore ladies' shoes and tops, but always he wore a dress. I never saw him in make-up or a wig. He looked no more effeminate in his getup than any man might look with a bath towel wrapped around his waist. His handsome, thoughtful face seemed to assure you he was performing some necessary duty, an honorable obligation he had long ago accepted. He did not seem the least bit crazy — that was what was most disconcerting. "He's not a homo," Ironsides explained. "He don't go for that kinda scene. I'll tell you, he's just as normal as you an me. When he come here, he wore pants an suits like everyone else. Had a job, doin okay. What happened was his wife died. He stayed up in his room a few days, alone and keepin to hisself. An when he come out, he was the way you see him now — all her clothes. You get the picture?"

CANDY MAN

"Wanna buy some candy?"
"I'm lookin man, I'm lookin."
"Tyrone's out front."
"Tyrone?"
"Light-skinned dude."
"Good shit?"
"Fly!"

GETTING BACK

Doc's canine teeth jut out over his lip, cracked and yellowy, like tiny scrimshaw. "I wanna get outa here," he says. "If I could just find me some work, I could get me an apartment an fix it up right."

A tiny woman with spindly legs and a sweet thin face sits beside him in a splotchy black dress. "You'll do it, Doc! You'll find somethin." She passes him her bottle of Night Train.

"Yeah," he sighs. "Only each time I try to make it back I see how far down I come. Seems like I'll never make it back."

"You will! You will! An you gotta start by buildin self-confidence."

"You're right, I know, but that hill I gotta climb — I look up to where I gotta go, and it looks more like a mountain to me now. I'm startin to think I ain't ever gonna make it back."

FED UP

"I'm fed up with Trinity House," Lloyd says. "They only take you when you're okay — won't let you into AA unless you've already stopped drinkin. They don't want you when you have problems."

INDEPENDENCE DAY

American flag drooping from a fourteenth-floor window. Candy and a few friends sitting on the iron steps of Freya's. Lady, Candy's plump little mutt, sprawled on the pavement, stuffed and drowsy after feasting on the huge pork butt that lies unfinished by her side. Slanting morning sun. The heat is already building. A young man weaves down the sidewalk wearing a hooded ski parka, sandals, and a checkered blanket fastened kilt-style about his waist. He looks like he's eighty.

"You cold?" one of the guys asks.

"Don't say nothin!" Candy warns.

"Hey man, where you get that fancy dress?"

"He's crazy!" Candy struggles to his feet. "You don't know *what* he's gonna do!"

Two fire engines tear down 100th Street and stop in front of the hotel. A police car shoots in from the other end of the street, followed by an ambulance. The kilted crazy takes off. Heads pop out of the hotel. On the seventh floor some guy leans way out of his window and points down. Other residents gesture in the same direction. "Second floor again," one guy says indifferently.

"Mental," Candy adds and moves up a step to get out of the sun. Lady flaps a leg. "Ain't wrapped too tight."

One of the guys tugs Candy's ankle. "Hey chief, gimme one of those!" Candy takes a pack of Pall Malls from his sock. His friend takes one and nods down the block. "That one ain't too brown either."

Walking up the middle of 100th Street, making his way around the fire engines, police car, and ambulance is a stocky guy in baggy yellow shorts, high wool argyle socks, and a black tee-shirt showing a deco Manhattan skyline. He smiles, beams radiantly. "Another mental," Candy says. "Actually, they don't like no one callin em mental. I got my VA trainin in nursing, an they don't like you callin em mental or crazy an stuff. 'Sick' is what you're supposed to say. Guy come in saying it's the end of the world an he's the first black Jesus — we gotta call him 'sick' like he caught a cold or somethin."

"You're not really a nurse, Candy. Nurses gotta be women, man. That ain't no thing for no Indian brave to be into."

"Goddamn right! I'm a nurse!" He takes a slug of Night Train and passes it on. "An those welfare people downtown want me sweepin streets. I'm not sayin I'm too good for it, but I'm a nurse. Got my certificate up in my room. Seems like with all the sufferin in this city they could find me work in some hospital."

"You goin to the fireworks?"

"If I'm not too drunk." The fire engines and ambulance leave. Two policemen step out of the hotel leading a middle-aged woman in a tattered house robe. She waves a taped finger above her head in triumph.

A few feet away, the guy in argyle socks is talking at the walls of Temple Beth Ansched. "I wanna get a shot at it! You tell him, you tell him, you tell him they can go FUCK THEMSELVES!!!" His voice drops to a confidential murmur. "No, no." his head shakes back and forth. "Don't let them . . . it doesn't . . . hold . . . I can't . . . Philadelphia . . . I WANNA GET A SHOT! A SHOT! SHOT!"

"Shoulda took him too."

"He's not hurtin no one."

"We got too many mentals in here. What I'd do, I'd get one of them tall ships with all of them sails an shit. Bring it right up to the dock at Seventy-ninth Street for July Fourth. Then get all the mentals, all of em from all the hotels around here an make like a big party for em. Beer an barbecue an reefers — whatever they're into, see. An I'd take the ship out in the river, right. Take em out so they could see the city, on around the Statue of Liberty an down under the Verazanno Narrows Bridge. Yeah, an then I'd take em out in the ocean an pull the plug. Like they do with all the garbage an shit."

"Broadway's givin a barbecue tonight," Candy says. "I'll be there if I ain't too drunk. But I don't like crowds. Makes me nervous with too many people."

A guy walks past them, gets as far as the man in argyle socks and turns around. "Hey man, there a numbers place around here?" He points towards West End Avenue.

"Other way. That grocery store."

"I asked in there and they didn't know nothing about it."

"It's Fourth of July, man. No numbers today. National holiday."

HEAT WAVE

A WONDERFUL AFTERNOON

Heat wave. Impossible to stay in airless rooms. Doc and Muriel find a shaded spot on the street, leaning against a parked station wagon as they wile away the steamy afternoon. Doc gestures at the next car. "That's a Toyota Lift Back," he says.

"Left Bank?" Muriel smiles. "Well, isn't that continental!"

"Lift Back. Rear goes right up."

"Washington plates! Now I wonder — is that our capital or the state?" Her most cultivated accent. The missing dowager.

"They'd have D.C. on it if it was the capital."

"Why of course, Doc! You've got such a good head for these things. Oh my! See that JLY in the corner? Do you suppose that could be a code for July?"

"Yeah. An look here — it says JLY 80. That means his plates is expired on him."

"Why Doc! You're a regular Sherlock Holmes!" Muriel is having a wonderful afternoon. And Doc is a gentleman. He knows how to listen. He appreciates clever remarks. "Why we ought to teach this criminal a lesson!" she says. "Lift his Lift Back! Confiscate it. Confidentially skate to the Cape." She giggles at her own fantasy. "Old Cape Cod! Oh, my land! I'll bet we'd be something new at the old Cape!"

Doc pushes out from the station wagon, teetering in drunken rhythm as he sings:

> In the Big Rock Candy Mountains,
> There's a land that's fair and bright,
> Where the hand-outs grow on bushes
> And you sleep out every night

"Oh Doc! You're being romantic! He lurches back against the car. "Or is it pedantic? Those mountains may be quite far away, you know. Your work is cut out for you."

"Washington's fallin in the ocean. Guy's lucky he made his getaway," Doc says. "That volcano out there, that's just a sign. Next time you're gonna have volcanoes along with them California earthquakes. Whole coast gonna split off an fall into the ocean. Listen, you ever hear of that big rock out at Niagara Falls?"

"You honeymoon there?"

"Need a woman first."

"I'd be delighted!"

"And what about that dam broke in Italy?"

Muriel ponders a minute. "Never heard about it. I feel so uninformed. I used to read *Time* and *U.S. News and World Report* and — "

"It never happened, maybe. I got so much on my mind, I don't always know which is news and which is somethin I thought of on my own."

Across the street an old geezer yells and curses at an empty phone booth. "Nazi butchers! Nazi butchers!" he screams. "Have to cut me open to get the names! I got em! I got em! Fuckin cocksuckers!"

"High," Doc observes coolly.

"Out of his mind," Muriel adds. "But not out of sight. Out of his mind. . . . But where could that be? Does that mean we're *in* our minds?"

"Oughta get him off the street." Doc does his best to impersonate a concerned citizen. "Disturbing my peace. I don't know what's happening to our neighborhood."

"I meant to tell you Doc, your hair looks good short." He pulls his cap off and rubs a hand over the stiff stubble. "Who did it for you? It must've happened very recently."

He rubs his scalp again looking genuinely puzzled. "I wish I knew. I wish I knew."

COMING APART

Five days is all it took. Five days of steady drinking and Lloyd Smith has turned his life inside out. His periodic binge. He tries to fold his hands but three broken fingers poke out at painful, impossible angles. They're swollen to ugly fatness, so impossibly bent that it seems they must have been clamped in a vise and carefully, methodically maimed. The room is in total disarray; Lloyd looks pathetic, utterly wasted. . . . I cannot take my eyes off these three fingers.

"I went to pawn my TV yesterday." Sheepish grin. In some way he relishes his humiliation. "This Puerto Rican guy saw I was having trouble cause of these fingers. That happened last night — I don't know, maybe the night before — and I was kinda hanging out, and these two guys start jumpin each other. I go in to break it up — so of course I'm the one who gets hurt. Anyways, this Puerto Rican guy carries my TV, and the pawn shop lady gives me twenty dollars. Okay, so now I buy him and his two Irish buddies a few pints of Thunderbird. Then they say they're hungry, and I buy some sandwiches. I don't now what I'm doin. I'm drunk. Someone does a little somethin for you, and if you don't give em somethin back they call you a pigeon. I'm fucked up, man. I'm drunk."

Bottles all over. Richard's Wild Irish Rose, Thunderbird, Night Train. Crumpled brown bags. Wrapping foil from carry-out sandwiches. Butts and ashes in the carpet. Soiled sheets stuffed in a corner. On the empty TV stand a large frying pan with bits of scrambled egg and feasting cockroaches. On top of the refrigerator is a pot with burnt spaghetti caked inside, filled with soapy water. . . . Deep in his anguish, self-destructive and out of control, Lloyd has remembered to soak his pot.

POKER GAME

Empty room on fifteenth floor. Formica table. A bunch of chairs. Refrigerator stocked with pony-sized Millers, house beer for tonight's game. Ironsides presides from his wheelchair. His head looks much bigger with his hat off — bald and pear-shaped like Jarry's cartoon of Pere Ubu. Clarence Taylor in his purple pants and purple flowered shirt. Pony tail. Eager to win. Willy, a large dark man. He was once a club fighter in Detroit; playing cards look like postage stamps in his huge heavy hands.

They play a variation of seven-card draw designed to keep everyone betting. Eight wild cards — and each new card is dealt face down. Dealer calls the wild cards. Almost every hand is twos and fives ("quarter's wild"), threes and fours ("thirty-four this game"), or sixes and nines ("awright boys, we're gonna do it down and dirty").

Eddie the bootlegger staggers in. Grey hair. Grey beard. Barely standing. He bumps the table and slumps into a chair. He pulls a crumpled ten-dollar bill from his pocket and begins nodding out before his change is counted. Cards are dealt but Eddie doesn't touch his hand till his head droops and clunks the table. "Eddie! Eddie! Your cards." He turns one over without bothering to look at the others.

"Dollar to you, Eddie."

"Yeah, yeah," he mumbles and shoves all his bills to the center of the table.

"Just one, man." Clarence pushes the bills away from the pot.

On the second round Eddie sees the fifty-cent bet, then takes his first look at his two down cards. "What'd yuh say was wild?"

"Threes and fours."

"This ain't worth shit!" He chucks his hand in.

On the next hand he antes his fifty cents, then turns his hand in and snoozes while the others play.

"You ready, Eddie?" Ironsides asks on the next hand. "Hey Eddie! We're here to play. Trying to run a game like gentlemen."

"Yeah, yeah." He shoves his pile of bills into the center.

"All right," Clarence says, "I'll take out your ante."

Eddie's lids fall. His chin rests on his chest. Shoulders drooping low over the table. "Your bet, Eddie."

"Yeah, yeah." He shoves two dollars into the pot. Everyone sees his bet. "Threes and fours wild, right?"

"No, Eddie. That was last hand. We're goin down and dirty this time. Sixes and nines."

Eddie's head snaps up straight. "Shit. I thrown in two dollars and now you go an change the wild card!"

"Hey, Eddie," Ironsides says sternly, "we don't need no one noddin through our game. We're playin like gentlemen. You wanna play, you gotta stay awake."

"Fuck that shit!" Eddie slumps back in his seat.

"Your bet Eddie."

"Fuck you!" He throws two dollars in the pot. "Fuck your fuckin money!" Everyone stays in.

By the fifth round Ironsides shows all diamonds, Clarence a pair of kings, Willy a pair of tens, and Eddie a hodgepodge of low cards.

There's over thirty dollars on the table when the players check their last cards. Clarence bets three dollars. Ironsides sees him, and Willy folds. "To you, Eddie."

"Fuck that shit!"

"Eddie, you in?"

He swats a crumpled five-dollar bill with the back of his hand. Clarence smoothes it out, sets it in the pot, and hands Eddie two singles.

"Fuckin money!" Eddie mumbles. "Take the whole fuckin thing!" He shoves the two singles back into the pot and drops his head.

Ironsides and Clarence see his two and call. "I got your diamond flush beat," Clarence says to Ironsides.

"You got the flush beat, but that don't mean you got me beat." Ironsides shows a full house — aces over eights. "You got any extra kings you feel like showin me?"

"Fraid not," Clarence replies. "Just a couple of sixes and nines." He turns the two wild cards and pushes them towards his pair of kings. "Four of a kind! That good enough?" He drops the used deck on Ironsides's losing hand and smiles. "Hey Eddie, you got anythin we oughta know about?"

Eddie's head is on the table again, forehead pinning his cards in place. "Eddie! Hey, Eddie! Whatchya got?"

"Let the cards talk!" Ironsides says. "Eddie! Eddie! Deal's over. Turn your hand!"

Eddie raises his head with great effort and flips his cards. "Shit!" Willy exclaims. "He's sittin on three wild cards!"

"Still gotta beat my kings."

Ironsides stares at the cards a moment, then pushes them in line like pieces in a puzzle. "What you say about a straight flush!"

"Shit! He didn't even know what was wild. Where all those threes and fours he was bettin on?"

"He ain't got no threes and fours," Ironsides says. "He probably been sittin on these sixes from the first cards. Puttin us on. Settin up the pot." Ironsides's spirits have soared considerably, but Clarence is not amused.

"An I been countin out his money," Clarence says, "makin sure he don't lose nothin he ain't supposed to."

"Yeah," Eddie says as he rakes in his prize, "sure do appreciate it."

WHITE PUSSY

Ironsides has this thing for white pussy. Or maybe it's an act he puts on for Lloyd and Chink and Bobby and Candy — whoever's out on the street when he cruises down the block to walk his weimaraner each morning. He's got this thing — turning on his love light as the morning procession passes from West End to Broadway on their way to work.

— Hey Baby! I got somethin good for you.

— Ooooooh, you look *nice!*

— Honey! hey Honey, I'm talkin to you!

— Mmmmm-hmmmm! Nice! Nice! Nice!

"Sheee-it!" Ironsides yanks the visor of his terry-cloth cap and watches his dog take a dump on the sidewalk. "White pussy! Gonna have me some white pussy!" The words gurgle low in his throat, like a death rattle.

FIRE SALE

Yvonne Mitchell has come by from the Regent on 104th to visit a while with Yvonne Smith. Yvonne Mitchell's eyebrows have been thoroughly plucked, replaced by a sharply rising pencilled line. Her eyelids and upper cheeks are colored vivid rose. "I don't wanna boast or nothin," she says, "but my momma didn't raise no ugly children." Barry, her six-year-old, clambers up the metal gate of an empty store. "Get offa there," she barks. "Who you think you are, climbin up where you can fall an hurt yourself!"

"Spiderman," he declares.

"Well you get yourself down, cause you just a boy. You ain't no Superman."

"You hear about that little boy who thought he was Superman?" Yvonne Smith says. "Right uptown in Harlem. Went out on his roof and jumped off five floors."

"That ain't normal. Boys'll climb an get in trouble, but no average boy's gonna jump hisself offa no five stories." Another woman comes by with a cute little girl. The child clasps a half-eaten bag of potato chips. "Hi, Ya-Ya!" Yvonne says. "How ya doin?" Ya-Ya waves her bag of potato chips and gurgles. "Hey, Barry," Yvonne calls, "come on over here an say hi to Ya-Ya."

Barry wraps himself around a metal stair railing. "Hi, pretty girl!" he says, averting his eyes.

"Ooooh, Barry! You got a thing for Ya-Ya."

"She better find her a man fast," her mother says. "Way she's eatin I can't go on feedin her. She goes in the Red Apple with me an starts cryin cause I won't buy her no bag of popcorn to eat at this hour of the mornin."

"Right," Yvonne Smith says, "an you know all about bein a good mother, don't you?"

"Come on, Ya-Ya," the mother says. "We got things to do."

"What's that about?" Yvonne Mitchell asks after they walk off.

"I wouldn't trust her with nothin," Yvonne Smith says. "She came to baby-sit for a friend of mine. Watched her baby for four days so my friend could visit her family, an she goes off an calls the police. Reports my friend for runnin off; says she's an unfit mother, like she abandoned her child or somethin."

"Barry! You get outa that garbage!"

"Look Momma!" Barry waves a brand-new shoe.

"Bet that's from the fire," the boy's mother says.

"We was there when the windows blew out," Yvonne Smith says. "Soon as people saw the smoke they was down there rattlin them gates. Doug come by an started yellin for everyone to get back. All them people could think about was tearin down those gates, but Doug kept yellin at em till they moved outa the way. An just as soon as they done it, the window explodes. POOM! Glass shootin out onto the street. These peoples was in there in a minute. Flames. Smoke. Nothin gonna keep them outa there. I seen this one guy, musta made twelve trips. Come out coughin on the smoke, put down a pile of jeans, an go back in for more. Blouses, shoes, underwear — you name it. Fashion Trap was empty in ten minutes. Police come but they didn't do nothin."

"Shit, those people got insurance. They don't want that stuff back after they just set a fire to get rid of it."

"Nobody loses. Peoples was sellin jeans up an down Broadway. You coulda bought anything you want right here on the street. An you know what I think — they been clearin out the Carleton Terrace all last week, an now the Fashion Trap burns down next door. I think they're plannin to combine em an put in a new supermarket."

"Fire's the fastest way."

"I wouldn'ta gone in there for nothin. Runnin in an outa them flames. But gimme another one of them blackouts, I'll be doin some fast shoppin in that supermarket. Get me enough to live on for a couple of months."

YVONNE SMITH'S STORY

Seems like I grew up so fast. And sometimes it seems like I never grew up at all. There was nine of us, nine children, and outa the nine I was the black sheep. Everything was decent in our neighborhood. People playin outside, goin to parks, family picnics, tennis, basketball, readin books. I'd get up in the mornin, get dressed — my mother would do our hair and send us off to school. But I'd never go. I'd run off to the park because my family — they were livin on a pedestal, thinkin they're high and mighty. That's a trip, and it wasn't my trip.

My mother and I argued every day. My father, he was a retired Army man, but he would never be home. Too busy gambling, bein with the fellas, lookin for a big time. And he didn't like my mother's *madness* — he called her that all the time. No love there. Neither of them ever took the time with me. I always wanted to talk to my mother, to tell her how I felt inside, but she was carryin on drinkin. Oh, man! She was very depressed, very emotioning — gettin in the car and drivin off drinkin. One time she didn't come back for three days. All of us walkin the streets lookin for her. Comes home and tells us she had an accident drinkin. She was highly emotional. Nervous. Very upset. Drinkin, drinkin, drinkin — always carryin on. She's where I get my high-strung nature from. And she's tryin to tell me what's right for me! I couldn't take it. I simply couldn't take it.

I was gettin older, growin up on my own. By now I was sixteen, havin dreams that I wanted a baby — wonder dreams, I call em — and my mother said, "You're not gonna have any of those dreams! You're gonna hurt, you're gonna hurt for a long time!" That's what she told me. . . . And that's what happened.

I'd see guys, neckin and carryin on. And I wanted to have this baby so bad. Ooooh, I'd just love to have me a baby! When I got pregnant I didn't know it — my mother had never told me anything. All I knew was I was sick in the stomach. When I went and had tests, the doctor said, "I'll call your mother to come get you. You're havin a baby."

"Keep her there!" That's what my mother told him. "I don't want her!"

They said, "Well, you just come and get her!"

I wondered why she brought my two sisters with her. I felt like they were plottin, like they were very evil. And we didn't go right home — we went to some place I'd never been. I was leery. But I couldn't think what was gonna happen, so I went along with it. . . . "We gonna insert this thing up her," this man told my mother, "and tomorrow morning the baby gonna be on the floor. No proof. No witness. Won't nobody know nothin, right?" I was a young girl — didn't know nothin about no abortions. They took me home and put me in my mother's bed. Paper runnin from her room to the bathroom. It was terrible. Six o'clock Sunday morning, I was . . . felt very . . . I'm soakin wet. Body achin. I said, "Maybe I should get up and go to the bathroom. Nobody there to help me. Left there by myself. I was scared to move. I felt my whole insides was gonna fall out. I could have died. Coulda went crazy. Hemorrhaged. I didn't know. I passed out.

Came to in the hospital. My family had called the ambulance and told them I'd miscarried — fell down the stairs. It was like a dream. I couldn't believe . . . I would never hurt my mother. Never. But she hurt me, tricked me out. I just couldn't stand up to her. And I'm sufferin now because. . . .

Got my freedom at age twenty-one. It was around the time everyone was rioting where we were in Detroit, and I was out there with them, lootin and carryin on. I wasn't really into it myself, but I was havin a good time helpin other people. Everybody runnin and hidin, duckin behind buildings. It was a big game for me. And when that got over, things sure enough changed for me.

That was when I met William Smith. He was a militant. Shaved his hair off. Carried guns in his side. I dug him. To me he seemed very strong, so at twenty-two I married him. Life with him was sort of a trip. He was always fantasizing, but things never happened the way he said they would happen. He had a full shelf of books he studied. He was reading about Vietnam, about politics, and Eldridge Cleaver. And he was a certain kind of Muslim. Not the Black Muslims, but this other type. They can eat pork, drink, smoke marijuana, party, commit adultery, do weird things — everything the Ten Commandments is for, they're against. So he was studying his group and the Black Muslims and trying to put all of it together. And you can't do that. You can't mix fiction with truth, hate with God, the Devil with human beings. It was sort of a mixed-up world for him. And I went right along with it, right? It seems like he had some kinda power over me, and I was living in a dream world. Like a book I could open up and see pictures of me like a lamb — surrounded by snakes, lizards, sea creatures — all the madness, all the things happenin around me.... But I knew reality was always there. I never forgot reality.

I tried to be a good housewife, but my husband changed from good to bad, from bad to ugly. Weeks passed. Years passed. William was pickin up men in funny bars, partyin, smokin herb, drinkin expensive liquor, tryin to set up freaky scenes. We kept on fightin, kickin, and scratchin each other, and I just got tired. I was gettin close to twenty-five. Fourth year of our marriage. Man, I just couldn't take it. Pressure. Always pressure. Seemed like the Devil was eatin me up on the inside. I started havin convulsions. And I was eatin a lot. Steady eatin. Gettin fatter and fatter. And sleepin, fallin out soon as I woke up.... And I just started cryin.

One weekend my mother, my whole family, had a big party. Me and William came, and something strange happened. I couldn't pop my fingers. I couldn't dance. I couldn't move my feet. I was just standing there. Then I started cryin and foamin at the mouth. Oh boy, my family wanted to kill William! They took me to the hospital and the psychiatrist told me, "Look, get away from this man. Get away from these nagging people — or you will always be like this!" I just couldn't believe that this was happening. But honey, the fifth year we was married I just changed. Got myself together, packed my clothes and told him to kiss my ass!

You guessed it — I moved back home with my mother. William called and told me, "Come home! Come on home!"

"I'm not goin nowhere!" I said. Hung up the phone.

Next day, "We gonna have black brothers in the streets! We gonna get guns! We gonna rob a bank!" All kinda weird things.

I said, "I'm not comin! You do your revolution without me!"

A few days later he says, "I want you to come here because I'm ready to be killed."

"Oh, you're crazy," I told him. "You're talkin shit!"

"No, I'm gonna get killed. Can't leave my house."

I said, "I don't want to hear it. I'm not comin there. I'm goin to sleep." So I hung up. Never heard from him again.

My sister called me about four o'clock in the morning. "Your husband's dead! Somebody stabbed him." When I went down to the morgue it freed me. We buried him, and after we put him in the hole I partied all night long.

I was twenty-six and I thought about New York. I loved the idea of New York; I always wanted to come here because there wasn't nothin in Detroit for me. And my mother was a trip. I couldn't stay there no more on account of her.... Well, there was this friend of my dead husband's, name of Jimmy Lewis, and when he came to New York I bought a train ticket to come visit. I arrived about ten o'clock that night, and I was real jittery. Jimmy said, "We got a nice place. You'll like it here." So we took a cab to the park Plaza on Seventy-seventh between Central Park West and Columbus — my first SRO. It was a pretty decent place. I had a small room with cabinets by the door. I didn't have no stove, but I had a hotplate. My own bathroom. Comic books. A TV and radio. I had everything I wanted. Jimmy sold herb, black beauties, acid, THC. He had a lotta mouth — after three weeks I knew everybody in that building. Everybody. Plus he went from market to market stealin. I thought it was a joke, but it wasn't — it was his life.

I was very dedicated to Jimmy, but we never went nowhere unless it was business. We started gettin in arguments, and he slapped me around. Before he met me Jimmy had a woman that was a prostitute, and now he wanted me to come that way. This other woman couldn't sew, couldn't cook, but she spoiled him her own way. Turnin tricks and payin the rent. Bought him clothes. Spent all her money on him. And when he got with me I didn't have any money to give him. Only thing I've got is my SSI check. Know what that nigger tell me? "Well, *all* my women got to give me a check once a month! Now you know that's not correct. Very insultive. Very insultive. So what I did was put the whammo on him. I told my girlfriend Chicky my problem and she says, "Well, I'm movin to Brooklyn. We can get you a nice place. You get yours and I get mine."

"For real?" I said.

"Yeah."

I say, "Cool! I'll do it." Chicky, she's a lady of the night. A real trip. Her mind's very weak; she gets mad too fast — way faster than me. But see, she's been misused. Her old man kilt her mother.

I was thrilled with my place in Brooklyn. I had a bedroom suite, a whole houseful of furniture, and a little cat. I gave Jimmy my new address, but he was actin crazy now that I had left him. He come out and lay a couple of nights with me and then started fightin. "Get out!" I said. "Just get out!" He took some scissors and cut my TV wire. He cut my clothes, my bodice — everything I owned he tore up. Cut my furniture. Took my watch. My shoes — he ripped my shoes up. Oh man, everything I had he just tore up completely, yellin, "Bitch! Bitch! I should kill you!" I was afraid he was gonna cut me up next. I left everything and ran out of the building.

By the time the police got there he'd gotten tired of tearing up my apartment. Police looked for him all over the city, but he got away.... He was nice lookin. Very intelligent. An A-1 student. Got a lot on the ball. But he got hung up usin those drugs. He went back to Detroit, started shakin guys down. Six months later some gangsters shot him dead in the head.

Well, by now Chicky had introduced me to Clarence Taylor. She saw that I was starin at him, lookin at his pretty hair. He was stayin in the Hotel Walden, and after we met I used to go over there and look for him. I wanted to get it on, but he was never there. People would ask me who I come to see. I'd say, "I come to see Clarence — Clarence with the ponytail."

They all knew him. "Yeah, yeah," they'd say. "You gotta catch him early in the morning."

But I never did. I wrote him a letter — he wants me, he gotta come to me. No sooner I put it in the post, here comes Clarence to Brooklyn. I was gettin ready for bed when I heard the buzzer ringin, so I put on my little negligee and made myself really good lookin for him. Told myself, "Oh, goodness! This is gonna be my man!" I opened the door and there he was. Looked the same way he do now only his skin was prettier. . . .

Next mornin he told me all the things that happened to him. He's Aquarius. He was rich three times. He smokes herb, drinks a little, talks and parties — and now he wants a housewife, wants to live like a normal man, wants to give me things I like. "If you want me," he said, "you better come to Manhattan." So I got ready to go.

Before I moved into Hotel Walden I went to the hospital for stomach pains. What really surprised me, they told me my tubes were tied. All these years I'd wanted a baby and couldn't — I didn't know what was wrong. And being childless had takin a lot outa me — a big gap in my life. I've always told myself that bearin children would make me more of a woman, make me see myself grow. I want to experience things with my daughter that I didn't have as a child. But see, in the process of me gettin the abortions they tied my tubes without ever tellin me. And I know my mother done it — tryin to control me, keepin me from being a woman. . . .

I come to Hotel Walden and moved in with Clarence. Wasn't no turnin back. He bought me a twenty-five inch color TV, a record player, speakers. Got me a refrigerator. A lotta new clothes. He does plaster, walls, plumbin — everything to do with pipes, he knows. And he goes upstairs every week to run the poker game with Ironsides. Never wants me to go with him. "You stay here," he says, "cause these guys in the building, I know all of em, and I know that they see you they're gonna be carryin on and flirtin. I don't want you around them. That ain't what it's about."

"That's cool," I'll say. "I'll stay right here." I'm a respectable woman, and I see where this hotel can be a lot of trouble. I don't feel insecure, but I feel Hotel Walden has a lot of effect on our relationship. It's not that we argue — we're doin fine — but it's this building. Everybody wants to bring the other person down. They don't trust each other. They want you to be the same way they are — insecure and layin up with this one, doin all kinda things. I'm not like that, but they done label me every trick in the book. People slippin up to me and sayin, "Clarence's gonna leave you. He did this and this with this other woman." I don't listen to that garbage. I know they're jealous of us — seein us make it.

I been here a few years now. I met a lot of people, but most of them are gone. They die. You forget them. Ones that are left are half crazy. Like Frankie — he's a playful dude. Should have been a mother instead of a man. Actually, he's a good person. He minds his business. Tries to treat everybody the same. But most people are crazy. White, Puerto Rican, Spanish, Greek, Latins, blacks, Haitians — these people are a trip. And you get some like Ironsides. Now there's a strange dude. One minute he talks good things; next minute he talks to another person about how bad you are. He's two-faced, very nosey. He screwed up a lot of people's lives. Him and his brother Jiggy. I call him the Devil, but he's cool too. A man of the night. A strange cake. And Eddie, bootleggin Eddie with the white hair. He's in a world of his own. So many people is wastin away. You see em everyday, but a lot of em ain't got nothin on the ball. Doug, Bobby — it may seem that they're together, but they fight, they argue, they throw things at each other, burnin each other up. They all crazy. Half this building's nuts.

Look, it gets to me too. I'm gettin too old for this. I can't take much more. I'm trying to find me a job, so I won't be sitting around here all day. Since I've been in New York I've worked in Prince Laundry on Thirty-fourth Street. I've worked at GHI as a homemaker's aide. I was a dancer at the Palace on Forty-fifth Street, but there were too many queens. I have a lot of respect for my body. I have no shame, but I couldn't see myself doin this type of life. I respect it. I understand it. But it's not for me. I was supposed to get a job in Burger King, but it didn't work out. Plus I baby-sits a lot. I just gotta see what kind of work I'm best in. Sometimes I sell dinners — cook a bunch of food. I'll cook fried chicken, potato salad, homemade string beans, pepper steak — sell dinners at the poker game. But now I was thinkin of sendin leaflets around. I'll have the chicken ready and people be knockin on my door. I could be sellin wine and liquor too. For every twenty dollars you spend, you can make twenty back. So that's not bad. I got to plan it all, get it together and put it on paper.

You know, I got these plans — and me and Clarence's hopin to get outa here — but so much of my life has been a rut. I hope, knock on wood, that I will never live like that again. And my mother — I don't ever want to be bothered with her. See, I've learned something every day I've lived here. And I got a chance to make a decent life with Clarence. I feel happy, I feel blessed, cause we got peace of mind. And if you got peace of mind, the whole world could go tumblin on your head but in the end you'll be all right.

HOUSE OF DEATH

Somebody named Jackie died last night. They took her away early in the morning, but word spreads. Out on the street, Candy pulls a corn chip from his pocket and extends his arm. Lady, his fat little dog, leaps up to snatch it from his fingers. "She was on our floor," he says.

"I'd know her," Bobby Carman says. "Hey, I know everyone in this fuckin hole. If you told me what she looked like — "

"She was way down the other enda the corridor. Right, Chink?" He nods — round boyish face with thin slanting eyes. He never seems comfortable when attention turns to him. "I never really got to know her," Candy continues. "She only come here in February."

It's August first. Check Day. Food, beer, cigarettes, reefer, dope, and settled debts. Three hours till the money comes. Jackie's name passes back and forth. Nobody knows much about her. "She was drinkin," someone says. "I saw her Friday night. Drinkin pretty good."

Yvonne comes by sipping Old English 800 through a straw. "Last day in this place! Last day! You hear about Jackie?" People nod. "She wasn't more'n twenty-seven."

"You knew her?" Bobby asks. "What'd she look like? Doug an I musta known her."

She gestures towards West End, the entrance to Temple Beth Ansched. "We played cards out there. We useta sit on these steps an play cards, an drink."

"H-e-e-e-e-y," Bobby says, eyes sparkling, "Dougie and I knew her. Sure. I saw Doug talkin to her like just a week ago. Right where we're sittin."

"Natural death?" someone asks.

"Hey baby, no one dies a natural death in here."

"A house of death," Yvonne says, "That's what this place is. A house of death."

"I mean like drinkin," the man explains.

"She was drinkin heavy last weekend, but I don't know that it killed her. Her old man, he give her a good beatin for it. Heard they're holdin him for questionin, but I don't think he done nothin to kill her. I'll tell you — it's this place. She couldn't handle it. A house of death. House of death. . . . "

COMING SOON

[Sign above the burnt-out entrance of the Fashion Trap]

```
COMING SOON
ANOTHER RED APPLE
SUPERMARKET
```

THE GLENDALE

Late night evictions. Management thugs kicking doors in at two A.M. Over fifty people homeless in less than a week. Doors nailed shut. All this just a few blocks away in the Glendale. The manager claims he only removed people who were behind in their rent. A few weeks ago a convenient fire broke out in the Glendale office, lasting just long enough to destroy the rent payment records. So now it's up to building management to remember the payment records of 200 people — and residents must trust management, go along with its decisions. At least, this appears to be how management sees it.

There are laws, of course. There are always laws. Eviction notices must be served. A relocation fee must be paid to each person sent away. And it is management's legal duty to find suitable living quarters for those whom it evicts. That is the law: yet close to one third of the hotel's population is sent scurrying before city agencies bring this wave of evictions to a temporary halt.

Furniture, mattresses, broken appliances, and personal effects pile up in the rear courtyard — heaved out apartment windows as part of the eviction process. Finally, four Dempsey dumpsters are brought in to haul the stuff away.

The city has vowed to take the Glendale management to court. It is dimly conceivable that management will have to pay a stiff fine. But how stiff? Look at it from management's position: if they remove sixty people by legal means, they have to fork up $30,000 in relocation fees. By intimidating these people with thugs and late-night harassment, management can reasonably assume that over half of the sixty will be too scared to ever file claims against them. The mathematics are simple. If forty out of the sixty evicted people disappear, that's $20,000 saved. If the city puts together an airtight case and actually takes the violation to court, a steep fine might come to $10,000. Management can pay its fine and walk out $10,000 ahead. But litigation is highly unlikely.

Tenants of Hotel Walden are wary. The principal owner of the Glendale controls their hotel as well as several other SROs in the area. The time is ripe, the money is right, to convert these buildings to co-ops and middle-class apartments. Daily rumors fly about the fate of Hotel Walden. This morning Candy is sitting on the Broadway island, sharing his pint of Night Train Express with two newcomers.

"Fifteen minutes!" one of the guys says. "I swear it was only fifteen minutes we'd been in our room." Soft chocolate skin. High pompadour, purple, like crushed blueberries.

His companion has handsome, tough features reminiscent of Eldridge Cleaver's cover photo for *Soul on Ice*. Light sandy-brown complexion with reddish splotches around his nose and eyes. Tired. Wasted. "You know what did it," he adds. "His daddy was movin us in from Teaneck, and he was carryin the TV for us. Well, see, he's got a bad back, so he sets the TV down in the entranceway an gives the fella behind the desk five dollars to bring it up to our room. Big, mean son of a bitch — he never shoulda showed him the TV. So we get our stuff moved in an go out to the butcher — "

"You're leaving out why we hadda leave Teaneck — how your drinking got on Daddy's nerves till we hadda move."

"If I didn't drink — listen, that man makes me nervous. If I didn't drink, I woulda killed him."

"An still he helped us move into this Glendale place. Drove us in from Teaneck an gave us that TV outa his basement."

Okay, so we came back from the butcher shop an here's our door layin out in the hallway. Bastards took it right off the hinges and walked away with the TV an all our clothes."

"Fifteen minutes!"

"Yeah."

"An we could still be in Teaneck if you coulda got along with Daddy."

"He may be your daddy, and he may look out for you, but I don't *ever* wanna see that man!"

"You'd rather stay in that hotel?"

"Not in that Glendale!" he says to Candy. "Listen, they weren't done with us. We went out, bought a second-hand TV, and we're sittin watchin it that night, and three guys come in an kick the door down. Guy puts a screwdriver to my throat an takes forty dollars."

"An then he tells us we should be careful or somebody could steal our TV."

"One of the guys was from behind the desk. I saw him there, kinda half smilin when we were movin the stuff out. Wasn't gonna spend no night in that hotel! Took every damn thing we had. I did my time in Nam, lookin for Viet Congs in the middle of the jungle — but I had men along with me, my own gun. Nothin like the Glendale."

"Didn't have nothing to move out except two empty suitcases, the TV, and our puppy here. At least I had the sense to leave my furs in Teaneck."

DADDY'S COMING

". . . Driving all the way from Florida."

"Y-e-e-e-a-h," Bobby says. "Seventy years old an he runs that fuckin car up here in two days."

"He done it before. We gotta get our suits cleaned an get ready."

"Nothin's gonna fit," Bobby says. "We lost so much weight since Daddy's last trip."

"It'll be okay. Get our suits cleaned and pressed. We'll look okay. Daddy understands — just so long as we show him we done our best to look right."

Candy shakes a Pall Mall loose and offers it to Doug. "He's got a beard, don't he?"

"We showed you the pictures," Doug answers. "All those orange trees. Swimmin pool. You seen his beard. You got a picture of Bobby an me in your room. When we were fat. Daddy sittin in the middle with a pointy beard. Candy, you remember."

And he does. He's heard their stories a dozen times. "Where's that place he takes you? You told me once. Some kinda . . . "

"Sun Luck East, man. Best fuckin — "

"Useta go there when we were kids," Doug cuts in. "Take us to Yankee Stadium, watch a few innings, then get a cab all the way down to Sun Luck East an have a big meal an watch the end of the game on TV. He had money. Earnin like $80,000 a year. Tip the cabbie five dollars. Give all the waiters an extra coupla bucks."

"Hey baby, Daddy knew how to live, you dig. He'd order — none of that one-from-column-A-one-from-column-B, egg roll, wonton soup, and chow mein shit." His mouth twists in a froglike scowl. "H-e-e-e-y, it was Peking duck, crab with black bean sauce, bass with ginger and scallions, melon soup — hollow out this melon an serve the soup right from there. Best fuckin restaurant in New York. An they all knew our Daddy."

"Still know him. We'll walk in there next Wednesday an they'll all say, 'Hello Mr. Carman!' He'll tell us to order anything we want. Anything. Stuff ourselves, and what we don't want we take home in doggie bags."

"You're lucky, man, havin a father like that."

"I'm gonna show him my pay stubs," Doug adds. "I want him to see I been workin."

"Y-e-e-e-e-a-h! An hey — like he's cool. He knows all about us. Nothin to be ashamed of," Bobby says to Candy. "He bailed me out when they busted me with 3,000 pills. An Dougie'll tell you — Daddy flew to fuckin Viet Nam for his trial. Pulled every string he could an flew around the world to be there. He seen everything go down — an baby, he still loves us!"

MY BROTHER'S KEEPER

The jacket looks fine. And if he keeps it buttoned no one can see how his pants bunch up under his belt. Face shaved. Hair clean and brushed back. Doug looks well. He orders a Heineken at the bar, rolls a Top cigarette, and does his best to relax while he waits for Daddy.

"Hey skinny!" Doug spins and spots his father at the entrance. They hug. Doug has played the scene in his mind a hundred times.

"Bobby couldn't make it," he blurts. "He had a coupla seizures yesterday. I took care of him. He's all right. But he's gotta rest." Sad acceptance on his father's face. No surprises after these many years.

Cool dark room. Bustling waiters. Men in suits. Daddy sitting across the table, talking softly about Florida. And the meal is fine. The way Doug imagined it. But no pleasure. Distance he cannot quite overcome. Like watching himself in a dream. "I brought you my pay stubs. That's how I lost all this weight." Doug spreads the slips on the table like a winning flush. "Here's one for ninety-two dollars. Bobby come up an worked two days with us that week." He'd planned this moment, seen it clearly. Daddy examining the stubs and smiling. Bobby, hair slicked back, telling some funny story. The three of them together, laughing, drinking, ordering course after course. Stuffing themselves. Doggie bags to share with Candy and Gerry and everyone back at the hotel.

But this is all wrong. Uneaten food. The room is dark and silent, empty except for Daddy's sad, familiar smile. Doug sips his beer, fights to force it down. He feels a rush of tears. "Daddy," he hears himself speaking. "I gotta get out! I can't do this anymore. I gotta go somewhere. Stop drinkin. Get into some kinda program. Daddy, I can't.... I can't...."

"Doug, listen." He leans across the table. "You're not helping anyone like this. Bobby can look after himself better than you think."

"I been tryin, Daddy. We eat good, an I'm there when he has his seizures. He got new glasses Monday...."

"Do what you have to do, Doug. You're not your brother's keeper."

"I can't keep goin like this! I gotta get out!" Busboys dispose of the uneaten food. He leaves his beer unfinished.

TOO MANY THOUGHTS

Bobby's out on the street with Willy and Buffalo and Ironsides, shuffling about, talking and talking. Eyes sharp and fierce — drinking since Doug left. "Come on," Doug says. "Let's get outa the sun."

By early evening, Bobby's back on the street. Wobbling. Mad endless raps. Doug takes his arm and leads him inside. An hour later, he's out again, arms flailing, body twisted like an angry marionette, cursing, defeating speech till he sinks to grunts and long bleating bursts of sound. Doug gives him a few minutes to wear himself down, then puts him to bed. This time he sleeps.

Doug leaves their stuffy room and walks down to Broadway

where he drinks a quart of Old English. Hands shake when he tries to roll a cigarette. He braces his elbows on his knees and puts it together. He unscrews another quart. It's not just his hands that are shaking — he's trembling inside. Head racing. Too many thoughts. . . .

A last long swallow and the shakes stop. Hotel lights blink out, one by one. The city is still. A cool breeze lifts off the river. For a few moments this tired, familiar street is almost consoling. The city is almost beautiful just now. And Doug — almost, almost now, he feels at peace.

BREAKFAST AT THE B-WAY

It will not go away. Morning beer and still it will not go away. Cramps. Racing thoughts. This morning, this one day, this room is hell. Unbearable. Six feet away, Bobby snores on soiled sheets. White and flaccid in his jockey shorts. Sleeping like a baby.

Doug rolls out of bed to fix strong tea. Nausea. Waves surging up from his gut. More than morning beer can cure. Gnawing inside. Horror comic years ago — man forced to swallow a starving rat. Lips sewn tight. Like that, eating him inside, relentless, devouring its way to daylight.

Hands shake. He can barely work the faucet. Cigarette — no way to light the match. *I gotta do something, get help. This life — I can't, can't keep on.* Scars. Deep stomach wounds where Bobby stuck him. Ambulance, cops, and lies. *Protect him. He doesn't know what he's doing. Helpless. . . . This is no life. No life.*

Dressed and out on Broadway to meet Daddy. Bobby's fine today — relaxed and sober and full of talk. Doug hangs back, fighting down pain. Lips sealed. Rats inside, feeding on him. More than he can bear. "Where we going, boys?" Daddy asks. "You name it." So far away.

"The Broadway," Bobby replies. "Only place around. Hey, I mean there's a lotta hole-in-the-wall places. We got Chinamen,

Cubans, Puerto Ricans, Indians, Haitians, we got this Italian place
run by an Egyptian dude — greasy spoons on every block. But —
hey Daddy, we don't wanna be with you lined up on these little
stools along some counter. Listen, the B-way's got booths. We can
sit down and talk."

"Fine!" Daddy says. "Okay with you Doug?"

Far away. For them to hear him, he'd have to scream. Words
and pain tearing inside. Hungry rats. "Yeah," he hears himself say.

Huge soggy pancakes. He cannot look at his plate. The first bite
of sausage tastes good, but when he swallows it seems to crawl inside him. Coffee cold and forgotten. Bobby talking about his
health, the lost SSI checks, about Candy and Eddie and Gerry and
all their cats. Stories. Stacks of words, like all those flyers. Doug
looks up, tries to fake interest, and sees his father's attentive eyes,
his helpless love. Wave of nausea. Pain through every bone. He
jerks his hand off the table and sits on his shaking fingers. *Hold on.
Concentrate.* Soggy pancakes. Brownish syrup like coughed-up bile.
Not in front of Daddy. Not here. Not here. Nausea and tears. Holding
back rats.

"Goodbye Daddy! Goodbye!" A cab stops, and Daddy's gone.

Broadway morning. Candy and Ironsides bullshitting by Freya's
Beauty Salon. Lady and Ironsides's weimaraner dozing at their
feet. Smashed bottles glinting harshly on the sidewalk. Hotel Walden looming against empty sky, huge and uncaring. It will crush us
all. . . .

HELP

Doug showed up at my door shaking and sobbing. "Bob, you gotta
help! I can't make it any more. I gotta stop drinkin. I know I
gotta — but you gotta help. . . . "

"Is he drunk now?" the man asks me over the phone.

"I haven't had nothin since last night," Doug tells me. "One sip when I woke up, but it made me sick. Bob, Bob, you gotta help! You gotta get me to a doctor!"

"Okay! Okay!" I pass the information on.

"Ask him if he's got Medicaid."

"He doesn't have it."

"All right, here's the situation. St. Luke's, Roosevelt, none of the good alcohol recovery programs will admit without health insurance. You say he's nervous. Stomach spasms. Shaking. Okay, but they won't take him in Emergency."

"Listen, he's right on the edge. He came here crying and — "

"Bob, Bob, I can't go back! You gotta get me in somewhere. I know what they're sayin. I know how they give the runaround."

"Dave, he's desperate. He needs help. He really wants to change. What are — "

"I'm just telling you the stiuation. Tell him to hang on. I'll be by in an hour."

Twenty minutes later Dave Mackey arrives. Field coordinator for St. Luke's Hospital Outreach Addiction Program. Stocky light-skinned guy in straw cowboy hat. Tough, battle-worn face. Ex-addict. Rasping, mellow voice that seems to come with the habit. Addict's sixth sense — mean streets, SROs, dope and drink and all the hustles, death and hunger, sad lost dreams — there in his eyes, the beat of his low rasping voice. Doug listens. "Look, I'll show you what the problem is." Mackey turns to me. "Bob, you call St. Luke's. Tell em you're a writer. Tell em about your work. Tell em you got Doug here and that he needs help. See if you can pull it off."

I do just that. "We can admit him," the voice says, "if you bring us his birth certificate, notarized proof of his source of income, and notarized proof that he's been paying rent at his declared place of residence."

"He doesn't have his birth certificate. He lives in an SRO. He's scared. He's desperate. He lives off his brother's SSI payments and that's a whole mess too."

"I understand," the voice says mechanically. "Maybe we can admit him in Emergency. When did he have his last drink?"

"Last night."

"I'm sorry."

"He had some this morning but it made him sick."

"Sorry."

"He's trying to stop! He's scared! He's sitting here shaking! He needs help!"

"I understand. But Emergency won't take him. People come in here with DTs. Come in with heads split open. They come in with seizures, rotten kidneys, comas. Emergency won't admit him."

"What I expected," Mackey says. "Okay, here's what we do." Doug listens like a frightened child. "I'll take you over to Central Harlem Sobering-Up Station. They'll put you up for the night. It's clean and you can watch TV. Then tomorrow you'll get yourself downtown to Bernstein Clinic. Be there when it opens at 7:30. They've got medical de-tox, and they'll take you in if they've got a bed." Doug's whole body shakes. "And listen, have a beer or two to settle down." Mackey winks at me. "I use unconventional methods."

The St. Luke's van is parked in front of the hotel. Someone waves at Mackey. They banter half a block apart. "Hey, Candy! Hey, Lloyd! Yeah, I know Hotel Walden. Know half the people here."

Doug is better now. Halfway through his second Bud. He spots Bobby seated on a car hood by Broadway. "Bobby! Bye, Bobby!" he calls. "Take it easy. I'm gonna get some help." He slides open the van door. Bobby sprints towards him in an awkward lopsided shuffle. He stops about five feet from his brother. "This is Dave Mackey," Doug says. "He's taking me to a place to spend the night. I've gotta de-tox."

"H-e-e-e-e-y, you gave me a card, man. I know you," he says to Mackey. "Yeah, I got it somewhere in here." He pulls out a fat split wallet, removing a wad of stuck papers.

"Bobby, we don't got time." Doug's voice breaks in a sob. "Listen, I'm goin. I gotta go. Defrost some pork chops. I'll call."

Mackey pulls the van onto the street and shoots up Broadway, radio blasting. "I'll be all right there, huh?" Doug's teeth are chattering.

"What?" Mackey cuts the music.

"This place we're goin. I can make it, can't I?"

"There's a nurse on duty. It's comfortable. You'll see."

"You know what they say at the hotel — they say me an Bobby is just like two niggers. We get along with everyone. You understand?"

"Yeah, sure." IRT tracks break through the ground just past Columbia, and as the street dips, the tracks shoot above us on lacy girders arching across 125th Street into Harlem.

"They'll feed me, huh?"

"Sure. Give you everything you need. But Doug, it's up to you. You've got to get yourself down to Bernstein tomorrow."

Doug slugs down the last of his beer. Chicken Delight. Baby Grand Bar. Blues and disco blasting from shop speakers, huge hand-held cassettes, and car windows. "I'll do it," he says. "I gotta do it."

"Five days drying out. Then you gotta look at yourself. You gotta hold on to yourself and get control of your life." He swings the van up Adam Clayton Powell Boulevard, west on 126th Street, and stops in front of a small brick building with a sturdy security screens over the windows. Inside, it's bright, air-conditioned, and orderly. Mackey says a few words to the nurse who lets us in, then he returns to Doug and shakes his hand. "Okay Doug, it's up to you." Mackey looks too big for the tiny space.

Exhausted countenance, body loose and stooped. Pink vest, pork-pie hat, and shabby pants — Doug stands in this bright empty room like a tired clown. "I'll do it," he says. "I gotta do it."

R U N A R O U N D

His Old English is warm already. Foaming and filling his mouth at every sip. It's 3:00 P.M. the following day. Doug is back on the street, sprawled on the pavement near my apartment building. "They wouldn't take me." Voice slurred, depressed and angry. "I went down to Bernstein an they kept me waiting till ten o'clock an then they tell me they're full up with Medicaid people an I gotta go somewhere else. Bob, they're givin me the runaround."

I extend a hand and haul him to his feet. He follows me back to my apartment. Tired, obedient gait. Muttering and cursing "the system." I make phone calls — hospitals, clinics, hold buttons, recorded messages — wondering how a distraught alcoholic could ever find help on his own.

A doctor friend steers me to a colleague.

"Does he have Medicaid?"

"No."

"What shape is he in?"

"He's shaking and scared. He's exhausted. He wants help. He's been trying for two days."

"Look, I know you've heard this before — but if he was dangerously drunk, if he was unconscious or hallucinating, you could bring him right in to Emergency ... "

Doug catches my expression and wrings his hands. "I can't do it. I'm trying but I can't. I oughta go out an stick up a store. Then the cops would pick me up an get me in somewhere. Or take some pills an go to Emergency for suicide. I'm tryin to stop, I gotta stop, an nobody gives two shits what happens. I'm a nobody! A fuckin nobody!"

I send him home to rest. More calls. The best I can do is another sobering-up station. This one is at Sixtieth Street and has some connection to Roosevelt Hospital. Doug can stay three or four days till he dries out. It's a nonmedical facility. In institutional terms this means that there are no doctors on staff, no medication dispensed — nothing but the chance to go cold turkey with the guidance of a few counselors. "Nonmedical facility" has an added significance to alcoholics in Doug's position. At a hospital, a doctor might examine him and decide that his physical or psychological condition rendered him unable to support himself. This medical opinion could be instrumental in placing him on SSI, entitling him to a monthly assistance check of about $300. At a nonmedical facility there is no chance for SSI placement. Still, Doug has given me no indication that he's trying to get on SSI. He wants to get out of Hotel Walden, go cold turkey, and straighten his life out. There's a bed waiting for him at Sixtieth Street. They tell me he has to show up within the hour.

Doug is frying pork chops when I enter his room. Bobby is on the bed, barechested, watching television. I tell Doug about the place at Sixtieth Street, that he has to be there within the hour. "I wanna cook these for Bobby," he says. "Then I'll get right down there."

"H-e-e-e-y, Doug! Did I show you this?" Bobby hands him a frayed calling card. "I knew I seen that dude Mackey before. Wears that cowboy hat like he thinks it's Tombstone or somethin. Yeah, like we're Indians or rustlers an he's fuckin Wyatt Earp. But he's okay, man. He's been out there on the streets."

"We talked," Doug says. "He's all right."

"Yeah, but like these doctors an social workers an shit — they never done anything." Bobby snaps the words through rotten brown teeth. "They act like they can barely stand the sight of you. Yeah, like you're a social problem."

"I'm goin, Bobby. I gotta get myself together." Bobby flops back on his bed and takes a long sip of beer. "I'm goin," Doug repeats, "but I ain't leavin till I finish cookin up your dinner."

"It's Doug!" His voice is distant and miserable over the telephone. It's 5:30 A.M. the following morning. "They wouldn't take me. I been out on the street all night waitin for them to open up."

"What the hell happened?" I ask.

"They said I was late."

"Were you?"

"I got there at seven-thirty. They said they were filled up. They wouldn't take me, Bob. They're givin me the runaround. They're all the same."

"Doug! I came by at five yesterday and told you they would only hold your place for an hour. You got there an hour and a half late!"

"I hadda cook Bobby his dinner."

"You didn't have to do anything except get down there on time!"

"I tried. I got there an they said they gave my bed away. They told me to come back this mornin. I been out here all night. Bob, I gotta get help!"

"Okay. Just hang on."

"You'll help, won't you?"

"I'm trying, but you've got to stop messing up."

"I need help. You gotta get me in!"

"Okay. Okay. . . . "

8:00 A.M. Doug calls from the sobering-up station. After his early morning call, I spoke to the counselor on duty, who assured me they'd look after him. But Doug is speedy now, almost screaming. "Speak to them!" he cries. "You gotta speak to them! They wanna send me on the street! I can't go back! I'm a nobody! A nobody! You gotta help!"

A counselor picks up the phone and tells me Doug should have medical de-tox. That's fine, I tell him, will he see to it that Doug is placed in an appropriate hospital program? No, he can't do that. I explode — two days of frustration and outrage all focused on this astonished man. I tell him what he must already know — that no hospital will admit Doug unless he's having DTs on the spot, that this sobering-up station is our only hope. Bitterly, the staff worker says he'll do what he can.

* * *

8:15. Doug sobbing. "Bob, they kicked me out! They wouldn't let me stay. I'm never gonna get better. They're gonna keep givin me the runaround. I'm a nobody. They can just keep movin me back an forth."

I jot down the pay-phone number and tell him to stay put. I call the director of the sobering-up station and ask her for an explanation. Doug demanded medical de-tox, she says. He didn't seem prepared for cold turkey. I tell her Doug was completely aware that this was nonmedical de-tox. I assure her he has the physical stamina and mental resolve to get through the drying-out period without medical supervision. I tell her he called me from the street, that he's desperate to come back. The director agrees to admit him.

I call the street pay phone. No answer. I call again and some man answers. I describe Doug and ask him to see if he's nearby.

Doug's gone.

Noon. Doug dozing on the pavement alongside Hotel Walden. The phone was out of order, he tells me, so he walked back uptown. I try to persuade him to return to Sixtieth Street. I promise they'll admit him. But he's dazed with fatigue, shaken by his last run-in. He refuses to set foot in the sobering-up station.

I make a last round of calls. This time I find the Holy Name Center for Homeless Men, a Bowery survival service that has been in operation since 1906. They work closely with Greymoor, a detoxification facility in Garrison, New York. The Greymoor program involves twenty-one-day stay at an estate run by the Franciscan order. After a sobering-up period, residents take part in daily chores. Counseling is readily available. There are AA meetings on the premises as well as prayer services, but none of this is mandatory. Also, for residents who show special commitment to recovery and rehabilitation, there's the chance for more extensive therapy, job placement, whatever the situation requires.

Doug likes what I tell him about Greymoor. I assure him that although Greymoor has a religious affiliation their primary task is to help people out, not to make conversions. Doug must concentrate on living without alcohol, recovering his health, and beginning to look inside himself to examine the causes of his problem. Okay. He understands.

Back in Hotel Walden, Bobby is watching the soaps with Gerry. He barely turns when Doug enters. Four shirts, just laundered, lay draped across the armchair. "Hey, you been cleanin!" Doug says.

"I got *all* our shit together. Everything. Yeah, every sock and shirt and towel. All that shit under the bed. Stuff the cats been sleepin on. Took it to that place on Ninety-seventh Street where they got them big motherfuckin machines an did it all in one big load. Shit, you could wash a whole — "

Doug reaches out to ruffle his brother's hair. "You washed your hair! You shaved an everything."

"Yeah." Bobby sounds reserved, self-absorbed.

"Listen, Bobby, I'm leavin. I gotta get outa here an get myself together. I'm goin upstate for three weeks. A place called Greymoor."

"Hey baby, that's where they keep them crazies!"

"That's Creedmore. This is somethin else. It's outa the city, where you can rest." Bobby nods, face empty. "I love ya, Bobby. I love ya."

"Yeah. Well, I'll be here."

"Take care of yourself."

Downstairs, Doug stops at the front desk. "Frankie, I'm leavin for a few weeks. I'll give you my number in case somethin happens to Bobby." Frankie slides a pen through the cage window. It's on a short chain and doesn't reach very far. Anyhow, it's empty. "I'll call when I get there," Doug says. "Give you the number then."

Frankie squeezes an arm beneath the window to pat Doug's hand. "Good luck, honey!"

"Take care of Bobby, Frankie. Make sure he comes in off the street at night."

"We'll keep an eye on him. Just you come back well."

Doug begins to cry.

HOME

Three hours later Doug's at my door.

"I couldn't do it. Listen, those people wanna brainwash you, turn you into some kinda Moonie. I got down there an there're all these people outside sellin flowers. Grinnin like Hare Krishnas. "Hey brother, this flower says that Jesus loves you!" Shit like that. Inside, there's two guys sweepin the floor like zombies. Everyone's eyes wide open. Weird. So some guy comes up to me an starts talkin about Greymoor. Brother somethin-or-other. He says how they got prayer services all the time, an how you gotta call everyone brother, an how the place is called the Holy Mountain. They brainwash you. I know that's what they do. See their eyes an you'd know I ain't crazy. I ain't goin nowhere where I come out like a fuckin Moonie. Listen, Reverend Moon's estate is right up there. I'll bet they got a thing where they brainwash everyone together. Getchya all alone up there, fifty miles away from home — they got control. Fifty miles! Fifty miles away from people! They gave me my bus ticket, but I ain't goin."

So Doug does not leave home for three weeks. He does not go fifty miles away. He does not go anywhere. He returns to where he began — with Bobby and his people. And oddly, all the fatigue and panic and childlike dependence seems to vanish. While Doug rages against the Holy Name brainwashing conspiracy, Broadway emerges from the hotel pulling a shopping cart packed with picnic gear. "You gotta relax an give yourself a break," he says. "Why don't you an Bobby join us for some barbecue? We're getting it set up right now."

"You sure it's all right?"

"We got plenty, Doug. You'll see — eatin somethin'll make you feel a lot better."

"You sure?" Broadway nods. "That's great! I sure need somethin. An I got some pork chops in the freezer. I'll get em when I tell Bobby. He don't know I come back yet. He likes barbecue. An these are good thick chops. Cook em an sit out on the grass. Fuck all of them brothers an Moonies an shit! It's good to be home."

A MATTER OF PRIDE

Muriel's curtains are knotted together to let in whatever breeze enters the courtyard outside her window. Bright green sumac fronds flap on her sill. "I'm down to ninety-three pounds," Muriel says. "The doctor tells me it's not enough, but on the other hand, maybe I get around faster now. I'm aiming for 100 — buying pork chops with lots of fat." She looks well. "I'm like that tree. In winter, I mean. Skinny branches and no foliage." She giggles at her simile.

Her room is neat. Jars of pills in even rows. Books and personal effects all in careful stacks. Floor swept. No more piles of rumpled clothes. Looped around her neck she wears a long brown shoelace knotted to form a necklace for her keys. "It's the only way," she explains cheerfully. "I think it's rather elegant. Actually, it's a matter of pride. You keep losing your keys and people look at you like you're crazy. If you don't care about yourself, you can't expect anybody else to do it for you. I get so discouraged sometimes. I have to tell myself, 'Clean your room; hold on to those keys; don't forget your medication.' But you'll see — pork chops and bananas — I'll be up to 100 pounds again."

Her post-card map of Cape Cod is missing from the wall. "Why, yes!" she says when I mention it, "I can't seem to find a way to keep it up." She takes the card from a dresser drawer and presses it futilely against the plaster. "It doesn't seem right keeping my home hid away in there. There must be a solution. . . . "

GOOD IMPRESSION

Mid-morning. Clarence Taylor and Yvonne Smith are moving out today, and they've gotten high to celebrate. Clarence moves down the street in a crazy stooping slouch. Like Groucho Marx. "Fucked my leg up last night," he explains. Beads of sweat cover his entire face, yet each droplet remains intact, perfectly stationary.

"You were high," Yvonne says. "Tripped on your own feet." Clarence doesn't deny it. A model of equanimity after a taste of methadone, reefer, and beer. He's around six foot two, standing tall, but this crazy slouch has cut him down a good foot.

"Movin out. Movin *out!*" he says.

"We be back though," Yvonne adds. "We ain't gonna forget our friends. We be back."

"You be back sooner'n you think," someone says, "with Clarence lookin the way he do."

Yvonne looks him over. "You're right. We're startin in with a new landlord. Here Clarence, chew this gum an mop your face. We gonna make a good impression. . . . "

TO KEEP A MAN

Ironsides is not pleased with Clarence Taylor's departure. The two of them had a good thing with their Friday night poker game. It will not be the same with Clarence gone. Ironsides is definitely not pleased.

"Clarence ain't been the same since he started goin with Yvonne," Ironsides says. "Man, you look at his eyes, you listen to him talk. . . . An some of the things he do — he ain't the same. Now I ain't sayin nothin against Yvonne, but this is true — you tell me if I'm wrong — all womens is gonna try an keep their man. It's in their nature, which is why I say it ain't wrong. It's just somethin they do, an you gotta keep your guard up or they gotchya like some little pet on a leash. Some womens I knowed, they'll squat over a bowl a rice an let the steam come up in their vagina so's the juices will drip back down. Feed that rice to their man, an he's her slave. I'll tell you another thing that works. They'll take their panties off an put it under your pillow when you sleep at night. Same thing. It puts that woman in your mind so's you always be dependin on her. Now I ain't sayin Yvonne done any of that to Clarence. I ain't sayin that. But you see what he look like now. . . . An tell me, tell me, would you let your woman go down an pay your rent for you? Representin you in public when she ain't got no self-control?"

THREE FINE GIRLS

Ooo-ooo-ooo! Snaps! . . . Three fine girls zip downhill, shimmying in tight shorts, little titties jiggling in tighter tee-shirts, bright plastic wheels floating them towards David's bench. Sweet round asses. They reach the bottom of the hill, shift weight, and come to sudden, graceful stops, laughing and giggling. . . . *Ooo-ooo-ooo!*

Lookin good, I'm lookin good. Got my new red cap, my People's Socialist Alliance button, silver shades. Yeah, and my Auxiliary Police badge in my pocket — that's something to show them. And later, maybe find someone with a cassette. Dance. Put on my best moves. Snaps! Nice girls. We'll all be friends, like. Skate all over New York, hang around together. And one night, things will just work out. I'll be alone with one of em an maybe show her my room. It'll be one of those things — we'll just kinda know the time is right. Something special. Of course, I'll still be friends with the other two. . . .

He smiles at them, then hurries up the hill. He clamps his cheap metal wheels onto his sneakers and shoves off. Straight steep drop. He picks up speed. Below, the three girls sit on the bench sharing a soda. One of them looks his way. *Gotta show some moves.* The path curves. David shifts his weight. The left wheels seem loose and wobbly. He struggles for balance but he's going too fast now — out of control. Off the pavement he goes, bouncing down the grassy hill. Three trees ahead. Iron fence. Garbage basket. Quick choice.

He tucks his head, lurches between the trees, and smashes into the garbage. RC Cola cans, newspapers, melted popsicles, Pampers, half-eaten Sabrett hot dogs — David rolling amidst the mess.

The bench where the girls were sitting is empty. He hears the fading whir of bright plastic wheels. . . .

MISSING

One of the Broadway benches is missing. Wooden slats, concrete frame — the whole thing is gone. People pass and stare at the empty space. In the hotel things disappear all the time — TVs, radios, clothing, liquor, hidden money. And people, too — packed off to hospitals, alcohol clinics, and psychiatric institutions; they die, land in jail, or simply walk away from their dreary rooms. But a concrete bench fixed in place with eight-inch bolts! There is no explaining it.

It disappeared overnight. The island looks empty without it.

HIGH SUMMER

Ironsides sits in his wheelchair like a little king, whispering come-ons at passing white girls.

Eddie the Bootlegger reels toward Broadway, bumping against the building every few steps.

Doug and Bobby stay inside a lot, staring at the soaps in their underwear.

Candy's face gets sadder and sadder. "I won't lie," he says. "I been drinkin. I didn't have nothin for two weeks — you can ask anyone — but see, I get these spells. I start shakin an I need some wine to steady me. . . . " For days, he's been trying to give away his dog. "Lady don't deserve to be treated like this," he says. But nobody wants a fat little mutt.

Everyone seems to be keeping off the street. Muriel, Fat Edna, Youngblood, Mr. Winslow — all stay put in their rooms. A kind of summer hibernation.

Gerry looks sad and puffy. A foot infection had her limping for awhile, and now she's put on twenty pounds. Someone says she's pregnant. Someone else says she has gout. Doug thinks she may lose her foot. Guesses and rumors. Gerry's drawn inside herself, and there's no one in the hotel to go on in after her.

Yvonne Smith shows up one morning, drunk and enthusiastic about her new place in the Bronx. Clarence Taylor's working as a super for three adjoining buildings, so they have a four-room apartment, rent-free. She's thrilled that he's working. Full of plans ... Clarence Taylor still comes by for the Friday night card games. And he still gets off on methadone. With grass and beer behind it, he shrinks a good five inches. After an all-night game you'll find him out on Broadway, shucking and jiving like any other dead-end buffoon. He sweats profusely, slaps skin a lot, stoops low to exchange confidences that he forgets before speaking.

And Lloyd Smith is hanging on after his drinking binge. His bent fingers are mending. He's taking it easy, watching a lot of TV, trying to keep the pressure off. But he feels like a werewolf under a waxing moon. . . .

Every week or so, a few people get together for a barbecue picnic at Riverside Park, but this time of year the broken glass and dog shit get pretty thick out there. One picnic night the George Washington Bridge — all lit and perfect in the August sky — makes everyone sad. Gerry insists that Manhattan is not really an island, that there's a way out through Harlem that gets you to the Bronx without crossing any bridges or tunnels. Everyone's puzzled that it seems so important to her. . . . Later, walking up the steps from Riverside Drive, the Fireman's Memorial looms above them — mother and child shining white in bright floodlights. Sad, Gerry feels, it is all so sad.

DEATH RATTLE

It's not the same today. Doug and Bobby sit in their underwear staring at the TV. They fidget, puff Pall Malls, grab quick slugs from their quart of Old English, and stare at the screen.

But it's not the same:

"If this is how you're going to treat me, then Angela was right."

"David's been telling you stories again. I still can't believe your mother put the trust fund in his hands."

"You always find someone to blame for your behavior. David and I are barely speaking. I don't need anyone to explain you to me!"

"Marge! Marge! You're always jumping on me before I have a chance to explain."

Dark empty screen. "Fuckin thing died on us," Bobby says.

"It ain't dead yet. We got sound."

"Baby, all we've got's a death rattle. Listen, that dude at the pawnshop said he'd give us a Philco or somethin for thirty-five dollars. And, hey! — the Democratic Convention's comin next week!"

"We don't need no picture for that. They take away all the movies for a week. Make us watch those assholes wavin flags an poppin balloons."

"Yeah, but we still got the soaps. Listen, we'll watch the soaps on our new TV, and save this piece of shit for the convention."

PEOPLE'S CONVENTION PARADE

"Yeah, I went down to the People's Convention parade," David says. "Took my bike and rode alongside keepin my eyes open. CPTF — that's Crime Prevention Task Force — we're supposed to spot any trouble before it happens. Wasn't no trouble though.

They musta had a thousand cops. Streets blocked off and everything. Besides, it was too hot.

"But it was beautiful! All the signs! JOBS FOR ALL; DECENT WAGES — made me feel good. Groups for everything: Communists — all kinds of Communists in their own special sections — Save the Whales; Save the Poor; Abortion; Puerto Rico; Faggots; a bunch of guys in white space suits and gas masks — anti-nukes; somethin about Johns and Call Girls; Welfare Rights; Women's Rights; PLO; all kinds of stuff about Cambodia and Iran and South Africa; and — oh yeah — this one guy, he was carryin a torn-off piece outa some carton that he'd written on — how he hated his wife and all his children and David Rockefeller and Jimmy Carter and a few other names I couldn't read. Walkin down the street all alone, and no one goin near him.... Crazy lookin, you know. Like he just come outa this hotel."

BLISS ON BROADWAY

She is fat and twenty-five, bulging in new Jordache jeans. Rich chocolate skin. Planted in her lap is a plastic container overflowing with an elaborate Carvel sundae. Swirls of vanilla like sculpted Crisco, sinking into a pool of chocolate-pineapple topping. Clutched between her legs is an open bag of Pepperidge Farm Fudge Nut Cookies. Her eyes are closed, clenched tight as a heaping spoonful enters her mouth; she relaxes blissfully as she swallows. She peeks for a moment to load up her spoon, then sinks back into her reverie. Over and over. No traffic, no city, no stuffy little room to press in on her. Just this. After a few more mouthfuls she digs into her cookies, gobbling a few in quick, hungry bursts. When the sundae is finished, she swirls her last cookies around the container, scooping up the last bits of her snack, eyes still shut — dreamer holding on to the last moments of a perfect, peaceful dream.

SWAMI

I haven't seen Youngblood in close to two months. "Takin care of business," he explains. "Uptown. Can't get nothin done sittin around in here." Whether he's high or just feeling silly today, I don't know — but there he is, towel wrapped around his head, bullshitting with a bunch of men on the stairwell between the fourth and fifth floors.

"Tell us, Swami," a guy asks him, "whattaya think of Carter?" They're smoking cigarettes, staring out at empty rooftops.

Youngblood bobs his head, beaming broadly. "He don't have that leadership personality. I'll tell yuh, it don't look right — his bein up there smilin all the time. Smilin! Man, what's he smilin about? We know he ain't done nothin."

"That's right!"

"So what's he got to smile about?"

"Yeah, he oughta cut that shit!"

"Nobody wanna see a man smilin when things goin bad."

"That's right, Swami! That's right!"

"I walk the line." Youngblood adjusts his towel. "You ask the Swami. He'll tell you no lies. You know Carter's getting set to cut back on welfare. Take away SSI. The man's got Reagan on his tail — gotta cut down his budget some ways. Carter's smilin, but we're the ones gonna lose. Poor people ain't got no say. You ask the Swami."

"What you think of that thing with his brother, Swami?"

"Libya give half a million dollars to Billy, and he's just a wino. You don't suppose some of that's goin to Jimmy?"

"Right!"

"You ask the Swami. Man's got a deal goin. He don't make no move till he's fixed his little deal. You take all them queers an killers an shit comin over from Cuba. Castro's payin him."

"Why's he doin that?"

"Where else Castro gonna put em? Ain't no jobs in Cuba."

"Right!"

"These dudes ain't got no money."

"Right!"

"Ain't got no friends."

"Right!"

"Carter'll keep em outa the way for a while, an then start slippin em in this hotel. We all be speakin Cuban next year."

"We don't need no more killers in here!"

"We got enough of everything already."

Youngblood raises his arms in a kind of victory salute. "Either way, Carter'll be smilin."

"You got any predictions, Swami? You got one of them crystal balls in your room or somethin?"

"I'll tell you about the hostages," he beams. "You know Carter got the Egyptians to kill the Shah — wanted to see if that'd free em, but the Ayatollah didn't make his move. Now, see, that Ayatollah's played out his hand — he's gotta free em before the election, cause if Reagan comes in he's gonna come out shootin. Ayatollah's holdin em now cause the country's fallin apart an he's gotta do some kinda cover-up. But now, if he lets em go just before the election, he can get Carter to bail him out. All that foreign aid an shit."

"How come we don't get no foreign aid, Swami? How come he don't give nothin to us?"

"Nobody's givin no one nothin for nothin no more," Youngblood proclaims. "You gotta be ready to deal. Like havin hostages — gotta have somethin the man wants."

SHIPWRECK PARK

Straus Park forms a quiet triangle where West End Avenue meets Broadway at 106th Street. Rows of shady trees and battered benches follow the park's outline, while a shallow pool sits empty in the center. Few people remember when it was last filled with water. Now it holds beer cans, broken bottles, newspaper, discarded clothing, and dry leaves which scratch and spin with every breeze. All this, and it still looks elegiac, peaceful.

Behind the pool a large memorial bench records Straus Park's origins:

> IN MEMORY OF ISIDOR AND IDA STRAUS
> who were lost at sea in the Titanic Disaster April 15, 1912
> LOVELY AND PLEASANT WERE THEY IN THEIR LIVES
> AND IN THEIR DEATH THEY WERE NOT DIVIDED

A statue of a reclining woman looks down upon the empty pool, and from the statue's base a lion's head pokes forth as if to nip the folds of her dress — or perhaps to remind us of the dangers of water.

All around the tiny park are "NO" signs prohibiting alcoholic beverages, dogs, bicycles, ball playing, and littering, but no one takes heed. The park is almost entirely given over to SRO residents, who come here to drink, get high, bullshit, read newspapers, stretch out and sleep on benches, mumble at private demons, or blast giant cassette decks. Trinity House is just a block away, and on her way home today Gerry pauses near the empty pool for a few sips of forbidden wine. . . . Shipwreck Park, some of the regulars call it, but it is more like a ship in motion than a ruined vessel — a bedraggled ferry shuttling equally bedraggled passengers across some still and sullen channel.

A few weeks ago there was a street fair. Screaming kids, tables of home-baked goodies, a teen-aged rock band, block association tee-shirts, home-crafted belts, and cartons of used books. Noise and gaiety cleared the benches — but that was a rare day. And today, while Gerry drank her wine, there was singing. The right combination of alcohol and people and good weather. A man started humming an old doo-wop tune, and soon two companions joined him a cappella. No one remembered more than a few words, but they hummed and faked their way through a rambling medley of tunes and phrases.

A rare day, a stolen day, at Shipwreck Park.

THE LAST OF CANDY

"He's back on the reservation!" Bobby says. "Hey, baby, he just said fuck it, told em to fuck themselves and split. You think those dudes on the reservation ever seen a street-smart wino Indian queer before? H-e-e-e-e-y, he coulda had a thousand bucks for giving up his room — that's what everyone was tellin him he should hold out for — but he just said fuck it, man, fuck this shit! Took the two hundred dollars they gave him, gave Lady to some dude that was goin upstate, and split for the reservation. Back to live with his mother somewhere in Oklahoma.

"H-e-e-e-e-y, he's beautiful man. Beautiful. You know what he said the day he was leavin? He tells me and Frankie, 'I been everything else,' he says. 'I been a junkie, a hustler, a thief; I been a wino — that is, I still am a wino but I got it mostly under control; I've run numbers, bootlegged, been a male nurse, been in the army; I done time and a few things I don't wanna talk about. I been everything else, so now I'm gonna let my momma cook for me while I get into bein an Indian.'

"We're gonna miss him, baby. But hey — he saw his chance and went after it."

And I'll miss Candy too. I liked his voice, his sweet sad eyes, his fat little dog bumping about his feet.

GARBAGE SYMPHONY

CRASH! Glass Breaking. Cans rattling.

PLOP! PLOP!

"Garbage symphony," Muriel says nodding towards her window. "I wouldn't stick my neck out. You get some real heavy stuff coming down that could take your head off. Of course, every now and then you get a head along with its body going out some window. They call them suicide leaps, but I have my doubts. I don't think that many people are so inclined. I mean, who wants to go out in such a big splash? I'll say this for my husband — he was neat about it. A phone call to his next of kin and a single bullet. Well, I guess he might have made a little mess — some blood and brains sprayed about — but it was a public phone booth, easy to clean. Nobody's carpet or anything. But these so-called leapers — who wants to end up mashed in a pile of garbage for someone to shovel up? That astonishes me — the way some people behave. Look at it! Look at all that garbage!"

A torn Flo-Sweet Sugar packet flutters to rest on her sill. Picture of an old sailing vessel — "The *Chebek*: used by Algerian Corsairs." Shredded clothing draped on the fire escape. Down below, a twisted bed frame rests against the sumac. Beside it, a torn mattress, pulled apart like a slice of bread. And all around it, the garbage symphony. Orange peels. Coffee grounds. Blue Adidas box. Green Pumas. Carolina Rice. Black plastic bag. Pall Malls. Insect spray can. *New York Post*. Irish Spring Soap. V-8. Colt 45. Old English 800. Welch's Grape Juice. Red Apple. Colonel Sanders. *People* magazine. Styrofoam cup. Bones and fat and soup cans. Wonderbread. Chicken of the Sea. Unravelled cassette. Newports. Yankees cap. Kiwi polish. Big Mac wrapper. Thick, putrid smell. A piece of something that must have been a doll. But no heads today. No bodies.

BIRTHDAY

Gerry does not bother looking at the clock. She knows it will be near nine. She's been sleeping late these past weeks. This is normal, her counselor at Trinity House tells her — normal if you're depressed, down on yourself for not finding work; normal if you're afraid you're in a rut that will go on and on and on. Her counselor says she has to put as few demands on herself as possible while she adjusts to living free of alcohol. "Do the simple things first, and build from there. The rest will come; but first things first." That's fine for her to say, Gerry thinks, but she's off in Bermuda on vacation.

Gerry pokes her head out the window. Bicycles, roller skates whooshing down 100th Street. Buses and cars and people with shopping carts out on Broadway. Everyone active and busy. Ironsides in his wheelchair, new red cap, gawking at white girls. Doc on the corner, sad-faced and wobbly. Drunk already.

Kittens nuzzling and scratching Gerry's legs. The second litter this year. She can barely keep track of them — crushed a little grey opening the door two days ago. She takes two cans of fish and liver bits and dumps them on a plate. The sharp smell makes the whole room feel old and worn — but the kittens are so cute. Blind and helpless. All need. Eating and whining and sleeping. Something makes her suddenly sad, cutting through thought like the cruel pungent smell of the fish and liver mush. She hurries and boils water for instant coffee and steals a glimpse at the clock. Ten o'clock. While her coffee cools, she snaps up the phone.

"Good morning!" She hears Frankie's voice down at the main desk.

"Hi, Frankie!" Her own voice sounds hoarse and tired.

"What number you want me to ring?"

"Oh, it's okay. I kicked the receiver playin with my cats."

"All right then."

So the phone is working. Well, there's no law that says a son has to call first thing in the morning. She flicks on the TV on the odd chance that her picture tube has come back to life. A bright white spot pops on the center of the screen, shrinks to an incandescent pinprick, and disappears.

The room stinks. Today would be a good day to replace the kitty litter, sponge out the litter box, clean the tub and toilet, do a laundry, put things in order. Her place has gotten so messy. Gerry knows it, feels ashamed. But this summer has been so hot. Just getting through the day seems an effort. Getting to the AA group is an effort. Feeding the cats is an effort. Filling time is an effort. Her counselor says this is all part of feeling depressed. The twenty pounds she's gained — all that's a sign that she's full of worry. The counselor wants Gerry to talk about it, but what's there to say? Every day is the same. Nothing changes. No alcohol. No drugs. Maybe an occasional drink, maybe pop some dope from time to time — but it's not the same. Every day's an effort. Dreary. Unchanging.

She brushes her hair and steals another look at the clock. Too early. She pulls up her sheets and smoothes them over. She turns off the TV, pets her kittens, smokes two Nows, and stares at her window — panes glare fiercely in sharp morning light. Clock again. 10:40. She decides to chance it.

Downstairs, people are milling in the hallway tearing open their mail, dropping advertising flyers on the floor, digging in envelopes for money, muttering and smiling and staring thoughtfully at these messages from the outside. Gerry hurries to the glass window and smiles as Frankie approaches. "Anything for me?" She tries to make it sound like the most ordinary request.

Frankie turns to check her box. "Nothing," he says.

"I'll wait till it's all sorted."

"That's it. Came in early today," he says. "You been gettin your checks all right, haven't you?"

"Yeah, they've been comin fine." Her voice seems to scrape against her throat.

"Well, you know how the mail is," Frankie says kindly.

"Yeah." Gerry shuffles back to the elevator.

"Gerry! Gerry! Hey, it's Faith!"

"Okay!" she mumbles and opens her eyes. 2:30. She picks herself up and unlocks the door.

"Happy Birthday, Gerry! Happy Birthday!" Faith gives her a quick hug, then pulls back. "Shit! You been cryin!"

"Yeah." She wishes Faith would go away.

"What's the matter, honey?"

"Nothin."

"People don't cry over nothin. What's the matter now?"

"My boy. He didn't call and he didn't send no card. He's all I got, Faith."

"He loves you, Gerry. You know, somethin musta come up. But that don't mean he don't love you."

"I know you're right but — he coulda bought some stupid little card with birds and flowers an put a stamp on it. He coulda stood in a pay phone for two minutes an said hello."

"Well listen, honey, you got friends right here gonna make you a party. We ain't gonna let you sit here doin nothin on your birthday."

Faith hurries out. Fifteen minutes later she returns with a bottle of blackberry brandy and some methadone. It helps. Gerry relaxes with the brandy, and after awhile the methadone rolls over her, gentle and numbing. Cats rub against her legs. She sees them, yet barely feels them — like something dimly remembered. Faith smiling, stretched back on the bed puffing cigarettes. But Faith, this room, the busy street, this long sad day, seem unreal now. Gerry is back in Newport News, standing on the veranda. Last customers gone. The girls giggling, sharing stories inside, while Gerry smokes a last cigarette. Damp salt air. Sweet magnolia rolled up in thick morning mist pouring off the harbor. . . .

"Howya doin, honey?"

Surprised by speech. Back again in this small sad room. "I was thinkin. . . . A place I use to live in. . . . "

"You okay?"

"Yeah." She smiles shyly and lights another cigarette.

A few minutes pass. Knock on the door. "Gerry! Gerry! Hey, it's O.J.! What's crackin?"

"It's her birthday," Faith says as she opens the door. "You got anything to help our party along?"

O.J. is short and a bit stocky. Unshaven. Watery eyes. "Well, yeah." He pulls back a step, staring at the floor. "I got a bitta coke here. Just enough for me and Gerry to get off."

"I didn't ask for nothin for myself. You got somethin for Gerry, you go on an give it to her."

Dull images. She could be watching some old television movie. Gerry smiles faintly and rolls up her sleeve. Watches from far away while O.J. squeezes up a vein and pokes in her shot. Current surges. Quick electric clenching, then the tension eases. Alive, alive, motion and heat, each cell beating with its own racing heart. "Good, O.J.! That's good!"

O.J. bobs his head to his own music, grins, flicks a thumbnail across a grey sore on his cheek. Faith is still there on the bed, but dim, like a ghost about to vanish. Kittens everywhere, scratching, tumbling, nipping one another's ears. Keyed to her energy. Alive, alive.

"Here, you kill it." Faith passes her the last of the blackberry brandy. Gerry gulps it down. It tastes too sugary. Almost backs up on her, but she forces it down. "See, Gerry, you got a birthday. You got friends here. How bout us goin to the park — smoke a few joints and see the sunset?"

O.J. still jerking to silent music. "How bout it, Gerry?"

"That'll be all right, I guess," she says. "I gotta change first." The voice is someone else's. She's almost startled to hear it. None of this is quite real. Even her body, charged and speeding, does not seem hers. Some part of her, some essential part, remains on that Virginia porch — alone and young and independent; blue morning glories oddly luminous in the false dawn, street lights blurred and nebulous behind the thickening veil of fresh sea mist.

Faith and O.J. leave the room to let her dress. She remembers her insulin and fumbles through her drawer where she finds two partly empty vials. Something's been wrong the last few weeks. Sudden weight gains. Feeling low. Gerry's been changing her dosage from time to time, seeing if that might make a difference. She fills the syringe and takes her shot. But something's not right. She senses it. Maybe those vials were empty. She barely felt her shot — no more than a pinprick. Concentrate, get this thing straight — she knows that, but her mind is racing. And what happens in this dreary little room does not much matter. She looks at the empty insulin vials. How could she be so stupid to imagine there was more than a drop or two in them? This time she takes a full dose, fills the syringe carefully, and watches the serum flow into her body. A tiny blind kitten nuzzles into her lap. She tickles the little thing on its belly. "Yes, baby. Yes, baby. . . . "

O.J. finds her flopped across her bed, kittens all around her, burrowing for some perfect cozy niche. "Hey, Gerry! You ready?" She doesn't say a word. He brushes a few kittens aside and sits down by her feet. A kind of gurgle comes from her throat. "You want some water or somethin?" Her body heaves. "Gerry! You all right?" He seizes her shoulders to raise her head. Bloody nose. Eyes clamped shut. Sheets puddled with blood. O.J. shakes her, raises her to a sitting position, then eases her down to rest.

He cannot revive her, and when the ambulance comes from St. Luke's there is little they can do. Medical science will keep her alive for two more weeks — alone in a corner of the intensive care unit, plugged into expensive life-support systems, wheezing regularly into a respirator. But today, Gerry's birthday, all that matters is already dead.

Gerry's cats have gone mad. During the two weeks she was up at St. Luke's dying, they had their own room at the hotel. O.J. looked in on them from time to time, and Doug and Bobby remembered to feed them pretty regularly, but now they shrink from human touch, retreating beneath furniture or scampering to inaccessible corners. Nervous movements. Eyes flashing panic. Wretched smell of putrid kitty litter. Cockroaches trooping over every surface, tunneling in cat shit, scurrying through every drawer, busy activity on the bloodstained sheets. . . .

"She was a pig!" Ironsides says. "And stupid. Fucked around

with drugs she couldn't handle. Hung out with trash. Didn't do nothin with her life except sit there with her cats an make a mess. Wanna kill herself, she can go right on ahead an do it — but I got the apartment next to her. She made a mess with them cats. I get her cockroaches spreading over to my place."

So Ironsides fumigates Gerry's room. He grabs a few of her kittens, dumps them in the basement, then sprays the room with full-strength roach killer. Four cats are still in the room when he locks the door. They struggle through a jammed window and leap for freedom — twelve floors down to the 100th Street sidewalk.

When the garbage truck comes by on its morning rounds, two kittens are still alive — broken and breathing irregularly, but still alive. There is nothing the garbage man can do. He chucks the ruined creatures into the back of his truck and turns on the compactor to finish off what Hotel Walden had so nearly completed.

AUTUMN

CHANGE OF WEATHER

Each day three cars pick up a bunch of people in front of the hotel and haul them uptown to the Harlem projects where they distribute Buy-Rite handouts. Doug's happy to have the job. Elevator to the top floor, a flyer under every door, floor by floor, until they're back at ground level. And now there's money to replace his silent TV. So Doug works, and Bobby watches the soaps and plays solitaire. "They're all into singing now," he says while some actor struggles through a miserable love song. "Singing, flashbacks, and Caribbean adventures. Lots of changes — and our TV was out only a couple of months."

David's stuck in his room. With this change in weather he's required to wear a jacket for his Auxiliary Police patrols, and the winter uniforms have not yet arrived at the precinct. He sits in his room listening to patrol-car reports. On his wall he's taped a map of the precinct, shading in the most dangerous areas and marking emergency call boxes with red Xs. Above the map is a xeroxed copy of a police form listing the contents of a wallet. "I found it outside," David explains. "They said the guy works for Senator Javits. Maybe he'll call me when they tell him how I recovered his stuff."

Ironsides is not out on the street much. "Workin things out with Francine," he explains.

Doc's gotten very shaky.

I ask around for Youngblood, but no one has anything to say.

Bamboo, one of Gerry's cats — a big tawny — shoots out of the garbage pile one morning, down a stairwell and into the basement. The basement is full of cats. People move on or get tired of their pets or run out of money to feed them, so they set them loose in the basement. A few people bring scraps or bones to leave at the top of the cellar stairs, but basement cats are always thin and hungry. Ten or fifteen of them living in semidarkness, fighting over rats and roaches and garbage. Eating their own dead.

Management starts piping heat to the rooms around Columbus Day. The dry steam air brings forth an overwhelming stench — as if walls and tiles, unlaundered clothes, and shit-stained toilets all at once released the filth of years. All over Manhattan you hear people saying, "It's a beautiful day!" But here people stay inside, close to their radiators.

SUITOR

"Anthony was courting me," Muriel says. "He spent the summer sleeping on park benches — trying to make his SSI go a long way, I suppose. But it's getting cold now, you know — Jack Frost, or Jack O'Lantern. Anyhow, there's a bite in the air, so he proposes that he'll sleep on my floor.

" 'I gotta make a call,' I told him. I think it's a little nicer to make some kind of excuse. A straight refusal can be so upsetting.

" 'I have money,' he tells me. 'This is just to get me through a temporary setback. I have property, bank accounts. I'm getting it straightened out. I've left messages everywhere.'

" 'Great!' I say. 'If you're worth so much, why'd you spend the summer in Riverside Park? What'd you do, buy a bench?' Oh, he was quite affronted! The expression on his face! You'd think I'd turned my back on royalty! 'Excuse me,' I say, 'I've got to attend to my shopping.'

" 'No problem,' he tells me. 'I'll come along and carry your bags. It's time I put on some pounds.'

" 'No thank you. The last time you accompanied me we got everything you wanted.' He was really getting on my nerves. 'You were going to come by last year,' I said. 'Well, I'm glad I didn't hold my breath. And now you're here to sleep on my floor and help me shop! You can't even afford a stick of chewing gum!'

" 'I don't have the teeth to chew it with.'

" 'You really are hard up!' I said. Then I beat a hasty retreat.

"You know, Anthony's not an idiot. Actually, he has considerable intelligence. It upsets me to see him make himself look ridiculous. I don't like being put in the position of feeling sorry for him; that's why I tried to keep our meeting as short as possible. It's not that I don't care, but I can't ignore past experience. If I haven't learned by now, then shame on me."

SCHOOL

YES! SEND ME YOUR FREE SCHOOL CATALOGUE: OPPORTUNITIES IN ELECTRONICS.... David pencils in his name and address in careful block letters. "The Cleveland Institute of Electronics," he tells me. "See, I'm doin things. I ain't gonna be in this place forever. Maybe I'll get a correspondence degree — where you don't have to sit around in a classroom. I could do the whole thing here at my desk, and then I could start doin repairs outa my room. Save until I rent a shop. Build up a whole chain. Custom stereo — with a special discount if you're Puerto Rican or poor or if I like you. D.T. Express, I'll call it! Snaps!

David tried school for a while last year. A special remedial program at West Side High School on Ninety-third Street. He keeps a folder with material he saved from the program. "Good to have you in our family group," the teacher writes on his program sheet. And under her note — "Welcome to West Side High. Hope to see you next cycle — Mardi."

"It didn't work," David explains. "I just can't do well in a classroom situation. It seems like too much is goin on in my head at once."

He shows me his vocabulary exercises:

> He *attest* the insadint to the police.
> He is allwas *badgerring* pepolie.
> The dog *beset* boy.

He actted to *buffoon* them.
When he is mad he gose through a *cataclysm.*
I am allwas triing to *circumvent* him.
The dog was *bestial.*

Was there anyone able to read this as the personal document it is? David does *badger* people, alienating them with his requests and commands, anxious to be heard. And more than once, he has created enemies by "*attesting* to the police" about minor incidents in the hotel. Sometimes he acts the *buffoon,* wisecracking and jiving till he drives you up the wall, but this is his way of *circumventing* the pressure he constantly feels. And he knows he must try to rein in his tension because "when he is mad he gose through a *cataclysm.*" David dreads the thought of committing another nightmare murder. It was a woman, the same age as his mother, that set him off. He still wants his mother's love, but he's full of rage at the way she once abused him, at how she still rejects him. His treatment of Lady, the beloved dog that he loses, recovers, and gives away repeatedly reflects his troubled ambivalence.... "The dog *beset* boy.... The dog was *bestial.*"

Words and ideas are a means of growth, but for David they are like baited hooks dangled in murky depths that teem with fierce, hungry emotions. They threaten to yank him away from his way of surviving — to draw him into a dreaded cataclysm of feeling and action. "It didn't work," David says. Better than his teachers, David knows the power of words.

YOUNGBLOOD

After all these months Youngblood is ready to talk about his life. He seemed to be steering clear of me, but apparently he's been watching and waiting. He's a cautious man — it's taken ten months for me to get my security clearance.

Youngblood's hair is cropped close and flat. His head stays

tucked between his shoulders — like a pigeon huddled against the cold. He carries himself in a permanent wince, as if recoiling from some unbearable screech. Usually, he's fastidiously dressed — neat pressed slacks, sweater, and sports jacket; but he has his share of dark days when his pants are unfastened, his shirttail flaps out, and he shuffles about with a pronounced limp. On days like this his talk rambles, and often he breaks into manic cackling that seizes him — eyes squinting, arms and legs shaking in spasms like a marionette gone berserk. He's like that today as we talk about Jack the Ripper.

"I heard he was a doctor," Youngblood says. "Like that Doctor Frankenstein — where he was ahead of his time and the law wouldn't let him go on with his work. This Doctor Frankenstein had to rob these graves cause they wouldn't let you cut up dead bodies then. Okay, so now Jack the Ripper went around cuttin out ladies' wombs — well maybe he was doin research on women, on their nature, so he just cut out what he needed an took it home to study. I'm not sayin it wasn't wrong," he cackles, "but it was wrong of the law to keep a man from his research. He mighta been tryin to find out somethin that was gonna help women — how their nature works — but see, they didn't give him the go-ahead, so he had to take matters into his own hands."

Youngblood's rap on Jack the Ripper puzzles me, until he sits down and tells me his story.

YOUNGBLOOD'S STORY

I come from a bad neighborhood where there was fightin all the time. People wasn't more or less civilized. You get anything decent, they want to take it. Understand? People in my neighborhood, they always had nothin. Weren't makin no money. Havin babies they didn't have no business havin in the first damn place. Everyone desperate for this, hungry for that. Well, my mother was steady workin most of the time. We wind up gettin an apartment uptown on 146th Street — in the middle of the ghetto. The fuckin jungle.

My father, he kidnapped my brother, so it's just me and my mother. My mother would feed me, clean me up, and go to work. Then I go on about my business — off to school. Come back, and I'm about so big, and people always tryin to take advantage of you, beatin you up. Gangs everywhere. No-mans, the Comanches, the Chancellors — all that shit. Learned what I could at school. As far as effort was concerned, I got A for it. As far as learnin something — now that's a different story. You try to learn something under all this pressure — fight on the way to school, more fightin at lunchtime, people waitin to beat you up on your way home.

That's what it's like bein poverty people. In order to survive, you gotta act just like the rest of em. There's certain things you gotta go along with if you don't want to turn out bein dead or bein some kind of homosexual. I had to become one low-down-dirty-rotten-top-of-nasty-shit-motherfuckin-son-of-a-bitch. I'm in the middle of the jungle. You can't take no lily-white cocksucker and stick him in the middle of the jungle. If he's gonna survive, he's got to get down there with all the animals cause, believe me, these zombies are gonna attack. This one dude, he and his brother were trying to make a faggot outa me. I say, "I gotta get this nigger's ass! That's all there is to it!" I whipped the shit off of his ass — all the way down the steps, really laid it on him. Then his brother come and I kicked his ass. "Goddamn! How'd you do that?" I say to myself. "I must be gettin mean. . . ."

Seein my momma goin to work — tired, half dead — I needed to finish school and try to get me a job so I could maintain myself. Get the weight off her back. I found me a barberin school — Vaughn Barber Academy — and I took to it well. I learned to cut hair just like that. Anything with hair on it I can handle. You'd be surprised what you have to study. Just like bein a doctor, because in order to be a full-fledged-master-craftsman-qualified-barber you had to study the whole body from the head down to the toes. So now life was gettin a little better. I'm comin outa the jungle. My idea was to sleep and eat, get up and go to school. I never was one to do but one thing at a time and try to do it well. Tried to avoid gettin involved in miscellaneous abstract shit — don't wanna deviate from the main event, which was goin to school. A lotta people, they know more about bullshit than the main event. When they get older, can't live off that bullshit, but that's all they know about. I wasn't like that. I knew that you gotta learn some kinda trade or fashion in order to make some money. Don't wanna be a commoner — washin dishes, scrubbin floors all your life.

When I got to my seventeenth birthday, I got my apprentice thing and went to work. High Hat Barber Shop on 134th Street — big sign with top hat and two canes. One of the most spacious barber shops in Harlem. Very high class of people came in there. Strictly barberin, manicurin, and beauty culture. No numbers. No bookies. The man run that joint like it was a church. Hang your coat up, then you got the shoeshine stand. Manicurist on this side as you come in the middle of the place. Then the sink and shampoo. You come in and get yourself groomed. When you go out of there, you was *correct*! You were shined. You was swished down and whatnot. Your hair slicked and shaved. You're manicured. And your woman — if she come, in the back they got a beauty parlor there. When you left you were first class — go right to the White House.

I took to barberin like a duck took to water. Workin hard every day, from 9:30 till ten o'clock at night. After a few years it dawns on me — "Damn fool! When you gonna wake up? Your whole life is here in the barber shop!" That's when I started to mess around with the girls a bit. Rowdy crowd. When I got outa work, ain't nobody on the street but the lowlifers, hustlers, prostitutes — so I got down with some hustlin. I met this girl, she said, "You gotta do somethin. What you gonna do to get me some money?" So we started this hustlin thing — her and some of the hustlin girls walkin up and down the street. If they hit on a thing, they say, "Would you like to have a little sport? Would you like to see a lady?" Tip them on the rates, and whatever he want to do he give her the scratch. She get into bed, do whatever they're gonna do. She get her money, come on out — goin on about business, that's it.

I didn't like the idea of that kinda stuff, but I was tired of workin in the barber shop. It was one big fat drag. Wrong trade. But in those days nobody would hire no niggers no way. So now I got myself outa barberin and into hustlin. It was a change — a way of gettin a buck without workin myself to death — but not necessarily a good change. I knew what I was messin with, the chances that you're takin. I knew I was in danger.... Everybody was messin with narco. It was impossible to make any money less you messin with it. I didn't care too much for usin it, but see, you gotta put somethin on the streets decent for people to buy. I'm tellin people I'm givin top merchandise, so I gotta check my merchandise. I never was a real wrongdoer. I was more or less tryin to stay alive — tryin to be a civilized human being. Those fuckin savage goddamn animals — I wanted to get away from that. But I became a slave and an animal. Terrible! Ain't nothing to be proud of. I was a lulu. All I wanted was to come outa the jungle. The world was an uncivilized goddamn place as far as I was concerned. Such a shitty-ass undecent place compared to where I went to barber school and the type of people I had been around. But when I come to be around these crazy-assed niggers in the jungle, when you really got to doin narco, I did it. It's that simple.

Sure enough, motherfucker — I had to let them know I ain't no punk. You look at my face, you'll see it's a little up on one side. That's from bein hit so hard. The one thing these niggers got is a whole lotta strength. They ain't got no sense, but they hit like a son of a bitch. All they got is a lotta uncultivated, unharnessed energy. Had a fight one time — this nigger hit so hard it was outrageous. I was semiconscious. I didn't have my piece, and I knew I had to keep this cocksucker off or he'd kill me. So I gets my knife and I starts cuttin him till somebody come and broke it up. See, what he did was attack my woman. I had to kick his door down and get my lady out or lose my business standin in the jungle. Another time this lady who worked for me come outa the movies, and the police beat her damn near to death. This nigger cop come into extortion and all that kinda stuff — think he can take my woman and get her hustlin for him. So I said, "If he fuck with mine, I'm comin down on him like rain." I went down there and found me that nigger and almost whupped him to death. Attacked his ass like a mad dog. I had to take him on. Didn't have no choice, cause what he did was outrageous. That woman's my business! You don't fuck with business. You knock her out, you're knockin *me* out cause that's where my money's comin from. So I took him off. Did my job, I did my job.

That woman he beat up was my daughter's mother. And what makes it worse, she had the kid with her at the movie. He whupped her, and she had the baby right there with her. Man, if that wasn't lowlife! Nigger like that should have been strung up by the dick. He distorted my opinion of the whole fuckin police. You just don't fuck with somebody the way he did. She was all bloodied up — marks all in her face, all over her body. They did a job on her in the hospital — she got well and didn't look too bad — but it fucked up her head, and that got her messed up on that narco thing. Finally, that killed her.

It's mean in the jungle. Nice quiet guy don't make it out there — not during that time. You have to be a man. Do what it takes to stay alive and get what you need. While she was in the hospital I come down on the city so goddamn tough. That nigger cop represent the city, an they didn't have no business havin a cocksucker like that. Ed Small, he started Small's Paradise, he recommended me a lawyer. He's old-time — worked right next to the barber shop. Little Caesar, they called him, and he called me Little Barber. He got me a downtown lawyer. Sued them and got the girl all kinds of money.

After that, the cops was out to bust me. To make a long story short, they sent a guy, an Irishman, to the house, and he claimed that I sold him some narco. I didn't sell no goddamn dope to no whitey! But how'm I gonna prove it? They sent me up to Sing Sing. I got in the prison barber shop and did my job. Didn't have no trouble.

When I come out, I got another lady and we started fuckin around for a little scratch. I wanted to get away from this old narco thing, but that's kinda hard to do. I didn't know nothin but barberin an racketeerin. So this time I went out to boost me up some clothes. Bought some hot shit in the street. Cops came to my house and opened the closet. This is when Nehru jackets and all came in — and I got a whole closet of em. "Damn, what's all this shit in here?" they say. I think they wanted to get me off the scene or something.

Went to Rikers Island, and they put me on welfare when I come out. Never been on welfare. Heard about it but I never been on it. Got my steady checks for awhile and got on a methadone program. I was all messed up, didn't know how I was gonna survive. I was livin clean, decent, but ain't nothin happenin, and I got tired of takin that meth. I stopped goin to the program — just stopped, and I like to died. My momma come home, she finds me on the floor in a corner. Cold gone. Like dead. I was in a coma for about three, four days.

Come off that meth, they send me to this SRO joint. Keystone Hotel. Forty-third Street or somewhere, between Broadway and Eighth Avenue. Goddamn! Ain't nothin but a shootin gallery. This is some kinda terrible! They must think I'm crazy to come to this motherfucker. I goes upstairs and here's this little room with a little stove and a cot in it. Ain't big enough for nothin. I ain't gonna sleep in it — or die in it either. This place needs to be condemned. You walk through the lobby where the office is. Nigger's sittin right there takin off. Dope. Everything. Nasty. Greasy. I can't stand this shit. I mean, I don't know what kinda dope fiend the welfare think I am.

"I'm not about to stand no shit like that!" I told the welfare people. "I'll go back to jail first. You all get something better than this or you all kiss my ass! You ain't gonna make no punk outa me."

Wind up gettin a place over on Twenty-third and Lexington. It wasn't too bad, but they don't let you have no company. Couldn't take my woman there or nothin — understand what I mean? That was my business, my life. Once or twice over the years I'd try to fuck around with just an ordinary working kinda broad. Couldn't handle it. Every time I tried, I got fucked up. Couldn't handle that shit, cause they was stupid, dumb, and I didn't understand what they was doin. Hustlin bitches had to be smarter. They had to have a little better on the cap than somebody just do what the boss tells ya — get paid at the end of the week. I couldn't get along with them broads. They tryin to see how jealous they can make a nigger. That's so stupid. It's outrageous. What the fuck is so grand about your ass? Man is the most important thing on the fuckin planet. He need a companion. Now if you don't know where it's at, what you doin? The only thing you got to offer is your fuckin ass, and if you're gonna fuck around with that, what I want with you? I'm puttin up with you and all this stupid shit you're doin, for what? Kiss my ass! Let me get a hooker where I know what I'm doin.

No ifs, buts about it. I take care of them. Know more about most of them than they know themself. Means I got to be together. Any time a nigger's fuckin around in this town — he ain't on welfare, SSI, or nothin and ain't gettin no gifts; he stay neat and clean and keep his house, stays fed and keep a buck in his pocket — boy, that's proof of the cold-blooded fact he know what he's doin with women. Yeah! You helpin em keep themself together — supervisin their business, managin their money, executin a service.

Couldn't live down there on Lexington without my business, so I come on uptown and moved in here. That's how me and Elaine got started. See, she'd been with Lewis, this heavy dude I used to know uptown. Well known dude. He got his leg cut off below the knee through some shit that he got in. He may be a little psychiatric, but the nigger's heavy upstairs. Know a whole bunch of shit. So he had her for maybe ten or twelve years. She was his woman — hustlin for him, tryin to make money. They combined their money, which he handled, and they kept a pretty good apartment — decent food, clothes to wear, go on vacations every now and then. See, this was during the sixties and there was money in circulation.

When he got done with her, he brought her down here across the street and dropped her. I ran into her one day and remembered seein her with Lewis. She had a nice lookin girlfriend with her, but when the deal went down Elaine had more on the ball. I knew that because she'd been with Lewis. Like if you're with him, believe me, you got somethin on the cap. He's a first-class nigger. Balls nigger. High-steppin dude. Automobile downstairs, waitin for him in front of the door. Nothin but the best clothes. Talk big shit and wear top jewelry. Yeah, he had everything. Wheelin an dealin. Sellin this here, buyin that there. Gimme an overcoat once. Good material. I still got it upstairs. Come in the barber shop and give it to me jus like that. You know, like he'd get a bunch of coats — sable, mink, seal, nothin but the best — an he'd be in the coat business til they was gone. Ten years, an my coat looks like new. An women, yeah, he had women like he had coats. The very finest. Lots of em. And they was *his*. Things you read about in history books — like some king sayin all the women on his land was his property — that's how this dude took care of business. Just another one of his sideline things. High-steppin dude, all right.

Anytime I mess with somebody I know is hooked up with one of these heavy-type dudes, I look into the situation before I move. You better believe I'm takin care. I say to Lewis, "Listen, man, I went talkin to this lady a little bit. Now what you all doin? I always been a respectful and polite dude. I don't want no trouble — steal your stuff or whatnot."

"Do what you want," he said. "If you want it, you can have it." So I went on and got down.

Elaine was oversexed. Terrible. She had a high nature. Needed men — that was her jones. It was drivin her bugs, goin off all the time. Man can't take but so much, and Lewis was gettin old. She was too much for him to handle. Just bein around them people is a hell of a problem. They can't hardly go and get a glass of water without fuckin up the whole kitchen — break the goddamn windows and shit. They that nervous and upset. Their relatives send em to the psychiatric hospitals, and then the hospitals turn em out — give em that little monthly money to maintain themselves.

She needed heavy supervision. Stark raving mad. This thing was botherin her so tough, she was runnin around foamin at the mouth. She'd have two or three hundred dollars in checks, and she's sleepin in the park. If they give her a place to stay, she's runnin around naked. They don't want people like that in these hotels. Makes the place look bad. The bitch gets cold in here — she so stupid and fucked up, can't start the stove to do something about it — she start a fire in the middle of the floor. The bitch was mad. In and outa the nuthouse. But with heavy supervision you can bring them around, and that's what I did with Elaine. Business is a lotta trouble, but this bitch put money in my pocket. When you take care of your business, your business will take care of you. Don't ask about affection. I ain't in love. I'm in love with business. I'm supervisin all the financial shit — seein that the rent is paid, seein that she got food to eat every day. Cook, clean up the place, do the shopping, get the shit in the cleaners — I just managed the whole damn deal.

What made the biggest difference — I sat down and took stock of the situation. First thing — she couldn't get enough sex. And that kept her frustrated and all fucked up — kept her nervous, tensed up so she couldn't hardly hold a glass of water.

I gave her all kinds of medication to keep that down, but it didn't do the job. Narco was the next resort — to keep her cool — and I wasn't about to give her no dope. So I went up and talked to the psychiatric doctors. Anything that I can't handle, I go to them in a hurry. All part of doin business. "This bitch is a heavy case," I tell them. "Ain't got no light action here. Her problem's in her sex, so we gotta remove that part of her nature." Doctor agreed — she gotta have a hysterectomy.

When they eliminated her sex, her problem got so she could get around to handlin it. She's nowhere like she was. After she got outa the hospital the sex thing was still in her mind — she felt like she wanted it, but it was just a mental thing. In a month or so it wore off, eliminated all the nervousness. She was serene. She ain't broke down now in a hell of a long time. Before, it was maybe every three or four weeks — month and a half at most — she's gone. Now, she goes maybe two, three years.

I've helped a lotta people straighten themselves out. This colored woman, I got her to have the same operation. She thanked me and every other goddamn thing else. Even dedicated a song to me — "I Wanna Thank You for Lettin Me Be Myself Again" — that's how grateful she was. She wouldn't have agreed to do this herself, but I got her to do it. Best thing that could have happened to her.

I've been with Elaine about five years now, maybe longer. It was a strain. See, you have to do a lotta things to keep yourself in shape so you can handle it. Average person can't handle it. It's too heavy. You gotta keep your sex down, and you sho nuff bein enticed somethin terrible. Some of those people are sexy as a son of a bitch. That's the only thing they know. But you can't fuck with it. Can't have a good time. It would be detrimental to business. If you give in to sex they figure you a fool — you get carried away, you like sex. They gonna overpower you instead of you overpowerin them. You gotta be the boss.

I don't know that Elaine's gotten to the point that she could manage her whole life by herself, but even if she did, even if I had my money, I wouldn't walk out on her. Ain't no way I'd do that. She's been too much help to me. I helped her a whole lot, but I don't tell nobody that she don't help me. Give me something to do with my life.

No ifs, ands, and buts about it — I know plenty, and I didn't learn nothin at school. There are people here in this hotel I feel comfortable talkin to because I can learn somethin from them — people who have studied all kinda things. Some of em, things got too heavy for em, and they didn't back up or leave it alone. That's why they have a breakdown. They're makin big sense today — talkin all that highly technical nuclear shit and tell you damn near how to put a spaceship together — and then tomorrow he stone crazy. What are you gonna do with a case like that? One time I started messin with somethin, I saw it was gettin to me an backed up. And still I had somewhat of a breakdown. Didn't go to the hospital or anything like that, but I got away from it — sure nuff. Takin care of business.

I mean, you'd be surprised what you can learn from bein around these people. Give you a better respect for life. I don't take advantage of nobody. I feel sorry for them and try to help them — and they're helpin me, cause I'm learnin a whole lot. You be around here a few years, you walk away from here — don't you make no mistake about it, you got a few things on the cap.

They doin all they can do for these people. Can't do no more or you'll have a lotta people that shouldn't be here. See, it's a psychological thing — you don't make things too convenient for poor people, cause then they blow all incentive, all their drive and everything. That's why I ain't on no welfare and shit. Sign up for alcohol program, drug program, methadone program — you get your monthly check. But that goes against everything I've been taught in school. I don't feel like joinin some program; don't want to get too comfortable with this thing. Go over there and give him something to eat, hand him what he needs — well, he's never gonna get around to bein a productive citizen. You've got to remember that. Now, my situation — I've been in business, I study hard, and I don't accept this level of life in the first place. I'm a productive citizen. . . .

YOGA

Drizzling autumn morning. Muriel's hung some awful plastic curtains against her grey window. Soiled turquoise, torn and yellowy. By her bed are some carefully written notes:

> From Beacon Hill
> to
> Nob Hill
> with a little
>   Tin Pan Alley
>   in Between!!!

"Oh, it's nothing," she says. "I thought I might write a little short story about my travels. By the way, what do you think of my new bowl?" It's simple and pleasing to the eye — a ceramic soup bowl with yellow and blue stripes around the rim, blue flower at the center. "I got it at Shopwell yesterday. I thought it was time to do some redecorating in here. Of course, a bowl's no fun without some soup." Muriel's feeling chipper today. A beige fur cap covers her thinning hair, framing her face, allowing something sweet and strangely childlike to shine forth.

"Ah, here it is!" From a mess of playing cards, papers, and grocery receipts she retrieves a torn label from a packet of Stouffer's New England Clam Chowder. "Now that's my cup of tea!" She loves her little puns. "I appreciate a company that makes a good product. And I don't care for the Manhattan style. I don't think this is really clam country. The clams are clammier in New England. And I know I was happy as a clam during my childhood on the Cape."

Recently, Muriel's returned to SPOP (Special Program for Older People). Two mornings a week a van fetches her and she spends the day in supervised group activities. "I'm doing a bit of farming," she says. "I started my own avocado last week. Of course, it doesn't take much work after you stick a few toothpicks in it, but then I wouldn't want to mother it to death. . . . And yoga, we do yoga too." Even today, when she looks as well and lively as

I've ever seen her, I doubt she could do a single sit-up or touch her toes. It's impossible to imagine her in a lotus position. The jerky hobble from her broken hip is permanent. Her left hand is still heavily taped from her last seizure.

"What sort of exercise do you do?" I ask her.

"This is my favorite." She brings the tips of her index finger and thumb together and moves her hand slowly past her eyes, as if studying some fragile struggling insect trapped between her fingers, noting its markings, holding it carefully, gently, so as not to cause it the least bit of pain. Muriel's eyes fix on this moving point, face relaxed, body perfectly still. For one moment, all else falls away leaving only this exquisite unseen creature, delicately held before her steady unblinking gaze.

Then her fingers part. Her shoulders sag. Muriel's face looks white and tired under her fluffy furry hat. "That's it," she says. "That's my yoga."

MESS

Stanley's a mess. Both legs gone below the knee, his artificial limbs are smudged and scratched, covered with swatches of tape and string. He drags himself around the hallway like a gutter beggar from another century. His clothes are filthy. Hands callused and black. His face though, is handsome — soft green eyes that seem to look out with confusion and wonder, as if consumed by such a large and pressing matter that the mere world before him no longer holds his interest.

Everyone is courteous to Stanley. The social workers try to be helpful, of course, but so do the hustlers, the winos, and crazies. He has everyone's sympathy. He seems to take all pain with him as he crawls about. Even Dorothy, one of the most ornery people in the hotel, listens attentively when he speaks. "What are you?" he asks her.

"What you think I am?" she snaps. "I ain't no fish!"

"You're colored, that's easy. But I think you got some Spanish in you. You got Spanish eyes."

"Well, I did have a Puerto Rican boyfriend who used to — "

"Yeah, see. I'm good at telling. That's cause I got some of everything in me." He talks eagerly, but his eyes look past her to some vast and empty space. "I'm half Jewish, half Polack, with a little Arab and Irish. Lamia Rappaport, that's my mother's name, and she told me where I come from — from Germany and Poland. They killed Jews wherever they found em. And trains in France and Italy, trains all over Europe with Jews — carrying em to be killed. That's why I won't ride no subway. I won't go down cause I'm a half Jew, a wandering Jew. You know what that is? What that means?"

Dorothy bangs the elevator button a few times and shakes her head.

"I had to move," Stanley says. "I can't stay in one place. I can't — like a rolling stone. It's something in me. Yeah, I'm a rolling stone — but not like Mick Jagger; I think he's the biggest fag in the world. Wears lipstick wherever he goes. Faggot! . . . Tell me if I'm wrong — every Beatle has kids. John and Ringo, George Harrison — they're all family men. And Paul, he's the one they busted in Japan. Stupidest thing. They were all jealous cause he had children and made all these albums, so they snuck up on him like — that place in the Pacific — like Pearl Harbor, when the Japs were helping Hitler chase all the Jews."

"Well, nobody's gonna come lookin for you in here," Dorothy replies. "Japs an Germans don't give a shit about you."

"You know, Dorothy was the name of that girl on the TV movie:

> We're off to see the wizard,
> The wonderful wizard of love,
> He's gonna sent us all to die
> And meet our God above."

Dorothy bangs the elevator button again. "You're off key."

"I thought I was dead once — right at the station, waitin for the train of heaven. I ran outa bullets. Kept pulling the trigger, pulling the trigger, and this Viet Cong put his bayonet right into my neck!" He cranes his head back to show a thin white scar. "He was on top of me! I didn't have no bullets!"

"That's how you lost your legs?"

"I was dead, ready for heaven, and they blew him away — Braaa-braaa-braaa-braaa! Machine guns. What a mess!"

"Your legs?"

"Oh, that came later. I got home and couldn't find nothin to do. I was workin down in Red Hook, but it didn't mean nothin. Drinkin a lot. I'd take some drugs, but it was drinkin that lost me my legs. I passed out in the snow. Five hours till my sister found me. It took three operations before they took my legs off — gangrene and everything. I don't mind so much. It's only stairs that give me trouble. An it got me off drinkin."

The elevator door opens and Dorothy steps in. "Yeah, well you take care now."

"It's not true what they say about my mother!" His voice is urgent. Dorothy sticks out an arm to hold the door. "They say I hate her cause I phone her and say weird things, but they forget how I had two dirty bookstores and sold em and gave her the money. And Lloyds of London — you can check on this — I got a $100,000 policy on her if she dies. You can't tell me I'm not thinkin of her!"

OCTOBER BUTTONS

[Here are the buttons David sports:]

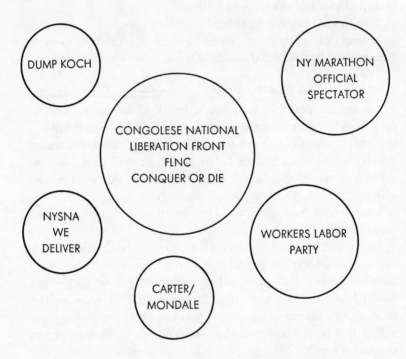

A FACE LIKE CHARLES BRONSON'S

A stocky Hispanic guy with a face like Charles Bronson's sits on a stool in the first-floor unit kitchen while Youngblood cuts his hair. Powerful arms propped rigidly against his knees. The Bronson resemblance is striking — Johnny must've heard it a hundred times — but he's short, and the macho image is spoiled by mournful, milky eyes. "You really needed it today," Youngblood says. "You had a clumpa hair in back stickin out like an Indian."

"Fuckin nigger!" Johnny says. "You gimme a haircut like last time an you gonna wake up scalped." His tone is appropriately threatening, but he slurs his words like a punched-out fighter.

Youngblood just laughs. "You been drinkin too much wine, Johnny. Too much for too long."

"You ain't never seen me drink no wine!"

"Sure, Johnny. How many tattoos you got?" Johnny pushes up his sleeves. On his left forearm is an American eagle grasping an unfurled banner inscribed with "Anna Marie." High on his right bicep is a blue heart with "Betty" on it. "Like I was sayin, Johnny, only a wino fool's gonna write his women's names all over hisself."

Johnny's busy fumbling with his shirt. "Dis one's duh best!" He spreads his shirt to display "Jeanine" arched around his nipple like a crescent moon.

Youngblood smiles his peculiar wry smile and steadies Johnny's head while he trims his neck. "You dumber than I thought, Johnny. How you gonna get a woman to stay in your corner if you got a list of names all over you? Tattooin is a wino scene."

"I *never* drink wine," he says. "I drink my rum. I drink vodka an whiskey. But you ain't never seen me drink no wine."

"Now you gonna run down that old shit again!"

"I got reefer. I shoot dope an cocaine. I'll get off on methadone, an I got Valium for fifty cents each — but I ain't no wino."

"All right, Johnny!"

"I *never* drink no wine cause it fucks me up. I done zero to five the first time I been in jail. I done five years hard time after that. They get me again and I'm gone. I ain't drinkin no wine. I ain't gonna fuck myself up."

"All right, Johnny!" Youngblood gives him a small hand mirror.

"Next time cut it like today," Johnny says after careful self-inspection. "Last time you cut it crazy." He hands him two bills and offers him a Pall Mall. "You got a match?" He looks down-cast, exhausted.

Youngblood cackles. He seems to be enjoying all this immensely. "Get outa here so I can clean up!"

Johnny waggles his cigarette pack at Youngblood, spilling a few Pall Malls on the floor. "Nigger!" he growls with feeble ferocity. "I asked you for a match!"

Youngblood collects the cigarettes and blows off Johnny's fallen hair before handing them back to him. "Take your fuckin cigarettes outa here. You ain't even got the money for a match!" Youngblood cackles at his put-down. A game of banter and insult, I know, but there is no play, no pleasure in it today. "You ain't no wino, Johnny? Well what kinda run-down garbage are you?"

SWEET FACE

Pretty, like Sugar Ray Leonard. Neat, cropped hair; lime-green sweatshirt; crisp new jeans. He leans back against the stair rail, facing the window to an empty courtyard. Twenty minutes and he hasn't moved a muscle except to adjust the slight, sweet smile he keeps fixed on his sweet face. At these moments the corners of his mouth quiver slightly — the way a ballerina might adjust her balance. His body stays perfectly still. Eyes turned down at the floor.

FLYING

"Hey, snaps! I can fly!" Forty-dollar polyurethane wheels — another check-day extravagance — but David's getting his skating act together. He can almost fly. He shoots smoothly down the corridor, coming to a perfect toe stop in front of Stanley.

Stanley's left his legs in his room today. He likes to crawl out into the hallway, sit near the radiator, and check out the scene. "Hiya, David! What's it like out?"

"Watch this!" David races toward the end of the hallway. Just before he reaches the front door, he spins around and does a sharp backwards loop.

"Yeah," Stanley says, "that wasn't bad."

David shoots off again. This time he zips outside and onto the street. He swerves and glides and springs up into his first leap. He lands awkwardly, almost cracking into a parked car, but he recovers and goes back to graceful looping curves. In two weeks he'll be hungry, bugging all the social workers, pleading and borrowing to scrounge up the money to get him through. But today he can fly, he can almost fly.

DISORGANIZED

Doc's carrying a Styrofoam cup with coffee sloshing over the rim. His shoelaces are gone, forcing him to shuffle rather than step, as though the force of gravity was just too much for him to handle. He's wearing his Boy Scout shirt, unevenly buttoned. His belt's flapping loose; a bobby pin holds his fly shut. He stops at a window sill and props himself against the ledge. He raises the cup to his mouth — but his hands shake, his wrist jerks in a sudden spasm, and the coffee spills all over his lap. Doc jumps up, slapping at his pants, inadvertently kicking off one shoe.

Youngblood looks on and shakes his head. "Doc ain't too organized."

WAGES OF SIN

Ralph's thick lenses create the illusion that his eyes have popped from his head and come to rest in the thick glass itself — like goldfish in a curved bowl. It gives him a peculiar intensity, as well as the sorry aspect of someone who's lost something very precious. "I get so angry," he says leaning forward on the edge of his bare mattress. "I see so many women that really need a man. I wanna give em sex, make em feel good, an they say they don't want it. They're crazy, those women. I'm tellin you the truth now — I got a pretty long rod; I been masturbatin so many years, it oughta be big. But I'm gettin worried. It's too long now an I don't want it to get no bigger. I'm afraid to do it anymore without a woman."

Ralph has so little to call his own that he doesn't bother locking his door. There's a dresser with two missing drawers and a small pile of dirty clothes stuffed in the open space. Four empty pint bottles of Abie's Irish Rose stand on top of the dresser, flanked by an empty gallon bottle of Coke and an empty jar of Tropicana Orange Juice. Off in a corner is a rickety table with a ragged overcoat on top. During my visit I try to keep myself balanced on a kitchen chair, but the seat keeps sliding off its frame. Beside me on a small table is a mound of wadded bags and wrappers from fast-food places on Broadway. Poking up amidst the bags is an empty pint of Hiram Walker anisette, dry as can be, but from time to time Ralph snatches it and takes an imagined slug.

"I'd be doin okay now if it wasn't for those crazy women," he says. "That and the voices. I have these days where I'll be sittin here hallucinatin with all these voices comin from the wall. I can't live like that. I know they're lookin for me for killin Frank Sinatra." He shakes his head and stares down at his feet, the perfect image of contrition. "That was a bad thing I done; I'm sorry for gettin so angry, but he woulda killed me if I didn't make my move. See, me and his daughter was havin sex. It was really somethin the way she took to me — dragged me down, and we're screwin all over the floor of their house. And Frank Sinatra comes home and breaks in the door — kicked it down and come at me — and I shot the hell outa him. It was pitiful, pitiful. You shoulda seen what he looked like. I know I shouldn'ta done it, but he said he was gonna kill me for fuckin his daughter. . . .

I hadda kill him again in Vietnam. I don't know how he found me, but I hadda kill him all over again. I know you won't believe me, but I don't even hate the man. I think he's the best singer there is. I saw him once on television — ole Blue Eyes is back — and I started to laugh. Well then he started to laugh back at me, right outa the television. That really broke me up. . . . But you shoulda seen the way he died, man. I didn't wanna do it, but he lives on hatred — that's his problem. An hatred'll kill you.

"Sometimes I wake up and feel angry. Red anger, Sunday afternoons — that's when this bishop named Ralphy comes after me on the radio. He's the older part of me — started broadcastin as I was gettin growed up — and my father gave him such a rough time, almost killed him. Well, Ralphy and this other dude, Bishop Wallace C. McCullough, come in and speak to me Sunday afternoons. Sometimes it gets scary — they can be a real pain in the neck. Mostly, I ignore them, but the Bishop is a hard guy to deal with. I saw him get angry once and kill this guy at a Sinclair station — fulla sin, like Frank Sinatra. I wish I could keep him away from me! I don't wanna hate nobody. That's all. If I could figure how not to hate nobody, I'd be a happy man. Like Daddy Grace — he was the only true healer — didn't hurt no one."

Under the jumble of discarded sandwich wrappers, I find an old book: *Rehearsal: The Principals and Practice of Acting for the Stage.* "I gotta read it," Ralph tells me. "I borrowed it from someone a year ago cause it looked good. Rehearsing. That's a good thing to do." He takes a deep swig from the empty anisette bottle. "That reminds me, you wouldn't believe what I did to Neil Sedaka. That was so pitiful I won't even talk about it!"

CLOSE SHAVE

Mr. Winslow ambles up and down the hall with seven slices of white bread pinched between his fingers. Smiling like the cat that swallowed the canary. "Goodness! You're looking well today, Mr. Winslow!" Muriel says.

"That's right!" He lumbers to within a few inches of her. "You see how I shaved?"

"Why yes!" You'd think she'd just caught a glimpse of the rarest marvel. "Right down to the last whisker!"

"You know, if you don't, if you don't keep your face clean, the d-d-d-director at M-m-m-men's Shelter puts poison in your food to stop you. He can send the FBI, the FBI to get you." The whites of his eyes are perfectly clear. It is almost impossible to turn away from him. "You see how I shaved my face? I didn't want any hair, no hair on my face. The d-d-d-director can poison your food if he sees one spot on your face. One spot. You see? You see? You see? I shaved three times today so he won't poison my food."

"I think a person should always keep up appearances."

"I don't want the FBI to take me, take me to R-r-r-rockford. I cut every hair, so they won't take me to R-r-r-rockford. There was some in my nose I couldn't get with my razor, but the d-d-d-director didn't, he didn't find them."

"It doesn't hurt to keep your nose clean," Muriel says with enormous pleasure.

"That's just what the d-d-d-director said, but he didn't, he didn't even look."

DAVID'S MOVIE

I was thinkin about the movie that I'm dying to make. Wow! This would make a perfect scene. . . . A guy goes to Central Park, rents a pair of roller skates — goes ridin outa the park, downtown. He puts on these headphones and this little radio, and he's playin the music loud. He doesn't care what is happenin — he just goes skatin down Sixth Avenue, and there's a whole traffic jam behind him. He's crossin through red lights, cars are going into store windows and flippin over; buses are hittin other cars — and he's causing this whole collision mess behind him. Doesn't even know it, because, see, he's in this whole spirit of his own — imagination and everything. He's just roller skatin downtown, doing all these moves all over the street. Then you got these police cars which are tryin to get to an emergency, and to keep from hittin him, they run into a doughnut shop and all these people get killed. And the only thing that makes the guy stop, actually stops him, is when he gets to Fourteenth Street he trips over . . . a cigarette butt. And all behind him you got the whole Sixth Avenue — store windows, people, the works — all smashed up. That's a hell of a movie if I could make it.

FRUSTRATED

"I lent this guy my blue suede shoes," Doc explains as he forages through the mound of clothes covering his floor. "An I was checking to see if he returned em. I found one here, but I don't know what I did with the other."

He sleeps without sheets on a mattress all grey and worn. Three hats hang over the back of the chair that serves as Doc's nightstand. A roll of blue toilet paper on the seat, along with a can of Campbell's Pork N'Beans and another of Hawaiian Fruit Punch. By the window is an old dresser crowded with books — *Godmen of India, The Perfect Crime for Two, Glass Inferno, Honor Thy Father, The Fourth Reich, French I,* and *The Story of Rome.* I ask Doc where he got these books, which ones he's read. Garbage cans, friends, hospital rooms — he can't remember. "This one is okay." He points to *Honor Thy Father.* "I was readin that last time in the hospital, but I can't remember a thing about it. Read maybe 100 pages, but my concentration don't hold too neat." He fumbles under his bed for a near-empty bottle of Red Devil Hot Sauce, pours a few drops on his hand, and licks them off. "That's my budget breakfast," he grins weakly. "Breakfast, lunch, an dinner till my next check comes."

Scratching, gnawing inside the wall. "He's already got a hole down around the pipes somewhere. Come up on the bed here an scare the hell outa me when I'm sleepin. Must be workin on a back door now." Doc pulls a large, rusted can from under his bed, wobbles to his feet, and pees. "Bathroom don't work too neat." He raises the flap of his Boy Scout shirt to keep it out of the can. A scabby pink rash stretches across his abdomen. He scratches it while he finishes peeing. "I gotta show this to the doctors. I put this rubber band around my wrist so I'll remember, an then I forget it's there." Weak smile again, as if he's musing on some poor friend who just can't seem to pull things together.

"One thing I know for sure is I'm gonna be drinkin. Stayin bombed out. That's all. That's what I do. I wonder, if I was to really try to get out of this thing and go back among people that are straight — I wonder how I would make out. That's one thing that's buggin me. But I come under the same wing as everyone else in this hotel, so there's no sense in my gonna say I'm different. It's very discouraging. I feel kinda split up — like in the mind. You're walkin around; you're doin one thing and you want to do another. And I'm wondering what kinda harm that eventually does to you. I mean, look at all this! A lost cause! What am I gonna do? The more I try to rumble outa this mess, the deeper I get into it.

"I been duckin loneliness for many a moon. What loneliness entails — you get hung up in your own sorrow and you get the droops. But it doesn't faze me. I can be happy-go-lucky wherever I am if I can have me somethin to drink. Like I remember when I was workin for Ward's Tip Top Bread in the Bronx. Each night we had to hose down the bakery room, squeegee all the water outa there. Now the only way to squeegee the water out was to push it down this drain, but the drain was up a hill. Imagine that! Pushin water up a hill, water runnin back downhill all the damn time. I used to ask myself, 'What kinda sense does this make? You've got to squeegee the joint every day, and every day you got to get frustrated.' And that's how I been feelin. Everything's buggin me. You have to forget a little, so that's when I start drinkin up. But it comes right back. It's like you're pushin water up a hill with a squeegee. The minute you let up, the water's gonna run right back down."

SIGN

```
LOOK
If You
Don't Live
Inside This
Unit
STAY OUT
by
Ralphy
```

NOVEMBER 4: BAD WEATHER

Muzak's rendition of "The Man I Love" pipes though McDonald's on Ninety-fifth and Broadway, two blocks from the neighborhood polling place. The Reagan volunteers are highly visible — a young man in a brown suit, a David Eisenhower look-alike in a Lacoste V-neck, and a young woman in plaid skirt and grey cable-knit cardigan. They fiddle with stacks of pamphlets and flyers set out on their mustard-yellow table. One of the tidy young men collects his coworkers' orders and heads over to the food counter. Mr. Winslow is already there, right under the Ronald's Party Room sign, lumbering back and forth as he counts his change. He looks particularly huge today — three bulky sweaters and a tiny blue baseball cap, which makes his heavy head look enormous. "TWO HAMBURGERS!" he bellows. "I want, I want two hamburgers and a Coca-Cola. And don't, and don't, I DON'T WANT ALL THAT ICE!" Ronald's Party Room listens in respectful silence. The Reagan worker surrenders his place and shifts to the far corner of the room. Mr. Winslow plunks his suitcase down on the serving counter and withdraws a couple of slices of white bread which he stuffs in his mouth all at once. "They said, they said you can't live on an empty stomach." He sounds like a grade-schooler reciting the Pledge of Alliegance. "If I eat I can be, I can be healthy. They didn't, on ward thirty-five, I say on WARD THIRTY-FIVE." His peculiar Jamaican-sounding accent gives the impression of some well-to-do gentleman lodged within his intimidating bulk. Heads turn, as if in search of this man, but there is only Mr. Winslow, cheeks swollen with bread. "On ward thirty-five they didn't feed me. And on seventeen and twenty-three. R-r-r-rockford doesn't, R-r-r-rockford kept me on that ward and didn't care if my stomach was empty. Twenty years, TWENTY YEARS — and they sent me back, sent me back another two years." People in line stare at the floor or turn with glazed attention to the pseudo-Wyeth and pseudo-Klimt that hang beside the counter. No one looks at Mr. Winslow.

The Reagan volunteer picks up his coffees and returns to join his coworkers. As they're prying open their plastic lids, David comes by and takes a sampling of the campaign literature. "Hey, look at this!" David says sliding into a seat across from me. "ONLY ONE MAN CAN PROVIDE REAL HOPE FOR HISPANIC PROGRESS IN AMERICA: The Committee to Support Reagan and Bush. . . . They gotta be kidding!" He turns to glower at the volunteers, but they already seem consumed with self-consciousness. "If Carter didn't need my vote," he says, "I'd vote Communist, but they said if it rains it's bad for Carter, and I ain't gonna let bad weather put Reagan in." It is David's first election — he registered at a desk out on Broadway — and to celebrate the occasion I'm buying him a McBreakfast-McMuffin and a miserable looking hash-brown potato patty that he seems to love. Carter will lose, I'm certain of it, but here in McDonald's the field belongs to David, loading up on junk food and expounding on socialist utopia while the Reagan volunteers sit uncomfortably with their stacks of promises.

"I'm Gonna Make You Love Me" jingle-jangles on the muzak

as Muriel enters in her Sunday best, cheeks oddly rouged in two russet blotches. The volunteers hand her a pamphlet as she passes their table. "Why, thank you!" she says with all the courtesy of someone who's never refused anything in her life. "I'm not voting," she tells me, "but they look like such nice young people!"

Across the room Mr. Winslow settles down to breakfast, biting alternately from each of his two hamburgers, supplementing them with a half-loaf of white bread he's unloaded from his suitcase. Like Mr. Winslow, most of the McDonald's regulars sit facing the large windows looking out on Broadway. But the Reagan people face opposite, against the mass of faces, and for this reason it seems Mr. Winslow is addressing them when he erupts into speech once again. "In R-r-r-rockford they put rubber in my mouth, and they gave me electric shock and I was just like, just like a dead person. I tried, I say I tried to put my foot RIGHT THROUGH THE WINDOW and get away! I didn't like nothin, NOTHIN they did to me! There was an Irishman with red hair, Big Tall Malloy with red hair, and he said, 'You better not tell any supervisor or no doctor you don't like it here or we're gonna, we're gonna tear your ass up!' They didn't feed me and they didn't let me go. I tried, I tried to put my foot through the window, but they kept me, they kept me. . . ."

While Mr. Winslow's talking, the manager approaches the Reagan volunteers and asks them to take their pamphlets outside. They seem relieved. Mr. Winslow is quiet now. He stuffs a few slices of bread in his mouth and mushes them contentedly while the Reagan people gather up their untouched materials. "It's still raining," David says as they depart. "This could be bad."

When David leaves McDonald's it's pouring. At the corner of Broadway and Ninety-sixth some Elizabeth Holtzman volunteers are handing out flyers, yellow ponchos flapping in the rain. "It's okay," David tells them. "I'm gonna vote for her." He rounds the corner into the gusting rain, then turns back to grab a handful of Holtzman literature. "She's the best for senator," he says. "She can do the most for the poor, an she can start helpin me right now." He creases the flyers and holds them over his head.

Down on West End Avenue, half a block from the polling place, a young woman stuffs a bit of Jesus-loves-you literature into David's hand:

DOES GOD
LOVE
NEW YORK?

If God really loves people, why does He allow all the suffering, crime, poverty, and sickness?

If you've ever asked yourself questions like this about God, you're not alone. Many of us often mistakenly blame the Lord for what happens in the affairs of men. We do this when we don't understand what the Bible says. It says that God isn't pleased with this world because the course it takes is contrary to the way He would have it. God created man with a free will, and it's man who has created our society for thousands of years, not God.

But God, who has seen our heartaches, failures, and struggle, sent Jesus Christ, His Son, to buy back this world and all its lost souls. He can save you and He can place His Holy Spirit inside of you.

Don't look at the circumstances of your life. Don't look at your job, your finances, and your romances, to discover the love of God. Good and bad things happen to us all. Look to Calvary where Jesus Christ shed His blood so you could spend forever in the kind of world He's prepared. God loves you more than you realize. Does God love New York? He loves everyone in New York. Ask Him into your life today and tell Him you want to experience that love.

He looks at the tiny piece of paper and shakes his head. "Shit! And she really thinks she's doin something!" It's still pouring and the Holtzman papers are not doing much good against the bursts of wind funneling up Ninety-sixth Street from the river. "I hope this rain don't hurt Carter too bad." He stuffs the soggy campaign flyers in a waste basket and rushes inside to vote.

THE MORNING AFTER

"Blew him away!" Ironsides says. "Beat him just like Holmes beat Ali. Carter got whupped so bad he come out lookin like an old man. You see him on TV? Gettin up an surrenderin before the votin's done? The man's been beat up — he been hit by a laan-slide!

"Now Reagan's gonna give the rich peoples a chance. Take care of some ecco-nom-ics. Carter, he said all the right shit — everything black peoples like to hear — but he left us hurtin. Reagan's gonna get his rich friends on the case. Gonna put money on the street."

YOUNGBLOOD'S POSTMORTEM

Carter didn't get the job done — that's why he lost. He wasn't tough enough. You gotta get down, low down with the nitty-gritty, to take care of business — an maybe he didn't know how; maybe he didn't have no stomach for it. But you ain't gonna get the job done unless you connivin with the folks that run the show. You got to have real cunning. Nice guys don't make good leaders. Reagan, now, he's slick. He's been out in California, and you know how slick they are in Hollywood. I ain't sayin he's not nice, but he knows how to hit low around your knees and ankles. You gotta have that in reserve if you gonna get the job done.

Look, who does Carter know? Who's anyone gonna know raisin peanuts an runnin Georgia down there in the South? He knows a few Georgia bankers who think they're somethin big and a few Navy men who mighta gone under the North Pole with him back in his submarine days. But he don't know the folks that count. He don't sneak over to your house and say, "Bam-bam-bam, this what we gonna do." He don't come by cause he don't know whose house he supposed to be visitin. Four years, an he's still a backwoods number. He ain't never learned who he should be raggin with. See, in California they know all about raggin. They got movie producers, an millionaires, an all these Arabs movin in now — everybody's wheelin and dealin in Hollywood, an that's where Reagan learned his stuff.

When you check, you see Reagan never went backwards in life. Take a good look at that cause it shows you somethin about the man. It takes a lotta scrutinizin, a lotta ambition, a lotta connections, an a lotta money. So he got it all together. An that's gonna help him along the way. I say he'll probably do all right with those foreign dudes. They don't know him, but they gotta respect him.

I go along with the Democratic ticket. They says they is for the poor — and that's the way it is — but I gotta say that the Republicans are the professionals. They got the business and management people an they gonna be the ones to make things move. Somebody's got to set the pace, organize the people, an show leadership, an that's the strength of the Republican party. Democrats say the Republicans are out for themselves, but the better the man do, the better you do. Take one of them Republican fat cats — say he plan to put up a nine-million-dollar house. Well, lookit all the jobs that means! That dude don't just hire Republicans — he hire anybody can get that job done. You get them Republican millionaires in a good mood — buyin and buildin and carryin on — an they gonna make it sweet for a lotta people. Reagan's gonna get them to put their money in circulation, an it's poor people it's gonna come circulatin through. Long as they don't put it all in the stock market, it's gonna bring work to somebody.

See, I voted for Carter. That's how my people vote, an I didn't wanna go against them. Carter was sayin how Reagan's a racist, but if he is, he handles it well. Poor people never gonna like the man. But if he get money circulatin, if he set the pace and get things organized, if he get the job done, you ain't gonna hear no complaints.

NEW REGIME

President-elect Reagan is beaming soundlessly through his first news conference. Bobby's way off to the side of his bed where he can barely see the screen. "H-e-e-ey!" he says. "I could hibernate the whole winter after the sandwich I just ate." Reagan is all smiles. Nice guy triumphant today, while Bush stands beside him, arms crossed with the rigid gracelessness of a bodyguard. "Big fuckin slices of baloney and good white bread. I put mayonnaise on one slice and Gulden's mustard on the other. Not that yellow French's shit — that's why people stopped going to Yankee Stadium. Lindsay and them put in all that money to fix the place up — they didn't know that no one could stand that yellow shit on their franks. H-e-e-ey, so listen — I got some tomato and lettuce and a few slices of pickle and stuck all of that on top. Greatest fuckin sandwich I ever ate! And mozzarella cheese. A couple of slices of that. H-e-e-ey, I'm talking about a sandwich!"

Somehow Bobby segues to a long rambling discussion of land-development deals in Florida. I keep sneaking peeks at our next president. Silence becomes him. "There was this dirt road out near Daddy's place," Bobby is saying, "all scrub and junked cars, swamps and mosquitos and shit. Even the blacks wouldn't live there, dig. So this Cuban dude — he's got a chain of laundromats and a coupla taco huts — he buys every inch he can get his hands on. And now they got suburbs. *Suburbs!* Fifteen thousand an acre and shit like that!"

Reagan's head moves with a slight Parkinsonian tremor. I can't keep my eyes off him. I'm astonished at how quickly he's been accepted, how easily his presence furnishes this room. The transition period is already over less than one full day after Carter's defeat. Easy as changing a TV station. "These people who bought motels in the fifties," Bobby rambles on, "they ran their Mom-and-Pop operation for twenty years, and now they're cashing in. Selling out to fucking shopping centers. Millions! Millions! Fuckin Florida's the Switzerland of the Caribbean!" As he says this, an Hispanic journalist is asking Reagan what appears to be a lengthy, rather obscure question. Little smirks break out on some of the reporters' faces.

"I wanted to tell you," I say. "I've been hearing a lot of talk about Hotel Walden being sold."

"We've been gettin rumors like that for five years."

"Well, it may be they've finally done it." I tell him what's been going on at the Glendale and remind him that this building has the same owners.

"I don't care about moving," he replies. "I wouldn't wanna go any further north than this — like Harlem and the Bronx — but I don't mind midtown, and I always liked the Village." You'd think he was a young professional speaking to a rental agent.

"You're not going to get a lot of choices if they have some thugs throw you out at 2 A.M." But nothing I say alarms him. His eyes drift to the president-elect.

"H-e-e-ey, you ever see this?" He waves a copy of *Jackie O.* "It's a piece of shit, but I read a chapter every month or so. Gossip and scandal — Lord Beaverbrain running off with Lady Pussy. Even if it's lies it's fun seeing the names of people you know. It's all fuckin lies anyway." He grimaces at the president-elect. "All the stuff they say in news is mostly bullshit. Doug and me been hearing shit about this building closing for five years and nothing's happened." He riffles *Jackie O*'s pages as though he's anxious to return to it. "Maybe something will happen, maybe someone wants to make this a condominium, but there's not a fuckin thing we can do about it!"

There's nothing else to talk about today. I leave him with his *Jackie O* beside the dim, reassuring flicker of his TV — our soundless new president.

A RARE JOKE

Frankie doesn't want to talk about it. "I work for them," he says, "and I don't want to lose my job. But it's started. They kicked two guys out last night, three the night before. They were no good — behind in their rent, drinking around the entrance and making noise. They're gonna get rid of a few more like them." A few people have drifted towards us; Frankie takes them in with a wary glance. "Hey, you know where I live?" He asks the question loud enough for everyone to hear.

"On the eleventh floor," I say.

"No, no honey!" He bumps against me flirtatiously. "Between Fruit Street and Gay! That's what I always say to people when they ask me where I'm from. Between Fruit Street and Gay! Fruit and Gay!" He skitters away — propelled by mirth, it seems. Nothing he's said can stand beside such a rare joke.

RETURN OF THE BISHOP

"This Sunday went kinda good," Ralph says. "But then these hallucinations caught up with me. The Bishop said I was ready, an he started laughin his head off at me. 'Ready for what?' I asked him. 'Ready for whatever I got to dish out!' he said. It got me angry. But shit — I can't even talk back cause he won't hear me anyway. He just likes to give pain. He's a rough guy. Rough. The others, they're ordinary people like you an me. People of his church —

Elder Crawford, Elder Bailey, and Elder Bolder. I ain't afraida them, but then on Sunday they look weird, real weird. They come an go, come an go. I can't stand to be sufferin all that time on Sunday. It's a waste. Don't have time for nothin but keepin an eye on them. I could be doin better things with my life — like buildin a bridge or somethin. . . .

"I'll tell yuh, I didn't have no trouble from the Bishop when I was in Westchester Hospital. The meals were better. The atmosphere was much better — like there was a mood over the place. I couldn't understand what it was, but it made me feel good. I woulda stayed there, but I made love to some female. They said she was innocent, but I don't know about this innocent business. She enticed me. She was the one that took the lead. I didn't know where she was leadin me. It was a case of stupidity on my part. She asked me up to her room an I went off with her. An when they kicked me out, they sent me here. An when I come up in this room, the Bishop was waitin to get me. . . ."

FRYING PAN

People are getting worried about Doc. They see he's losing control. Muriel drops by one day — she helps him wash his face; she combs his hair and persuades him to change into some fresh clothes from the outreach office. Doc sits there, dazed and patient. When she's done, Muriel asks him how he's feeling. Doc doesn't answer. "It's me, Doc. Muriel. Can't you speak to me?"

"I'll tell you," he mumbles. "I'll tell you." He gestures towards the heap of filthy clothes spread around him. "See that?" The handle of a cast-iron skillet pokes out of the mess. "You look familiar, but I don't know you. You might as well be that frying pan."

CAPTIVE TV

For a few months now, the social workers have been holding back
on the TV. They keep it locked in their office for most of the
morning; then they bring it into the lounge for a few hours in the
afternoon. They say it provokes way too much commotion — people squabbling over program selection, people talking when others
want to watch, people flocking in to stare at the tube and jamming
up the office area. Some tenants complain; but in truth, most people do not seem to miss it very much. They still file in and take
their seats. Some of them look off in the corner as if the TV was
right before their eyes. But now the TV is missing. The lounge is
oddly silent.

Enter Youngblood: plaid pants, blue turtleneck, and brown
jacket bunched up around his stooped shoulders. He places his
chair directly in front of the empty TV stand, crosses his legs, and
begins his rap. "Hey, any of you see this movie, *Angel City,* on TV?
There's been this atomic war, see, an all of California's pretty
damn fucked up." The room is filled with familiar faces. Ralph,
Fat Edna, Sugar Blue, Muriel, Mr. Winslow — all of them perk up
as Youngblood begins his story. "So the whole state is fucked up.
Hollywood and San Francisco and all the surfer beaches — blown
away." He laughs, then scrunches up with pleasure like a mantis
rubbing its mandibles over a lump of sugar. "Well, just about everyone's dead, you know. Either the bomb got em, or all that ra-
diation dust, see."

"That's right! That's right!"

"Shut up now, so I can tell yuh! Well, this black lady is travellin
around with this white guy an another black dude. An with everyone blown up or rotting along the highway, naturally she an this
black dude is makin love an shit every chance they got cause everyone that's still alive has got to save the human race, an besides
there ain't much else to do at night with no televisions an movie
shows an shit."

"Like here," someone adds. He looks eagerly to Youngblood for some response.

"Yeah, but in here it's a money thing. Shit, you got money in your pocket, there ain't nothin you can't do in this town. Now in this TV movie they ain't even usin money cause there ain't no banks, no payrolls, no SSI, nowhere to spend it if you had it, and nobody to take it from you. You hungry, you jus walk yourself in some supermarket an pick up a few cans of anything you want, or get yourself some steaks outa a deep freeze where it ain't contaminated. So anyways, these three peoples is drivin around California havin adventures, an the black dude an his lady is doin their thing together. You know, like right before the commercial come on they show him easin up to her an makin his move; and after the commercial, sure nuff, it's been nine months an she's havin a baby.

"They find this other woman to come in an deliver it, an the two men is sittin outside, sweatin and worryin — is it okay an all that kinda shit. So the baby gets born an these two dudes hear it screamin an complainin. This other woman come out wipin her hands on a towel. 'Is it okay? Is it okay?' these two dudes is sayin.

" 'Jus fine,' she says.

"The two of them's shakin hands an yellin an carryin on. 'An what is it?' this dude asks.

" 'A baby boy,' she says. This black dude's so happy he's cryin, an whitey's got his arm around his shoulder congratulatin him. 'Jus one thing . . .' the nurse says.

" 'How's my woman?' Black dude's all concerned, you know. 'Nothin's happened to her, has it?'

" 'Oh, she's fine. She come through all right,' the nurse says. 'But . . .' she don't look too happy about what she's gotta say — 'but the baby's *white*!' "

Youngblood's head tucks deep between his shoulders as he shakes with laughter. Around the room everyone joins him. At least, almost everyone. Mr. Winslow seems unable to laugh. The mood seizes him though, and he smiles his biggest, broadest smile.

All eyes are still on Youngblood. Squinched up and cackling, hands rolling over one another, he looks like a melodrama miser. But for these people in this room, Youngblood's story, this moment of shared laughter, is a rare and generous gift. And no one misses the captive TV.

UPTOWN

Bobby is stoned and drunk and sprawled out on his bed in raggedy underwear. Doug's frying some pork chops and taking solid slugs from a quart of Old English 800. "Big news," he grins. "Bobby went to work with me today."

"H-e-e-e-e-y, you gotta be a fuckin Hercules, motherfuckin Captain Marvel or somethin, carryin all that shit down all those steps."

"We did the Harlem projects today." Doug pokes the chops. "We figured Bobby'd behave himself surrounded by a million spades."

"H-e-e-e-e-y, man, they're lovely. Doug knows they're lovely." Bobby's jowls sag when he's drunk. He looks wasted, sophisticated, and heartbroken all at once. "These are our brothers and sisters, baby. Shit, me and Doug been livin like fuckin white niggers since we got here. But — hey, can I talk to you for a second? Can I say a few words? I'm thinkin about Uncle Sam and Mayor Koch and what's goin down uptown. I mean, we were *way* up there, man. UP-town, dig it — these projects stickin outa the world. Twenty stories high, some of em. Takin up several blocks. And we're distrib-utin door by door, motherfuckin floor by floor. Children cryin in-side all these little shitass rooms. . . . All these projects stickin outa the world and — "

"He's excited cause he put in a day's work, earned some beer money."

"No, no — come on, Dougie, I gotta finish. You know, man, you know what I'm sayin." He sits up on the edge of his bed and crosses his legs in a gesture of unexpected suavity. "Motherfuckin bar on every corner. Goddamn drug pusher every three feet. Do you know what I mean, baby? Booze and drugs — they're keepin em like children. Think about it. I mean, black people are sophisticated as hell, but they're bein kept from the mainstream of life. We're keepin them in these projects. Keepin em intoxicated. Lettin the dope scene run a little bit. Hey, you don't realize what it looks like up there!"

The frying pan is sputtering, but Doug is looking at Bobby, nodding in agreement. "Tell him Bobby — ten-year-old kids gettin a bottle of wine."

"Twelve-, thirteen-year-old girls walkin down the street puttin their bodies up for sale. Jesus H. Christ! Our black brothers and sisters! Fuckin Harlem! Fuckin Uncle Sam! I swear to God, man, it made me feel . . . I felt like cryin."

NOVEMBER 18:
GREENSBORO

"You hear about Greensboro? They let them fuckers go!"

"They're never gonna put none of them KKK boys away. They got a deal goin. They got government protection."

"But how they sayin they ain't done it when they got pictures an witnesses?"

"Don't have to say nothin. Their lawyer just give the sign to the jury — they go off, chew the fat awhile, come back an say 'Not guilty.' "

TOO VIOLENT

Stanley went out of control last night. He smashed his window, and when people looked out into the courtyard to see what was happening they saw Stanley struggling to shove his mattress through the jagged glass. They yelled for him to stop, but he seemed too absorbed in his task. He had not thought to strap on his artificial limbs, so he wobbled around on his stumps, cursing and pounding the cumbersome mattress which kept snagging on little bits of glass that poked from the window frame like teeth.

The mattress was gone, his bed frame half in, half out when they busted down his door. The first people to reach him tried to calm him and assure him that everything was all right. But Stanley didn't see it that way. Something terribly urgent was still unfinished. He returned to his task. When they tried to restrain him, he punched back. They offered him coffee; he threw it in their faces.

Frankie called an ambulance, and they hauled Stanley off to Roosevelt Emergency. He was so full of his fury that no one picked up much of what he said except for curse words and some stuff about Jews. But few people ever listened when he spoke calmly. Before, he was too crazy, too sad. Now he's too violent too.

DISCOURAGED

A stained grey tee-shirt is all Doc's wearing when he lets me in at noon. "I been up half the night," he says. "Don't exactly remember what I been doin out there, but I rolled over this mornin an I couldn't get up. The damndest things seems to be happen to me." Doc looks unmasked without his glasses, younger and more desperate. Every part of him seems hurting. The skin between his toes is split and white with fungus; his ankles are swollen; open scabs run up one leg; little ashy spots show on his arms and belly; and lice are driving him crazy. I offer to take him to the medical clinic, but he firmly refuses. "Last time I went there for somethin, they spilled the beans to the whole world. Had a big discussion with them about it — their lettin loose personal information. I put em in their place, let em know they was hangin way outa line." He rakes his nails over a sore on his calf. "Can't figure out why it's itchin so much. I oughta see the doctor. I can do it most anytime I want, but in the background I don't have faith in these people, bein that they blurted everything out that time before."

Empty cans of pork and beans, mustard greens, and turnip greens lay on his bed table. The turnip green tin he uses as his drinking cup. The other two cans still have bits of food caked inside; roaches scurry in and out like they owned the place. Doc's clothes are all over the floor, and near his feet I spot his Boy Scout shirt, soiled from tan to dirty brown, almost black in spots. He gazes down on it as he speaks. "I never been in a hotel where you catch bugs like this. I tell em at the desk but they don't seem to wanna listen." His curtains are stiff and filthy, as if they've always hung closed. "I want a whole lot, a whole lot," he says. His voice grows hoarse; his eyes never rise from the filthy shirt. "Every damn thing I try for, I don't get it. I get halfway done and say, 'Shit, I'll do the rest some other time.' The few things I did see through, they turned out beautiful. One time I decided to get me a little wardrobe — like three or four suits, two coats, a few pairs of shoes. I had to calm myself down, cool what I was doin, an hold onto my money. Finally, I did it. 'Damn!' I said, 'I got me a fine wardrobe! I'd wake up each mornin and do some *selectin* before I get my clothes on!

"But you know, you accumulate things here and soon somebody's comin by to relieve you of it. Somebody stole my radio last week. I was cookin in the kitchen down the hall an left my door cracked. I thought I saw this dude make a funny move near my room, but I didn't check it out. I finished my cookin, walked down to my room, an surer than hell — there was my radio missin! I'd shoot the dude if I see him again, but then it's me that loses." He shakes his head slowly. "It's crazy here — hard times lately. I catch a good spell when everybody's lendin me money, don't even have to ask — hell, they're practically givin it away. And then, like now, they all clamp up at the same time." He picks at a bright red sore high up on his thigh that shines with some kind of oozing fluid. "I tell yuh, I'm fallin apart in this room, an I'm jus lookin on. I get discouraged. I'm getting more discouraged every day. It's been a long time since I had respect for myself."

ROUGH BIRTHDAY

"It's gonna be a rough birthday," David says. It seems that a lady upstairs passed her daughter, newly arrived from the South, off on David. Sherry invited David to her room a few times to watch TV. David hung around and sort of got to know her daughter, Magnolia. She was two years older than him and probably outweighed him by thirty pounds. Somewhere back in North Carolina someone was taking care of her five children. After a few days of watching TV together, Magnolia offered to pay half of David's rent if she could share his room at night. They were not lovers; they were not even friends really, but David let her move in.

"Why do you ask me about it?" David says. There must have been hopes, new possibilities opening in his mind. If not love, then sex. If not sex, then new prestige around the hotel for having a woman living with him. If not prestige, then the ninety dollars he would save each month by having her share of the rent. "It wasn't nothin, I told yuh. She had a very nasty attitude like that. Like she used to bump me off onto the floor when we were sleepin. I couldn't take it. I just gave her the bed. I been sleepin on the floor for the last week.

"I tried to get along and make her comfortable, but there was too much verbal abuse. She didn't like nothin I did. . . . 'Turn that music down! . . . Don't open that window! . . . Stop playin with your roller skates! . . . Stop rollin on the bed! . . . Oh yeah, 'Take off my boots!' . . . That was the best one. She had these kinda fat legs, and her feet would swell up so she couldn't get her boots off. So I was doin that. I was doin everything, and she still kept abusin me. I don't even want her to pay. I just want her out."

He opens the top drawer of his tiny desk and takes out a manila folder with MAGNOLIA pencilled across it. "I got a file on her," he says. "I'm gonna keep a record on all my girlfriends from now on. Maybe someday I'll get one of them home computers so it will all be at my fingertips." He laughs at his own fantasy and hands me a Human Resources Administration personal history report sheet — copped, no doubt, from the outreach office downstairs:

> NAME: Magnolia Johnson
> CATALOGUE NUMBER: 48763492
> CASE NUMBER: 34175473

"That's how they do it," he says, "with all these numbers. I haven't begun to write down her case history, but now I got her on file. Soon as I get her outa here, I can write my report.

"By the way, if you wanna get me somethin I really want for my birthday, let me show you this." From his desk he pulls out a Radio Shack Sixtieth Anniversary Catalogue, riffling through the glossy pages till he comes to his dream machine. "Here's what I want — a VHF-UHF Police Scanner, high-low frequency with fire department frequency extra. Snaps! Tune in to everything. It'd be the best birthday I ever had!"

SLOW

Ralph's ground to a halt today. Overmedicated, depressed, some vexing thought — there's no way of knowing. And Ralph won't tell. He's turned off, tuned out, closed down. He stands in the hallway, directly facing the elevator, eyes fixed on the call button. A red arrow blinks when the elevator's rising; a green arrow blinks when the elevator's going down. When the elevator's stationary there are no blinking arrows to stare at, only the button itself. Once or twice, the elevator door opens. People step out, greet Ralph, and walk right past him. He doesn't bat an eye.

Sometimes he sticks a finger up his nose, digging eagerly. For a moment he'll abandon his vigil to inspect the results of his probe. I stand with him for a half hour, till staring becomes a kind of numbing meditation. Only once does he speak. "They fought too much," he says. And that's that.

BAD ELEMENTS

Frankie's been away from the front desk for a few days. "Jury duty," Doug's been telling me. Now there's a new guy to take his place, and a few more hotel residents have been booted out. "Bad elements," Doug says. "They were behind in their rent and some of em were drinkin in front of the building." I remind him that he and Bobby have sometimes fallen behind in their rent payments and that just about everyone has slugged down a beer or shared wine and liquor in front of the building. "We're not like them," Doug insists. "It was good to get ridda them. . . ."

A few days later, new hand-lettered signs go up in the entrance-way:

NO VISITOR
AFTER
10

PLEASE NO
HANG OUT
IN LOBBY

"Frankie's out," Doug informs me. "He was overchargin customers, siphoning off money. An they say he was lendin money when people run out and takin interest outa their SSI." I ask him how he feels about it. "Last night, Cappy started up on the fifteenth floor and come down from room to room tellin everyone it would be okay." I remind him that Frankie was his friend, that he loaned him and Bobby money when they were broke, that Doug was crying when he said goodbye to him this past summer.

"All I know is they caught him," Doug says.

"Did you know he was doing the things they accused him of?"

"No, but they caught him doin it. Cappy says they'll be fixin up the hotel now. He says maybe they'll raise the rent ten percent or somethin, but we can all stay."

"That means if you're paying $180, it'll go up to $200. If someone's getting $300 from SSI, that doesn't leave much to live on. They'll have half of you out of here in six months."

"I got my job. Bobby an I can make it."

"What about everyone else?"

"They're gonna upgrade the hotel, get ridda bad elements. Look, if they fix our place up, it's worth it."

THANKSGIVING

[Thanksgiving card on Doug's and Bobby's dresser]

> Ahhhhhhh
> Those Great
> Thanksgiving
> Dinners
> Of Yesteryear
> Where
> Have They
> Gone?

[Inside: the punchline]

> some to the hips
> some to the waist
> some to the chin
> Oh well,
> Happy Thanksgiving
> Love
> Mom and Dad

"H-e-e-e-y, I just cleaned the floor an did the laundry," Bobby says. "You caught me on a good day." He picks up a belt I gave him some months ago and stretches it across his knees. "I was checking this out, man, seeing how it was put together and all that shit. I always wear it when I put on my red shirt."

Bobby's always there, sitting quietly on his bed, TV purring. "I've been getting flashbacks today." He sounds cowed, an edge of speedy tension. "Like mescaline or a fuckin LSD trip. Man, walkin across this room is a goddamn experience, like black magic or somethin. Christ, I got so much buzzing through my mind — every fuckin circuit, like a fuckin long distance switchboard on Christmas morning. But — hey, they probably send all that shit by satellite now. Happy Thanksgiving! Merry Christmas! Yeah, like a fuckin billiard game — pop it into the ozone, bank it off the satellite and back into your living room.

"You know — h-e-e-e-y, I know you know — the human mind has more circuits than any fuckin computer. And listen, this is what I'm sayin — I had five fuckin seizures Thanksgiving. One after the other, Doug said. Sure as shit, I wasn't counting. I was in a fuckin trance. Like some medicine man, yeah. When I came to, my fuckin jaw ached from grinding my teeth. My tongue is still kinda bit up around the edges. And hey — my fingertips, my legs, eyes, every cell in my fuckin body's been on a fuckin trip. A trip, baby, like Marco Polo or fuckin Buck Rogers.

"And I wanna tell stories, like them Indian witch doctors that go off in the wilderness to dig on the Great Spirit an shit. I wanna tell stories, and then I'll get halfway through, an there's too fuckin much to say all at once, an I lose my main point.... Fuck it man — that's the problem in America — 'What's your point? Get to the main point!' You know what I'm sayin? It's the fuckin American way. You gotta have a main point. Put some dude on television runnin for president — he's got two minutes to get to the point on the economy, ten seconds for the main point on nuclear arms. We're programmed, man. I'm serious. They want a main point every minute — fuck em, they oughta let McDonald's run the country."

"I Love Lucy" ends, followed by a succession of noisy commercials. "We don't need this shit!" Bobby says as he flicks off the sound. "Commercials are like fractured glass, man. These seizures, you get where you can see how many pieces these images are made of — like acid, when you start seeing every cell, every motherfuckin molecule. I mean, the human mind is a *receiver*, a receiver, dig? You can tune in to everything, *everything* man, if your mind is open. And this TV is nothing next to it. Like you're seein this in black and white, right? Well, hey — I'm catchin it in color. Not complete, not all the time — but it comes through after my seizures.

"And hey, they lay shit on us with every image. I see things on TV and I feel I gotta have it. I *gotta*!" He stands up, jams his hands in his pockets, and pulls out the empty linings. "I know what they're doing. I see it, man, and it still makes me feel like shit. I'll tell you how the programmin works — just the act of buying gives you a kind of status. Nobody needs all that shit. You can leave it in the store, for chrissake, just as long as you *buy* it, as long as you're *seen* buying it, so you can *feel* that high, get that rush.

"There's emotion, emotion everywhere — that's my point, maybe — but you gotta open your mind to see it. I watch TV for emotions. Anna Magnani — she can screw you up till your spine's about to snap. Black magic. *Wild Is the Wind*, when she was beating on this guy and yelling — some of the faces that came through, I'd never seen that except when I was high on drugs. But like that's real emotion. Now they're tryin to put over a new era of wholesomeness — game playing, tinsel froth, cotton candy and shit from Hollywood. And Reagan — what the fuck is he all about? They're doin it, sending out this new emotion and programming us to buy it, to need it in order to feel good. But there's no real emotion in it. It's yellow. Fuckin weird. I mean, I almost couldn't look at Anna Magnani some of the time. The intensity! All those changing faces — like looking at fuckin Vishnu, man. And like my main interest — I know I like to drink and party an shit — but my main thing is trying to expand my fuckin consciousness. People who haven't taken mescaline and acid don't know, but after one of them jerking seizures, every muscle, every cell in your body is tingling. It opens you to things you wouldn't have imagined. And see, what I'm saying, with this new programmed cotton-candy shit, like with Reagan — I look and look at the man, and all I see is my TV screen."

LOST

"You hear?" Ironsides says. "Doc got lost." He and a few other men are sitting around the sixth floor stairwell, passing a bottle of

Irish Rose, bullshitting their way through another Sunday afternoon.

"How's he gonna get lost when he can't get outa his bed? He probably slipped inside that pile of clothes he got heaped up on his floor an nobody's got the stomach to go in there after him."

"No man, he's *lost*. And he's not just lost from here. They lost him downtown at the hospital."

"I saw him yesterday."

"Sure you did. I'm not sayin you didn't. But last night they took him down to the hospital. He hadda go — sittin out on the stairs all hours, drunk as hell, hallucinatin an mumblin. Didn't sound like him. Wasn't takin care of himself. Ambulance came an took him off."

"So he ain't lost." Ironsides's friend has a hard knobby face, but now his features smooth out in an expression of real concern.

Sprawled on the floor, Buffalo reaches up to grab his turn on the bottle. Years ago, Buffalo was a middleweight boxer; today he's too drunk to stand. "He was a man," Buffalo says. "A hell of a man!"

"So he ain't lost," Ironsides's friend persists.

"He sure as hell is! What I heard from the social worker is that the folks at the hospital started complainin when they saw Doc with all his lice and raggedy clothes an shit. So while they're standin around arguin what to do with him, Doc picked hisself up an walked out."

"He was a helluva man," Buffalo says. "I was a helluva man too. I had lice an mites too — in the war. Japs had us pinned to the beach an we was gettin low on rations. Sergeant says to us — big motherfucker from Decatur, Georgia — he says, you boys is part — "

"The war don't count, Buffalo. Everybody had lice in the war."

"What do you mean the war don't count! They sent me halfway round the fuckin world!"

"I mean it don't count *now*. You got all them lice off you, didn't you? They all dead and gone."

"The war counts. It bein over don't mean it don't count."

"Doc's lost! That's what we was talkin about," Ironsides reminds them. "He spent last night out in the streets. He mighta slept under some bush in the park or down in some cellar freezin an catchin pneumonia." Even before Ironsides is done speaking, his companions nod and mumble acceptance of the familiar vision.

"He been in bad jams before," Buffalo says. "Doc's gonna come outa this."

"He shouldn't let himself fall down like that."

"Man had too much time. How you live depends on how much time you got an what you gonna do with it."

A lively black mutt comes bounding up the stairs followed by its owner, a gaunt black man with the craggy features and pointed beard of Uncle Sam. "Down! Stay down!" he orders.

"She's all right," Buffalo says.

"Down you black bitch!" Uncle Sam stomps menacingly. His dog shrinks down on her haunches.

"Why you use that kinda language?" Buffalo asks.

"What kinda language you mean?"

"Yellin 'black bitch' at some little animal. That ain't no kinda Sunday talk."

"That's what a black bitch *is,* brother. Unless you'd rather hear me say how you been goin about with that white bitch."

Buffalo shows no sign of anger. "Why can't you just say *woman?*" Ironsides says. "Color don't matter."

Uncle Sam pats the wide window ledge and stares at the other defiantly. "Get up you bitch! Up! Up! Come on you black bitch, or your tail is mine!"

"Doc was always afraid of dogs," Ironsides's friend says.

"He was a man," Buffalo adds. "He was a man just the same."

HOLIDAY

SEASON

FUN AND GAMES

[From the *New York Times*, Sunday, November 30, 1980]

Game Satirizing Life on Welfare
Draws Criticism, but Sells Well

ARNOLD, Md., Nov. 21 — "This is going to be a fun Christmas for the Republicans," chortled Ronald W. Pramschufer. "Republicans love this game."

He was moving a plastic piece across the game board that he invented with a neighbor here and acquiring his fifth "illegitimate child," which, according to the rules, was worth $100 a month in play-money "welfare payments" plus a $50 donation for "obstetrical costs" from each player unlucky enough to have "a job."

Illegitimate birth is the most likely way to win in playing "Public Assistance," the bitterly satirical board game conceived by Mr. Pramschufer, a 29-year-old printing salesman, and Robert B. Johnson, 37, a West Pointer and retired Army captain who became a critic of American "war crimes" after serving in Vietnam.

The 'Working Person's Burden'

A player of this game, which has been denounced as racist and callous, is also likely to draw a "working person's burden" card that says, "Your son is beat up by ethnic gang while being bused across town to school. Pay hospital bill, $200."

Controversy over the barely concealed "black welfare" image of most of the game's chance situations — "pitch pennies all day," "Lincoln needs a new paint job" — has brought high-powered notoriety to it. The first order of 10,000 games is gone, at $15.95 a copy, and a reprint will include 50,000. There is an order of 5,000 just from a California distributor. Games industry analysts say the figures represent good but not great sales.

Denunciations of the game reached national proportions last month when Patricia Roberts Harris, the Secretary of Health and Human Services, criticized the game in a speech as "a vicious brand of stereotyping," "callous," "racist" and "sexist."

Mr. Pramschufer and Mr. Johnson, political and social iconoclasts of the Archie Bunker persuasion who say they voted this year for Ed Clark, the Libertarian candidate for President, deny emphatically that their game is racist.

"We're all from somewhere, we're all ethnic," Mr. Pramschufer said.

"We didn't invent this game," Mr. Johnson said. "Government liberals did. We just put it in a box."

R. E. A. C. T.

"PA COPS KILL MAN IN BUS TERMINAL," the *Daily News* headline reads. "I picked that up when it happened," David says as he slips the clipping back into a fresh manila folder. "I get things over the police channel they won't even let em print in the news. Here's another — two-alarm fire I picked up in New Jersey. "17 HURT IN BLAZE," the second headline reads.

I ask him why he spends half his waking day listening in to CB calls. He give me an incredulous stare and opens his desk drawer. "Here's my new file." He tosses the folder in my lap like Kojak among his flunkies. "RIVERSIDE R.E.A.C.T.," it says on the cover. "That stands for Radio Emergency Associated Community Team. I made it up myself."

"Was that *community* or *communications*?" I ask.

"Communications, yeah. I like that better."

Taped to the left side of the folder are six police sketches of wanted men. On the right side are three complaint forms from the Twentieth Precinct, each one filled out in David's hand:

> COMPLAINANT'S NAME: David Torres
> COMPLAINT: Assault
> DATE: 7/9/79

"That was when the guy next door came in and broke my stereo."

> COMPLAINANT'S NAME: David Torres
> COMPLAINT: Petty Larceny
> DATE: 7/10/79

[Across the sheet *WANTED* is written in quavery block letters.] "Things were gettin bad then. This is when some dude took my bicycle."

> COMPLAINANT'S NAME: David Torres
> COMPLAINT: Assault
> DATE: 8/26/80

[*CLOSED* written across the page.] "This one worked out good. I showed em what'll happen if they push me around."

David closes the folder and puts it back in his desk. "I did my R.E.A.C.T. file on Thanksgiving. I've been saving this stuff for awhile an this seemed like a good time to do it. When you're poor there's nothin special about Thanksgiving. The one that hurts is Christmas. It hurt last year and it's gonna hurt again."

THE SUNDAY PROGRAM

Sunday again. The weekly broadcast, and Ralph is powerless to tune it out or turn it off. "Trippin my ass off," he says. "I could be buggin out, but I'm not. I fight it — just lay here till it subsides. That Bishop's a nut, a real horror. Likes to see people sufferin. Always knows where to find me." Ralph shakes his head like a concerned citizen deploring rising crime. "The Bishop knows his way around. He's a sly one — worked his way up through the ranks. I can't beat him alone. You can't fight the power unless you tell somebody, but you start tellin folks about the Bishop, they throw your black ass in jail."

ON DOC'S CASE

Doc may not have been as lost as people thought he was. On Monday afternoon, a day and a half after Doc's disappearance, I run into the social worker who's been on Doc's case. "They've got him," he tells me. "I just spoke with the hospital. He's resting and seems to be under control. But can you believe this — they say he was never missing!"

Mr. Bollatine has not had time to straighten out the confusing story, but this is what appears to have happened. "I was here late the night Doc went to the hospital," he begins. "People came to my office and said he was sitting out on the sixth-floor landing, muttering incomprehensibly and looking strange. I didn't know whether he was having a seizure or heart attack or what, so I called an ambulance for Roosevelt Hospital. He was so louse-ridden I'm surprised they took him. Usually they don't with alcoholics, but they must've realized he needed help immediately. See, it puts the ambulance out for the rest of the night. They've got to fumigate it, clean the whole thing out, before they can make another pickup. Well, the ambulance ran him down to Emergency, and they refused to admit him. They're very tough on alcoholics. If he's not hallucinating on the spot, he's not a medical emergency — that's their rule of thumb. They'll send him home and tell him to seek admission to an alcohol treatment program. And then they say Doc has no medical insurance. Well, he has Medicaid, but he's sitting there unable to speak, and they're preparing to discharge him. I was on the phone with them, but I try not to argue; if we fight, it's our clients who lose. I asked them to send him back here by ambulance, and they refused. I asked them to call the police. They said he must go home on his own. Finally I told them I'd pay for a cab myself — and here's where it gets muddled. We thought Doc either walked out on his own, or someone booted him out. But now it seems a new shift came on duty in Emergency, and they saw that he was hallucinating. So apparently what happened — I'm still not sure, because they only just called me — but what could've happened is that they reevaluated his condition and took him into Emergency without letting us know. A day and a half we've been worrying about him and had police out looking for him, and no one in the hospital bothered to let us know. It's so crazy. I still don't know if he was ever lost. Well, he's resting and doing better, they say. That's the important thing."

Hospital Report

"Harris Young was brought to us at 11:40 on November 25. He appeared to be extremely intoxicated. He was very sick. Terribly out of it. We would like to take in all these street persons — the hospital would like to — but we just can't. We don't have the facilities or the financial resources. We'd be overwhelmed. Our procedure in cases such as Mr. Young's is to do what we can without admitting him. Mr. Young was deloused; we gave him nourishment and clean clothes. Our usual procedure is to let these people rest for a few hours, then give them a subway token and send them home. In Mr. Young's case the social worker at the hotel requested that we return him by ambulance. I can understand how he feels — it seems heartless to send a feeble alcoholic home by subway — but again, it's a question of limited resources.

"Well, Mr. Young was simply too weak for us to send him home. He had acute dehydration, which is common among serious alcoholics — he couldn't rise from his chair — so we kept him at the hospital overnight. On the morning of November 26, as arrangements were being made to release him, Mr. Young seated himself on the floor of the Emergency Room and began eating imaginary things and conversing with nonexistent people. DT's, you'd call it. With the onset of hallucinations we reregistered him at 10:47 A.M. and admitted him for treatment.

"Per nurse's request he was taken to the medical ward and given a series of diagnostic tests. Blood tests were not possible the night before due to the high alcohol level in his system. The tests indicated partial kidney failure, pneumonia, and severe anemia. There was no question of sending him out on the street in this condition. I can't explain why the social worker and the police couldn't find him for two days. He was right here. It's in our books. But these things happen. It's unfortunate. It's just a wonder things work as well as they do."

RUN DOWN

"For a while I didn't know how it would end up." Doc sounds like a spectator when he talks about himself. He's weak and pretty dazed, but it's a great relief to see him shaved, deloused, resting safely in a clean hospital bed. He does not look quite himself without his threadbare Boy Scout shirt and crazy hats. SRO life had formed a crust around him, and like Doc himself, I'd come to despair of ever seeing it peeled away. "I'll tell you," he says, "I'd never have brought myself here. I get that bug sometimes, and I wouldn't budge for I don't know what. I don't really know how I got here. Everything's so fogged up — I don't know what happened.

"I got jammed up. In the back of my mind it worried me, cause every move I made was a step down. Now I'm tryin to nurture myself to health. Feel much better already, now that I'm not gettin to the juice. I mean, this is what I really wanted — to get a rest — but I fight against it till it happens. It's just the way I am. Gotta run me down with a jackrabbit to catch me. Thing is, once I pull in here I'm gonna stay. Ain't gonna do me no good bein back there passin Night Train around with the boys. They're headin in the same direction, fast and furious, like a car goin to a wreck — rushin to get there, speedin down the highway; and fast as they're goin, this wreck is rushin to meet em head on."

Doc's doctor tells me that along with his dangerous alcohol addiction Doc is seriously anemic, that he has pneumonia and "horrible skin." "I like him," the doctor says. "And I'll tell you, he was burning himself out fast." I ask what a phrase like that means to a doctor. "I mean it literally and figuratively," he says. "You drink like he does and you destroy a lot of brain cells. And when they're gone, they don't come back."

YOUNGBLOOD'S ANALYSIS

I know what Doc's been through. You get to a point where you know you gotta pull yourself together, but once you feel yourself in trouble, recuperation is a lulu. It's your own conduct — ain't got nothin else to blame it on. You gotta keep your head above the water an make sure you don't fall down on some of the don't's you gotta deal with. One false move an you're defeatin your own purpose.

It's a helluva hole to crawl out of. An there's this whole hotel here pullin you back down. It's a dangerous situation for me if I don't handle myself right. See, I don't have no drinkin problem like Doc, but we all gotta keep control of our conduct, hold it together or pay the price. The main thing about makin a comeback is executin mental strength. You handle that, you got a chance of recuperatin. You fall outa that, you in outer space and driftin.

And you can't let sex mess with you. You gotta have the mental strength to leave it alone. You fall into some sex thing that's gonna make demands on your nature an you get to the point where that's all you think about. Then some situation comes along: everything you been workin on is down the drain cause you lost your mental concentration.

But the main thing is not to go backwards. If somethin come up and you don't advance — *stand still!* Hold on to what you got. Pick yourself up an get yourself ready to make your next move. *Stand still!* You ain't losin nothin if you're standin still — but don't go backwards!

DURAN POSTMORTEM

"He hadda shit, man! That's what it all comes down to."

"Weren't nothin wrong with him cept that Sugar Ray had him beat. Leonard was teachin the man a lesson, sayin, '*Hit me! Hit me!*' Duran couldn't touch him, so he picked up his money an went home."

"Duran wouldn't walk away from no fight. He's a dirty street fighter, an boys on the street got heart. Duran come up hungry in the street, an that's what beat him. Grow up hungry an you *always* hungry — that's a fact. Two steaks for breakfast an another little one before the fight — fillin up his stomach like he didn't have no ten million dollars to spend when he's done with Sugar Ray — got in there to fight the man, an sure nuff, he hadda shit. That's what beat him, what it all comes down to."

A SUITOR,
A BLACK MOMENT,
AND THE ENERGY CRISIS

"Things didn't work with me and Anthony," Muriel explains. "He seems inclined to take me off the deep end. 'Let's get a jug of wine and talk it over,' he says. That's his solution for everything. I tried his way. We drank our jug and we weren't getting anywhere. So he said, 'Let's get another!' From one jug to another — jug, jug, jug! If they had a marathon for juggers, he'd be champion. I said, 'I'm tired. We're not getting anywhere.' And he kept telling me he was making such an effort to change. I said, 'You know, you're not helping matters when you say have another jug. All it leads to is another jug.'

"He's awfully nice. Always a gentleman. I feel sorry for him.

He's trying, but he's going about it in a haphazard manner — leading me into disarray. I still like him, but heaven sakes, he doesn't seem to be trying to help himself. He knows my weaknesses — smoking, drinking, and always having to apologize for myself — and how to play into them. I don't need any encouragement in that direction.

"By the way, don't think I got this black eye from him. Anthony would never do that. There was an argument in the lounge between Edna and some other lady. I was sitting there and one of them rushed over and grabbed my cane. I was holding on so tight she pulled me right out of my chair and I went headfirst on the floor. I came to with a black eye, the cane still in my hands.

"That was a black moment, I can tell you. But things have been going so nicely in the SPOP program. They gave us such a nice Thanksgiving! I can't seem to recall just what they did, but we seem to have gone somewhere in a van." She wrinkles her brow in a pose of intense ratiocination. "A van.... Yes, a van for sure. And ... well, it was a nice Thanksgiving.

"Another day we went to the Metropolitan Museum of Art. We saw that enormous Christmas tree they have." She hands me a fund-raising pamphlet from the museum. "This rather amused me," she says. "Become a Patron for $2,500! I don't have twenty-five cents to my name, let alone $2,500."

She hands me a second pamphlet, this one from the Con Edison Energy Conservation Exhibit Center: *Solar Energy for Today and Tomorrow.* "Now where did this come from?" she muses. "I guess someone picked me up to go there. In a van! Of course! Oh yes — and I got a little nasty at this one." She sounds enormously pleased with herself. "They had this kind of fun house with little models of factories and houses and things, and how we could all help America if we cut back on energy. I told them I don't pay any Con Edison bills. I have one light bulb in my room and I use it as much as I need to. I might wake up in the dark and not know where I am, so I often sleep with my light on. I told them this, and I said I didn't see where solar collectors would change my energy future. 'I live in this one little furnished room,' I told them. 'I don't have a fridge or television or electric range. Just one little light to burn. I don't see where I'm wasting all that much energy.' They got quite upset with me. They all seemed to be insisting I participate, but I didn't know where I fit in. It just didn't apply to me. Living in this little room you're not using much of anything."

TOO WARM

Youngblood's head is tucked deeper in his shoulders than usual. "I lost in cards," he says. "Wasn't much money, but this dude took me fair and square. I'm not sayin he was better than me, because he ain't — but I was off my game, wasn't concentratin, an he beat me. I had on too much clothes. Too warm, I think that mighta been it. I had on my heavy jacket, a sweater over my shirt, an in this little basement room uptown everybody was smokin; the air felt close and there wasn't any windows."

While he's explaining all this, Elaine slips up behind him and hooks her arm in his. He gives her a brief sidelong glance, tough-guy reticence — hardboiled as the Heartless Lion. "Daddy! Daddy!" she says. "I been looking for you." This is the first time I've laid eyes on her. Often I've knocked on their door and spoken to her quavering voice inside. She always seemed to be in bed. Faint light and musty smell; I'd begun to imagine the worst — some gothic, "A Rose for Emily" revelation. But here she is — a nice Jewish girl. Forty years old, maybe. Sweet round face and curly hair. She looks weak but well. Her dark room seems to have given her skin a funereal pallor. But what strikes me is the warmth of her greeting to Youngblood. "Daddy! You gonna fix me some lunch?" She rises on her toes to kiss his cheek. A nice Jewish girl.

Youngblood recoils slightly, but he loves it, or at least he needs it. "Sure. Just gimme a few minutes."

A few people in the hallway look on with amusement but no surprise. "My Daddy takes care of me," Elaine says for our benefit. "I don't know what I'd do without my Daddy."

"I'll fix you some eggs in a few minutes." Youngblood shakes his arm free and steps away. "Maybe I'm gettin a fever or somethin. I don't know — I'm feelin warm."

CHRISTMAS IS COMING

It happens every year, Buffalo tells me. Sometime between Thanksgiving and Christmas, Sugar Blue loses control. He drinks, takes drugs, gets in fights — whatever's coming down, Sugar Blue catches a piece of it. This time it started with Mookie. She's been living with Sugar Blue, and he began suspecting that she was slipping off with another man. That put him on edge. Then on Saturday night this white lady came screaming down the hallway on the eighth floor, naked and freaking and a little drunk, crying that Sugar Blue raped her. Someone found a sweater and draped it over her shoulders, but she was shaking and gesticulating so, that it kept falling off.

When a woman with liquor on her breath cries rape in Hotel Walden, people usually assume she had it coming to her. But Sugar Blue's Christmas rages are well known; everyone agrees he probably did exactly what he's accused of doing. Nevertheless, no one, including the social workers, wants to know too much about what happened. They're afraid the facts of this case would go against Sugar Blue. He's just too vulnerable to go to prison. And he's okay, he really doesn't act up; he's harmless and kind of amusing all year — except when Christmas is coming.

A few days later Sugar Blue comes parading down the hallway, resplendent in a red plaid suit, rainbow shirt, and brown polka-dot tie. His hair is wildly frizzy, what a cartoon cat might look like after poking his paw in an electric socket. He looks handsome and

sad, infinitely gentle. And crazy—you can see it. A kind of
nimbus. "They got me in court," he says like a child scolded
unjustly, "but I didn't do nothin, so there's nothin they can do to
me. Ain't that right?"

"That white lady says you raped her," Buffalo replies.

"That wasn't nothin. She asked me to her room. No, this court
thing was Mookie's mother. She says I come back an beat up
Mookie. She's suin me for assault an battering."

"So you're sayin you didn't do nothing to her?"

Sugar Blue smiles his sweetest smile. "I didn't do nothin I wasn't
supposed to."

A LOTTA HATE

A little dead mouse is lying in a puddle of sticky liquid just outside
Ralph's door. Inside, Ralph sits on the edge of his bed, talking
down at his cupped hands as if he expected them to catch his
mumbled words. "Anytime you see red so much," he says, "there's
gotta be a lotta hate."

ANOTHER DEATH

"Remember Magnolia?" David asks. That girl I kicked out a coupla weeks ago? Well, her mother died. Last Thursday. Thanksgiving, I guess. She fell and collapsed. Somebody was with her when it
happened, but she died right off. They called it a heart attack or
somethin like that, but it was drugs that did it. Cocaine. Got her
through her illness a while ago, an she's been doin it pretty heavy
since.

"It didn't break Magnolia up much. The old lady was a pretty
nice woman, but Magnolia never got along with her. She didn't
shed no tears. All she wanted was the valuables."

HAIRCUT

Gamine haircut exposing Muriel's thin white neck — her head small and round and vulnerable. It has the startling effect of making her look like an adolescent suddenly turned fifty. "Oh, what a day!" Muriel says. "SPOP took us all to Wilfred Academy Beauty School and I had my hair shampooed, cut, and blow dried. They really do a job on you. It cost a couple of dollars, but it would've been worth it even if they didn't do a thing. A whole day away from here! The lady who cut my hair kept asking me questions, and I just said, 'Do whatever inspires you. I'm going to sit back and enjoy myself.'

"Of course, the minute I set foot in the hotel, Youngblood comes up to me. 'What happened to your hair?' he says. 'You need a haircut!'

" 'I just came back from getting one.'

" 'Well, that's where you got yourself in trouble,' he tells me. 'You need some work done.'

"By now Elaine's getting into the picture. 'Your hair's a mess!' she says. 'You better let Daddy do what he can for it.' I'm just shaking my head. I don't know if I'm going or coming. I haven't even seen a mirror. But I like Elaine. I know she's not just saying all that to drum up business. They're close, I know. Calling him Daddy all the time — apparently that pleases him. They rely on each other for moral support, I guess. Well, Youngblood went off and got his scissors and did a clean-up job — trying to smooth it up a bit. He does good, thorough work. And when he finished, Elaine said I looked chic. *Chic!* That's a word you hardly hear around here."

COLD SNAP

Cold snap. Everyone indoors except for Ironsides. He swings his wheelchair wide to avoid the broken furniture, mattresses, and old appliances of evicted tenants. No one seems to know the departed persons. Bad elements, the ones who deserved to go, Ironsides says. This time of year he has a bad word for everyone. Yet even in this penetrating cold, he still pauses to loll after any passing white woman. Frosty puffs of breath hang in the winter air like cartoon balloons with no message. Lust made visible.

CORNUCOPIA

Cold, cold, cold. This is the week they've planned to stock up the new Red Apple. For four months now, ever since the two convenient fires, they've been gutting and wiring and plastering and cleaning and painting behind the boarded-up storefront. This week the boards come down; long rows of shelves rise in a matter of hours; and, while a guard stands by, loads of produce are wheeled inside. A security gate has been installed, but there are no windows yet: you can almost reach out and touch the food. People from Hotel Walden stand outside, stomping their feet against the cold as shelves fill up: cases of Oscar Meyer Bologna, Hormel Luncheon Meat, Swiss Knight Cheese, and Rice-a-Roni; Kraft Jelly, B & J Hot Pepper Rings, Mueller's Rigatoni, Uncle Ben's Converted Rice, Chicken of the Sea Chunk White Tuna, Lipton's Onion Soup and Dip Mix, Rokeach Borscht, Goya Guanabana Nectar, Nabisco Nilla Wafers.

Buffalo grabs hold of the new security gate, tests it with a good shake, then fires a wad of yellow phlegm up against the grating. "Shit!" he says as the blob oozes down the metal barrier, "you'd need a tank to crack that gate!"

ALL THE GIRLS

Doc's been in the hospital over two weeks now. He's weak, but he hasn't had a drink since Thanksgiving. One day, the social worker from the hotel dropped by; another time a few friends from his old neighborhood looked in on him, but mostly he's been on his own, laying around and remembering bits and pieces of his past. "I was in Knickerbocker a few years ago for TB," he says. "Five and a half months I was there recuperatin, an they cut me loose. I think I made the doctor mad, cause I wasn't even cured when they put me out. I had all the girls. He just couldn't stand that."

Doc's head turns dramatically to follow a cute young nurse. He gives me a quick wink. "When I come in to Knickerbocker, the doc said, 'Mister, you got TB up to your asshole!'

" 'Man, you can't be serious!' I told him.

" 'I never been more serious in my life. Don't you cough or sneeze?'

" 'Yeah, man. Don't *you* cough or sneeze?'

" 'Look here, I'll show you the chart.' He shows me this X ray, an shit, one of my lungs is collapsed! Here I am, runnin up and down the street, drinkin an whatnot, not even knowin I'm in trouble. . . . I got to thinkin seriously. I told the doc I wanna get better. Well, when this dude tells me I'm all winded up at Knickerbocker, I thought they were kiddin. I didn't think they'd have an attitude like that. 'We gonna put you outa here,' the doc says. 'You gettin all the girls. Middle of the night — all the girls callin your name.'

" 'Hell, I'm just here to cure my TB,' I told him, but he was already shakin his head and fillin out the forms.

"I was kinda mad. Bet some of the girls was, too. . . ."

SCARY SUNDAY

It's noon. A runty German Shepherd slinks about Ralph's room, underfed and nervous, looking as if it were ashamed of some undiscovered act, waiting to be beaten. "He's been runnin up an down the halls all week," Ralph says. He looks dazed and empty. "Nobody's given him nothin since Low Down went to jail. Always looked the criminal type anyway — sayin what he done and how cool he is an stuff. Now they put him where he can tell gangster stories all day. Let him show off — he wasn't much good around here. The worst thing is, this dog don't know what to do without him. Some guy named Lyman's supposed to keep him, but he just runs up an down the halls, eatin garbage, pissin and shittin all over.

"I thought if I kept him here he might look out for me when the Bishop came, but it didn't work. I got up this mornin, went to McDonald's, and then come back to lay down. There was snow comin. At first I thought it was ashes or somethin someone threw out their window, but when I saw it was snow, I lay back an looked up at it. Then the Bishop — his voice was kinda mellow, he can change it to anything he wants — he started harassin me. I felt very afraid. The dog wasn't no help to me, and I was too scared to move. . . . There wasn't nothin but patterns goin in my head. Just patterns. What was scary was the way they kept comin an comin. I couldn't stop it any more than I can stop the snow."

SIX DAYS TILL CHRISTMAS

"Six days till Christmas," Doug says. "You know, people get crazy this time of year, an when you're out there delivering flyers it's like you run into all of em." The mouse under his left eye is purple and mushy looking, like a piece of rotten fruit. A line of stitches runs along his cheekbone. A yellowish welt shines on the side of his face.

"We was distributin flyers on Wall Street — this guy Mike I work for on Wednesdays and Thursdays. You should see all the dope dealers down there! One old building's a regular shootin gallery — 200 people in an outa there every lunch hour. Suits an briefcases. Coke, dope — they're the only ones can afford that shit. So we're out there distributin *Our Town* — you know, one of those neighborhood newspapers they stick in your building lobby — an this black dude comes up an asks did I wanna cop. I tell him I don't have that kinda money, but thanks, maybe when I get my Christmas bonus, an I start to walk off. . . . He was all over me in a second. Didn't know what the fuck he was doin — who he thought I was or what I done to him. He hit me with a rubber blackjack or somethin, an I started to go down. Comin at me like he was gonna kill me, so I threw the stack of papers at him an blacked out.

"Next thing I knew, Mike is draggin me to the van. 'I fixed that nigger good!' he says. Mike's this stout little guy, looks like a guerrilla fighter for the Israeli army. Musta hit him with a two-by-four or somethin, cause when I looked back this black dude was flat out in the gutter, *Our Town*s flappin all around him, blowin all over fuckin Wall Street." One of the cats springs from the bathroom sink into the Kitty Litter, then comes roaring into the room, hot on the ass of its companion. Freaky energy today — rolling and nipping, scattering Kitty Litter all over, scrambling in and out of the empty dresser shelf.

Bobby's bed is stripped bare. Deep cigarette holes spread like gunshot all over his miserable mattress. "He's in the hospital," Doug explains. "Had another seizure an fell on his head. He's okay, I think, but they wanted to do a brain scan before they let him go. Usually, I'm there to keep him from hurting himself, but this was late at night and we was sleepin. He wasn't drunk — we'd had maybe three quarts of beer — an around 2:00 A.M. he musta felt the seizure comin on an tried to get up. He got tangled in the sheets an fell over. I heard this thump an found him all tensed up right here on the floor. I was up to see him this morning —

brought him tobacco an a coupla books. They say he'll be out in a day or two.

"I don't know, somethin always happens near Christmas. I was hopin we could take the bus down to spend a few weeks with Daddy in Florida — he sends us the money an picks us up at the depot — but his wife's sick now. He says maybe Easter. If we was down there for Christmas, we'd get ourselves together. But Christmas here — they show carols an specials on TV, an I sit here cryin."

Knock on the door.

"Doug! Hey, Doug!"

"Yeah?"

"It's Luis! Carlito!"

"I'm talkin to a friend."

"They want you down at the desk."

"I'm talkin to a friend! I'll come down later."

"They wanna see you *now,* man!" Doug unbolts the door and swings it open. Two young Hispanic men fill the narrow alcove. "Yo, Doug! Howya doin?" They seem to be on friendly terms with one another.

"What's goin on?" Doug's voice is hoarse, apprehensive.

"Don't know, man. They jus wanna see you."

"I'll be down, okay?"

"They tole us to bring you wit us."

"Alright, gimme a minute to change." Doug shuts his door; he puts on a shirt and fumbles with the buttons. "Shit!" he says, "Bobby's got the rent slips up at the hospital!" He pulls his hair back in a ponytail, snaps a rubber band around it, and puts on his porkpie hat. "They ain't gonna kick us out with no bullshit!" he says defiantly. But I know he's scared.

Luis and Carlito are waiting down the hallway by the service elevator. We get inside. Nobody speaks. Downstairs they lead Doug through the lobby and usher him into a large empty room. Some furniture is stacked in one corner. In the center, under a lopsided chandelier, is a small wooden table and two chairs. I stay close behind Doug but a guy at the door shakes his head. "Manager don't wanna speak to nobody but Doug."

Five minutes later, Doug emerges. Cheerful, obsequious chatter as he says goodbye to a thin man standing behind the desk. "What a lotta bullshit!" he delcares as we head up the back stairs to his room. "He says the neighbors claim Bobby an me was fightin an disturbin the floor. That's just bullshit! You know, the cops was up there to take Bobby to the hospital, an that makes everybody nervous. They don't like to see the law walkin around in here. I told the manager what really happened, an I told him if we ever did fight it wasn't none of anybody's business. Shit! Jay an Tracy are fightin every night right above us. Throwin furniture an screamin an rollin around the room. An what about Stines, next door? They know he's sellin dope. All those cars double-parked out there from New Jersey an Connecticut — they know where these kids are goin. So what're they comin down on us for? Bobby has a fuckin seizure an cracks his head on the floor. I don't want a bunch of cops comin in my room, but that don't mean I'm gonna leave my brother layin out to die." His voice is tough and angry now. "We're savin our rent slips. They ain't gonna pull no bullshit on us!"

Bobby is fast asleep in the hospital bed. Thin grey strips of roast beef and pasty mashed potatoes uneaten in the plastic tray before him. I dread hospitals, yet each time I've visited an SRO friend — Doc; Bobby; even Gerry, comatose and dying — I've felt the same relief: *Clean sheets. People to look after you. Nothing to do but rest. Here you are safe. You will not suffer here.* I leave a note by his bedside and stop at the nursing station on my way out. I'm a friend, I explain, and I'm anxious to know what the results were on Bobby's brain scan.

"Brain scan?"

"I was told they wanted to check him out just to be safe."

"Brain scan?" The head nurse looks perplexed.

"Robert Carman, we're talking about."

"Yes, but there was no brain scan. He was in surgery this afternoon — a knife wound in his leg."

The nurse tells me that Bobby has to be wakened in a few minutes for a blood pressure reading. I'm there when he wakes up. He coughs and spits and pees and lets the nurse check him out. "Y-e-e-eah," he drawls after we're left alone, "just missed the main artery. Cut up a few veins an shit — bleedin all over the place — but he didn't hit the artery." Fatigue has left his features perfectly relaxed: angleheaded hipster if ever there was one. "It was nothin, man." He shrugs as if recollecting some childhood injury, long forgotten, long forgiven. "We were cookin dinner. I was peelin potatoes, or some kinda shit like that, an I don't even remember what Doug was doin. You know how it goes — I said somethin, he said somethin, we both got mad an jumped each other. I throw a beer bottle in his face, so he sticks me. It can be like he wants mashed potatoes an I want home fries, or he says I'm not peelin the potatoes clean enough, so I call him a fuckin son of a bitch an he says I'm a crazy epileptic — some kinda bullshit like that. But when we fight we — h-e-e-e-y, that knife was a foot an a half long — what you'd carve a roast with. Mighta been the same knife I stuck him with a coupla years ago. Yeah, it musta been, cause we only got one motherfuckin knife like that.

"These two detectives were in to see me, and I was tellin em how these guys broke in an jumped me. 'Whose knife is that?' one of em says. I tell em it's ours, that these guys grabbed it when they came in. And these two cops, two Irish guys — real pros, decent, woulda been perfect for some TV series — this one cop says, 'Come on! you and your brother had a fight!' I told em I had nothing more to say. He kinda winked at me and told me he hoped I'd be better soon. I'll speak to him when I get out. Doug an I'll go over there together an tell him we just have these fights sometimes. They can't do anything if I don't press charges. And they understand — they don't wanna get us kicked outa the hotel."

Bobby stabs a fork into the mashed potatoes and watches the gravy ooze through the crevice. "Who can eat this shit?" he asks. "We just bought twelve dollars worth of pork chops this week. Doug breads em and southern fries em; he's perfected it over the years — can do it better than any spade I ever met. Y-e-e-e-e-ah! Cooks the chops nice an slow, pours off the fat, makes a great gravy for the rice. I sure hope they let me home for Christmas. Makes me hungry just thinkin about it."

HOLE

The tree outside is grey and somber. Some knotted cord, an oily rag, and a black shirt hang from its bare branches. "Looks like the ghost of Christmas past," Muriel says. "Well, it fits in with the rest of the decor."

Her maps of Boston and New York have peeled off the wall, revealing the holes left by her seizures. Plaster has crumbled into the cavities, doubling their size. "This heat dries everything out," she says. "Scotch tape won't hold my maps, and these postcards are always flying down on me." Through the enlarged New York hole she notices part of a door. Unfinished pine, solid, with raised panels. "Why look at that!" Muriel exclaims. "Who would have imagined!" Weak winter sun casts a soft shadow on the old wood. "This probably was a wonderful place at one time," she says. "I'll bet all these rooms were huge apartments. This door might have opened from the parlor to the dining room. I'll bet there were grand receptions — at least, I like to think there were. Look! There's another door!' She brushes away chunks of plaster from the Boston hole and another pine door appears. "Now isn't that something! This hotel must have a real history!" She shakes her head to bring herself out of her sudden reverie. "It's awful, you know. A real horror to wake up with mysterious holes in your wall. Six months! You'd think they'd find time to fix it by now. The first thing I see when I wake up. Ugly, it's so ugly! I remember Halloween — I'd look at this wall and I knew there were these holes behind my maps. I'd imagine a skeleton or something coming out at me. . . . After that, I decided I'd better look at it with humor instead of mystery."

For a few moments she studies the hole and the shadowy old door. "Here! I know what to do with that hole!" From her dresser she takes an art project from her SPOP class — a collage she made a few days ago. It's a magazine color photo of two cats to which she's glued bits of dried leaves. A piece of fuzzy weed forms a mustache for one big tawny, and a pale yellow leaf provides a ladylike fan for the fluffy white Burmese. She sticks the collage in the Boston hole, taping it to the pine door so that a mustachioed cat and his fan-bearing lady look back at us through the gaping, accidental space. Old pine door to other times, other lives. It is like those fairy tales where one passes through some charmed closed space into a world of wonders.

"Well that ought to keep the mice away!" Muriel giggles. "Two bodyguards keeping watch on that hole." She giggles again as she admires her handiwork. "I like it," she says. "It really does something for the room."

MAGIC

Red lines drawn across Ralph's forehead and cheeks. "I put em there myself," he says. "Some day I'll explain. It's a kinda magic. Only good break I'll have. . . ."

POWER SOURCE

"Goddamn! Get outa here!" David plucks a fat roach from the pork chop gravy. "I spray an they still come back. Only way to get ridda them is to get water bugs. They love eatin roaches, an when the roaches is all gone I could get me a mouse to eat the water bugs. End up with one big mouse. That'd be a lot better than all these roaches. Shit! Lookit that! They got to my bread!"

He shoves the unfinished meal aside and opens a fresh manila folder. "I could be burnt, fried, or electrocuted." Sounds like a top-level intelligence briefing. "See, I'm workin on plans to turn my TV unit into an oscilloscope so I can monitor things and track down secret power sources." He spreads some sketchy blueprints on his desk and tries to explain. "See, on this side I'll have my digital scanner wired in to my frequency ground an — shit! They're all over my pork chops!" Two roaches slough through the congealing gravy. David pushes the plate farther away and turns his back on the mess. "So over here is my high-voltage ground wire, and right now I'm workin on my power source. This could be really great! See, the last few weeks somebody's been jammin fire department frequencies and also a coupla amateur two-meter stations — DHF Repeater and an FM Repeater. My mission — find em!" He says these last words like an avid follower of "Star Trek"'s Captain Kirk. "If I could find who's doin it, if I could find that secret power source — dontchya see — they'd see they could really use me. Special investigator or maybe technical advisor. An my name would be in the paper! Snaps! DTEX ENTERPRISES CRACKS FREQUENCY JAMMERS. I'd have more business than I could handle. I can do it! I know I can with my oscilloscope, but first I gotta put together my power source. . . ."

SIBLING RIVALRY

The guy beside Bobby has a bad case of the runs. Smelly stuff. And the nurse is slow on the bed pans. The guy across the room is dying of cancer. He hangs over the side of his bed gasping into a breathing apparatus — hospital gown hitched up, flashing his ass in Bobby's face. "Nice view," Bobby says. "Pull up the blinds, man, and check out the cathedral."

St. John the Divine sits huge and unfinished across the way. Towerless. Great limestone blocks stacked up along its sides. Winter light. Grey sky. The cathedral a mottled sooty brown. "Better than lookin up that guy's asshole," Bobby says. "Poor bastard's not gonna make it. Can't breath without that machine. Hey, as long as he's showin his butt like that you might as well take a look at my wound. Let me know if it's oozing or anything." He turns on his side and hitches up his robe. It's a mean cut. Another inch or two and it might have gone right up his rectum. "Fuckin sibling rivalry!" No anger in his voice — more the pity of a concerned observer. "We didn't know what we was doin. He was bringin home money from his job and we were drinkin it up. H-e-e-e-e-y! You know in the movies how a guy comes in the saloon and breaks a whiskey bottle over some dude's head? Real macho thing. Well, baby, you can really cut someone. I hit him with a beer bottle. I was a fuckin wild man. Glass all over the fuckin floor. And blood — Doug says there were puddles all over. Inch deep on my bed.

"Listen, I don't blame him for this shit. We were both outa our minds. Who I feel sorry for is the cats." He grins. With his tired round face and jagged line of ruined teeth, he looks like a Halloween pumpkin that has begun to turn. "Those poor little fuckers — they don't know what's goin on. Doug and me jumpin around, screamin and tearin the place up. Blood and glass everywhere they move. And — h-e-e-e-e-y, you know what I'm sayin — they're innocent. Like little kids. All they know how to do is love us, and we're trashin the place with our sibling rivalry."

CHRISTMAS LETTER

"I got some work for you." David opens a folder and hands me a sheet of DTEX stationery like a busy executive pressing work on his subordinate. "You gotta type this for me, Bob." His voice changes, full of feeling. "I've come to the point where I need my family to achieve certain goals. My brother — I gotta speak to him. I gotta clear this up. When I got outa Creedmore — right after I moved in here — I spent a weekend at his place. They have a girl, she was four or five then, an I was sleepin on the couch. She came in in the middle of the night an curled up at the other end and went to sleep. And then in the morning, my brother's wife said I was foolin with her. Touchin her, you know. Tryin to molest her. It's not true! I know it ain't true! An she says her little girl waked up an come runnin in to her room an told her all these things. My brother came in and started yellin at me. He didn't ask me if I done it — just yellin at me about how terrible I was. I couldn't talk. I didn't say a thing. I run outa there cryin an never come back."

David shakes his head and hands me the letter he's written. "I thought about it. You know, people sometimes do these things an black out, don't remember nothin. But I didn't forget the murder. I know what I done — I remember everything that happened — an that murder was the worst thing I ever did. So I know I didn't do this. She was just a cute little girl. I was sleepin the whole time. I gotta speak to my brother an tell him. I need my family. I done as much as I can on my own. It's like — on Eyewitness News last night they had this family up in the Bronx, burned outa their home, everybody out on the street cryin. I knew what they were goin through, but it just didn't break me up. They had each other, see — the whole family facin this together. If I'm gonna cry about somethin, I'd start with everything I gotta live with right here, everything I gotta take care of alone. But I don't let nothin get to me like that. If I started cryin I'd never stop."

David's Letter

Dear: mr & miss Torres.

Congradulaytions on your new baby boy   May he live in the best of helth

I also want to say I mis you both very much my love is still with you both and all of the fameley and best of luck to your wife in her school work.

I think of all of you every day   IM righting a book about all of you and the whole fameley and the real story about what happen on Jul 19, 1976 11:55 pm, wich is a shoking story an what reley happen that night   I WANT to see you and your wife to sit down and talk you both like fameley becaus deep down inside we all love one another and we can rech an understanding of one another because we are frome the same BLOD, and we will be fameley for years to come.

My girl frend lives 3 bildings away frome you every time I walk to her house I pass you bilding and think of all of you with tears in my eyes.

I will be stoping by you house to see all of you with a copey of my book I dont know when but plese exspect me soon, I just want to see you all to talk so we can be like we use to be, FAMLEY!   Love you all may god blese you.

MERY CHRISTMAS, with a happy new yer
David M. Torres

REFLECTIONS ON A GOLDEN ARM

"I don't know," Muriel says, "whether I've got a Mickey or a Minnie, but this little mouse has been coming to visit. My thought is it comes through the floor." She hobbles to the hot-water pipe in the far corner. The floorboards have shrunk and cracked all around the base, leaving an opening the size of a rabbit hole. "My mouse dropped by quite regularly until somebody broke into my room — took my winter coat and birth certificate. Not the mouse," she quickly adds, "I know he's innocent. But after the robbery Mickey or Minnie must've moved to safer quarters. Then one day this little grey scurry caught my eye. *Oh! Minnie's back!* I was so delighted!

She's just a tiny thing. Needs a square meal. I always try to put a little cheese out to make sure she doesn't go hungry."

Muriel's been fiddling with an unopened jar of capers. Now she inspects it with great interest. "I remember having capers with lamb once in Boston. Oh, that was so good! I didn't even know what a caper was at the time, so that impressed me even more. I think mysterious ingredients add a little something extra when you're entertaining. Well, there I was in Red Apple yesterday, and I saw these capers and decided to fix them with some lamb chops. Then I saw the price of lamb and couldn't believe it! . . . It was such a beautiful meal. . . . Well, now I've got my seasoning without the meat. I don't know how people afford to eat anymore. I should raise my own sheep."

She sets the capers down with her spices and picks up a book. "Do you know *The Golden* . . . golden . . . gold — I remember there's gold in the title. . . ."

"*The Man with the Golden Arm?*" I offer.

"Why, of course!" she says delightedly. "So many things seem to slip my mind."

I'm pleased that Algren's book has found its way back to a place so like its sad, seamy setting. "It's one of my favorite novels," I tell her.

"There's so much in it!" she says. "I read it little by little. So many lives, and you care about every one. Everything seems so real. Even a light bulb or a dirty plate looks interesting. And every page is another story."

"Is that Algren?" I point to the book she's holding.

"Who?"

"*The Man with the Golden Arm?*"

"Oh, no," she replies. "I read that years ago. SPOP took us to the library yesterday, so I thought I'd try one of her other books." She hands me her copy of *The Member of the Wedding*.

"This is Carson McCullers!" I'm still in my Algren reverie and rather confused.

"Yes, isn't she wonderful!" Muriel hands me the book. For her placemark she's using a block of Christmas seals — LIGHT THE CANDLE OF UNDERSTANDING: EPILEPSY FOUNDA-TION OF AMERICA. "I sent them a couple of bucks," she says. "Without their research I'd be a lot worse off. . . . Oh, now I re-member! *Reflections in a Golden Eye* — that was the book! I guess all that glitters is not Carson McCullers. But the book you mentioned sounded so interesting. Why don't you tell me about *Reflections on a Golden Arm?*"

So I tell her about Frankie Machine and desperate Sophie's twisted strategy of keeping him. I tell her about Schwiefka, Spar-row Saltskin, drink and drugs, the deck shuffled and dealt through a hundred Chicago nights. Old cuckolded Stash fleeing to the broom closet. New Year's Eve, when Frankie lives his dream for thirty precious minutes. Prison. Flight. Molly-O Novotny and the Pink Kitten Club. "Oh, that's good!" Muriel says. She takes back the McCullers book and opens a marked page. "I had a can of beans last night and listened to the radio till it ran out on me. I had nothing but this book — it seems I must've loaned my playing cards to someone — and I realized I hadn't properly concentrated the first time I read it. It studies a member of a family who's trying to figure out about weddings. She's very confused about men and husbands. She doesn't know what part they play in a woman's life. Evidently, she's very naive. But she never gives up. She's trying to reconstruct memories, put them together logically, find out why certain problems preplex her."

Muriel turns to her marked page and reads with enormous con-centration:

"Frankie," said Berenice, "Awhile back you started to say something. And we veered off from the subject. It was about something unnatural, I think."

"Oh, yes," F. Jasmine said. "I was going to tell you about something peculiar that happened to me today that I don't hardly realize. Now I don't exactly know how to explain just what I mean."

F. Jasmine broke open a sweet potato and tilted back in her chair. . . .

"This is a real jigsaw puzzle. This F. Jasmine — I've been trying to decide if she's connected to Frankie. I think she is. It seems Frankie's gone undercover, worked up this change in preparation for the wedding. It's very interesting. For heaven's sake — you've got to read slowly and enjoy each little piece like it was a story all by itself." She thumbs ahead till she finds a dog-eared page. "Here! This is my favorite part: 'Grey eyes is glass.' *Grey eyes is glass*," she repeats. "You must really study life to make a statement like that! *Grey eyes is glass*! There's so much deep thought behind it. Does it mean eyes are like windows? That you can see right through them and into a person's thoughts? Or is it some kind of trick? Eyes can be like glass mirrors, you know, and cast back a reflection — *Reflections in a Golden Eye*, for instance — so maybe what you're seeing is really yourself. . . . Oh, it's so fantastic! *Grey eyes is glass*! Like those cats' eyes looking out from that hole. I see stars, beautiful bits of light in the dark!"

Knock on the door.

"It's Benny," she says. "I just know it's him. . . . Yes?"

No answer.

"What do you want now, Benny?"

"I'm making tea," his muffled voice announces.

"Fine, Benny. Fine."

"I want a tea bag." He sounds gagged.

"Later, Benny. Not right now. I'm entertaining a friend."

"Later." He shuffles away.

"It's too bad," Muriel says. "If he could read, if he could just enjoy something like this, it would do him a world of good." She returns to her book. "Here's another part that struck me:

"Now I am here to tell you I was happy. There was no human woman in all the world more happy than I was in them days," she said. "And that includes everybody. . . ."

Muriel closes the book, setting it down gently beside her un-opened capers. "Now isn't that nice?"

EMERGENCY POWER SOURCE

"Yeah, my brother called." David's voice is hoarse. Eyes glisten with pain. "He won't see me. His wife won't let him. He says she started yellin an screamin just from seein my letter — how I could never set foot in her house again. My brother says she's goin through a nervous period, but that's not it. She's tryin to destroy me. She's tryin to keep me cut off from my family. I — forget it! I don't wanna talk about it."

He lights up a Newport and pulls out a new file folder. "Here's what I'm workin on now. I'm buildin an emergency power source — a 100-watt transistorized converter that'll hook onto any car battery. I was watchin this TV movie a couple of nights ago — *The Night the City Screamed.* You shoulda seen all the killin an stuff when the power went out. Dontchya see? If there's another black-out this hotel — all these hotels — will go wild. Robbin, beatin on people, rape — they'll tear the West Side down. An whataya gonna do? Everyone in the dark. No identification. Just think of it. I'd be the only one in the whole building, probably the whole area, with light. Everyone in the dark and me with my own power."

THE BISHOP SPLITS

"He's not comin! He's not comin!" Ralph's in the hallway to greet me. "He knew we were gonna catch him! He knew it! He couldn't stand the heat — the way I been exposin him for your book. . . . I got suspicious at ten this mornin. At noon I knew he was scared of us. No hallucinations! Nothin! I'll tell yuh, that Bishop can — " Fat Edna waddles past, laughing like a little girl who's just said a dirty word. "I wouldn't go near her," Ralph says. "Horny as I am. She's a nut, man." He twirls an index finger near his ear — the crazy signal — and breaks out into wild laughter.

Benny shuffles by, tugging on his unfastened pants. He's wearing a handsome purple blazer the social workers found for him, but the pants are pitifully small — the best the staff could come up with after they threw his louse-ridden garments away. "You see my shirt?" Ralph's wearing a new corduroy top. "I went by my mother's house and she gave it to me. My hands were dirty, my underwear and feet were smellin. I took a bath an I came out a clean boy again. I'm going back on Christmas. My mother loves me, she really does, but I'd rather live on my own. And now that the Bishop's outa the picture I can be in my room without him rushin in on me. At two I knew we had him on the run. Man, I was feelin good! Red-eyed devil is what he is. Red-eyed devil, an he didn't come."

Benny shuffles back, coming to a stop like a toy with a weak battery. "Gimme one!" He points to three rolls of coarse toilet paper stacked on the stairs. "Gimme one! I ain't got nothin."

"No, man! I need *all* these rolls," Ralph says expansively. "I'm a big wiper!"

HUNGER

"I say there, old bloke!" Muriel managed something like an English accent to show off her new eyeglasses. She's pleased as punch. "They wanted to give me bifocals, but I didn't like the idea of seeing everything two ways. I told them I already see too many ways, so they gave me these. Why, I can read my own writing now! You know, I have a tendency to forget things, so I'm in the habit of leaving notes around the room. I wake up, find these notes to myself — at least, I presume they were to myself — and now I can read them, find out what they say. It opens up new lines of communication."

She's enormously cheerful today. "All these clothes and nowhere to hang them." She points to a small heap of clothing at the foot of her bed. "I should have a bazaar to get rid of this stuff, but it's pretty bizarre around here already." She's delighted by her joke. She nods at the cat montage inside the San Francisco hole. "That's the cat house! Of course, we run a good upstanding establishment. Only the best customers and all that." Mr. Winslow lumbers past the open door, a leather handbag under his arm. "Why hello, Mr. Winslow!"

Mr. Winslow flashes his best grin. Then his face hardens with anger. "I should report, I should report Mrs. Talbot." Blunt staccato jabs of speech, as though he has to seize each word from a maelstrom of jabberwocky. "She's not, I say she's not feeding the people. I could report her for not feeding the people. I have to, I have to have food in my stomach. Ain't that right? If you don't have food in your stomach you can, you can die from star — from starvation." Mr. Winslow's arrival throws everything out of proportion, like a giant Magritte apple that fills a whole room. "It's a good thing, a good thing I can go to Mc-, to McDonald's, cause Mrs. Talbot, she's not — "

"She's not supposed to take care of you," Muriel cuts in. "You've got to take care of — "

"In R-r-r-r-r-ockland they gave me — "

"Let's not talk about Rockland. All right?"

"All right!" His face snaps to that wonderful child's smile. "I gotta, I gotta take care of myself. An I gotta, I gotta have food in my stomach." He says this like a kindergartener reciting his ABCs.

"Mr. Winslow, why are you carrying that purse?" Muriel winks at me, as if to assure me that I can sit back and let her take care of the questions for me.

"This bag, this bag — I got my silverware and candy here. The spoons, the spoons I say, the spoons and forks they got at McDonald's are too skinny. They are not, they are not, I can't eat cause they are not strong enough. I got my silverware in my bag so I can eat at McDonald's. I won't, I won't let Mrs. Talbot starve me."

"You'll never starve." Muriel sounds fed up with Mr. Winslow's intrusion.

"Everyone says you gotta have, you gotta have food in your stomach or — "

"These Irish prisoners went forty-five days without eating." Muriel grasps her pocket radio and gives it a pat. "I heard it on the news and then the battery ran out."

"What's that, what's that you say? These Irish, these Irish you say — somebody didn't eat for — how long did you say somebody didn't eat for?"

"Forty-five days. Just water."

"You say, you say they had water." Mr. Winslow seizes on this as a fact of some importance.

"It was a protest. They're having a war in Ireland."

"And you say they starved these soldiers. They starved them to — "

"No, no! They pushed their food away. It was a protest."

"They made a protest, you say, they make a protest and they pushed away their food." Mr. Winslow pauses to marvel at this incredible idea. "Forty-five days?"

Muriel nods. "No breakfast. No lunch."

"No supper?"

Muriel shakes her head.

"Not even a cookie?" Just asking the question seems to pain him.

"Not even a cookie."

Mr. Winslow winces. "I let, I let the girls wait on me at McDonald's. The boys, the boys there — Mister José put another fella in front of me to keep me from getting my food. They don't know how to treat, I say they don't know how to treat a customer."

"Maybe you should go get something to eat, Mr. Winslow. You look hungry."

"I look hungry, you say. I look — Mrs. Talbot, she's not here to feed us, you say. I gotta find something at McDonald's." He backs out of the room, pressing the handbag against his belly. "Do you think, do you think — " he can barely bring himself to pose the question — "do you think I could go forty-five days without eating?"

He leaves without waiting for a reply. "He really is something," Muriel remarks. "I don't think he could go forty-five minutes without stuffing himself."

AN AGE OF MIRACLES

Ralph and Sugar Blue lean into the stiff wind like hikers working up a steep hill. Sugar Blue's wearing an elegant frayed cashmere overcoat and a carefully tied scarf. Ralph walks beside him with no jacket on at all, pace changing with every step, drifting away, then veering back and brushing against him. Sugar Blue's laughing, looking straight ahead and laughing. Ralph's face is fixed in a fierce scowl. "How long we gonna live? How long we gonna live?" he mutters. "Cause if I gotta live like this much longer, I'm gonna be outa my mind. I shoulda died when I was sixteen."

"The Bishop?" I ask.

"No," he beams, "I think we got him."

"I was sleepin," Sugar Blue laughs at the passing traffic. "I was sleepin an now we're goin to church."

"I could use some words of wisdom today," Ralph says somberly.

"Church before Christmas," Sugar Blue says. "That'll be nice." They turn the corner and enter McDonald's. The place is hung with red-and-gold holiday tassel and two "Noel" plaques. "I gotta call Lorraine," Sugar Blue says and goes back outside to find a pay phone.

Ralph buys one giant Coke and slurps it down in seconds. "I jus don't know why they wanna keep us alive. Welfare an doctors an all that shit. They must be doin it for some reason, but I don't know what it is an I got no reasons of my own. I stayed up all last night. That was pretty good, cause I knew the Bishop would try to

break in on me today. Amen! Sometimes when I stay awake I —
aw shit!" One of the McDonald's girls is herding Fat Edna out towards the door. Edna likes to cop food from abandoned trays, and
now the girl is cursing, periodically shoving her, while Edna just
waddles at her own pace, tittering like an embarrassed child,
sloshing a half-filled cup of coffee all over the place.

"Where'd you get that!" the girl scolds. "Did you buy it?
You can't come in here and do that! We don't want you here!"
Fat Edna giggles like she's pulled off some fantastic hilarious
prank.

"I bought it for her!" Ralph says. "You don't have to shove her
around like that. I bought it."

The girl pays him no mind. She holds open the glass doors and
waits for Fat Edna to make her exit. "Goddamn nut! We don't
want you! Understand? Stay wherever you stay! Keep out of
here!"

"She never bothers nobody," Ralph tells me. "She waits till they
leave. Food's just goin to waste. It's not like she's stealin. She's not
takin nothin nobody wants." The theme from *Mondo Cane* pours
through the muzak. "I got the Bishop stopped an now I gotta deal
with the whole rest of the goddamn world — that loudmouthed
girl. . . . So I was sayin — sometimes I stay awake all night an feel
the power growin in my forehead. I meditate. Sit an clear the mind
an feel the power. Then if I see blue an red stripes — if I see the
hallucinations comin — I'm ready."

Sugar Blue hurries in, sliding into his seat, brimming over
with excitement. "I took the phone off the hook! It's hangin right
outside! They told me to hold, but I'm gonna make *them* hold
for *me*!"

Ralph's not listening. He's entertaining a cute boy at the next
table. "I am the greatest!" Ralph waves a fist, laughing wildly.
"Rope-a-dope, Ali Shuffle, fly like a butterfly, sting like a bee. I *am*
the greatest!" The boy turns away, then spins to face him with an
open smile. "You eat your McMuffin, boy! You eat all your fries

an maybe you'll grow up an be champ like me." The boy's father arrives with a tray of food and gives Ralph a baffled stare.

"I'm gonna check the phone," Sugar Blue says. "Maybe they're waitin for me now."

Ralph's still trading smiles with the little boy. "Seventeen years she's been in Manhattan State," he says after Sugar Blue leaves. "Calls her every day an she's not even family." He feints a jab at the boy. "Some week I had. I was goin home, but I didn't. I don't remember why, but I didn't go. An Friday somebody stole my winter jacket. I been wearin three shirts when I go out, but it's cold just the same. I guess I'm gonna have to lock my door."

Sugar Blue comes hurrying back to the table. "They wouldn't let her talk to me," he declares. "She's havin lunch an they say it's the rules. But look! I got my dime back! I hit the phone an this dime come right out! I don't understand, cause what I put in was two nickels. It's an age of miracles — it really is. Somebody read me that in the paper yesterday."

"There is a reason for everything," Ralph says.

"You still wanna go to church?"

"I'm ready, brother! I'm ready!" Ralph pops from his seat like a Holy Roller. "Amen! Amen!" He looks back to shoot a parting scowl at the McDonald's girl. "Somebody better tell me what I'm doin on this earth cause I'm not gettin no answers back in my room."

THE GOSPEL ACCORDING TO YOUNGBLOOD

You know why Jesus was so damn slick? He hung around people like you find here. He knew too much about too many type of things. Now where'd he get it from? You don't learn nothin around average people. Hustlin people, narcos, and psychiatric types —

that's who he got to, that's who talked to him, and that's how he knew what he knew. You got to get to the heavies.

STREET PREACHER

Revelation through a bullhorn. Squat Hispanic lady piping forth. Tan boots, skimpy plaid overcoat, fuzzy knit cap with a brown pompom that bounces as she speaks. Dark glasses on this grey, raw day. A newcomer to the hotel, but she's right out in front, preaching in speedy Spanish to the unredeemed. "Shut up, you bitch!" someone yells from the entrance passage. She redoubles her efforts.

She is preaching to no one, wasting her batteries. Cars slow and stop for the traffic light on Broadway. She points her bullhorn towards closed windows and raises her voice. But it is too cold. The sidewalks are empty. Buffalo hovers in the doorway, checking her out, then stumbles outside ready to take her on. "There's gonna be a war if Jesus comes!" he says. "War! You hear? If Jesus Christ comes there's gonna be a war!"

Two neighborhood kids bundled in down parkas stop to stare at the lady. They come right up to her and then freeze. She aims her bullhorn down at them, inches from their upturned faces, like an elephant begging for peanuts. "It's in the Bible," Buffalo persists. "Arma — Arma — Judgment Day. It's all parta the same deal. If Jesus comes back he's gonna tear the place apart. Ain't leavin nothin the way it is. An that means *war,* hear!"

"Dat in dee Bypull?" she rasps through her bullborn. "Dat no in dee Bypull. In Matthew 25 he say — "

"It's in the goddamn Bible! It's in every Bible. Arma — Gabriel gets the whole thing started, an then they come on down — horses, swords, heavenly angels, lightnin bolts — bringin in the heavy artillery."

"What Bypull dat? What Bypull?" The bullhorn is on the blink.

Her voice is her own now, a paltry scratchy thing beside her former amplified self.

"They *all* talk about war. All that preachin's no good unless you got the army behind you. Any fool knows that, an Jesus wasn't nobody's fool!"

"What Bypull?" she repeats, and the bullhorn snaps back to life. "My Bypull dee book of Moses an Solomon, dee prophets an Jesus." The amplifier squawks back at her. "Bypull dee book of love!" she yells over the noise. "Not war! Not like you say!" The bullhorn blinks out for good, and the little street preacher sets it to rest on her shoulder.

Buffalo has plenty more to say. He lurches towards her but veers into a parked car, clinging to the door handle for support. The two children are not interested in his arguments. They stare into the silent bullhorn, more wondrous to them than any of the great and terrible prophesies made here in front of the hotel. Armageddon, the Second Coming, the advent of universal love — it will not take place. Not this Christmas. Not here at Hotel Walden.

THE BISHOP'S BLESSING

There's a new hole in Ralph's wall. Shards of glass on the floor amidst ashes and cigarette butts. "I'm twenty-six!" Ralph shakes his head. "I'm tired! Fuck it, I'm tired! I've been wise — I'm not stupid — when I came here I didn't go around hurtin nobody. I didn't smoke marijuana. I was scared of all that. But I ain't gettin no results. I ain't gettin enough sex. I still got the Bishop on my back, and I can't control all this hatred." He looks up at the hole in the wall and shakes his head again. "Like that. I threw a beer bottle last night. I just got mad. It wasn't the Bishop either — it was me. I just was feelin funny, full of hatred like the time I killed Frank Sinatra — when it was either him or me. And I felt like if I didn't throw that bottle I coulda done something crazy. . . . I know

I can't give in to my hatred. I know. I know. But then somethin comes over me, like I'm gonna explode. But I know. That's why I'm plannin on doing some good for myself."

Ralph has been speaking out of an intense daze, like an accident victim recounting his misfortune. Now he snaps out of it. He grabs the filthy sheet bunched up against the drafty window. "You know what my mother did with this sheet?" His voice fills with wonder. "She took it to church and had it blessed by the Bishop. Took it right to the United House of Prayer for All People on 125th and Eighth Avenue, and the Bishop blessed it for me. He's a pisser, that Bishop. A pisser. See, I get angry at him when I'm hallucinatin, but I gotta learn to not hate him. . . . So this sheet — when my mother give it to me, I just got this feeling. I got in bed and wrapped it around me. I was angry at everything. But then I felt warm; I felt the Bishop's blessing and I knew he cared. I tucked myself in, and I didn't feel no hate. . . ."

DOC'S CHRISTMAS EVE

"Somebody always dies aroun Christmas. Least that's how it went in my family. Nobody could put much oomph into Christmas cause somebody'd be poppin off. Way back when I was little, Christmas was beautiful to me. A joy. My mom gave me anything in the world I wanted, any fuckin thing. Bicycle. Skates. Plenty of clothes. There was nothin that I asked her for that she wouldn't get me. Domestic and factory work — she did whatever she could to make it. And she promised that if I was to finish school, she would buy me an automobile. But she didn't make it that far — she didn't live to see that. And I didn't finish school either. The fact that she died put a hell of a damper on me. . . . She was only ill three days. Died December 23, 1944. And, man, she was gettin things ready for Christmas. The house was bein decorated — all of a sudden she just didn't feel well one mornin. To me it was a mystery. I got the death certificate, but ... what did she die of? I don't know. I hate to even. ... It was gruesome. ... Memories can be tearjerkin. It's a three-sided horse, I guess. You want to cherish those special feelings, yet there's still so much in there that you don't want to remember. It's a problem. Leaves you with a bad feeling. Oh man, it's hell!"

Doc's sitting in a hospital armchair. Plastic tray in his lap with two roast beef sandwiches he's saving for a midnight snack. It's Christmas Eve — his birthday as well. His eyeglass frames have cracked and been repaired with thick wads of adhesive tape that cut his view by half. They look awful. He looks awful. The room, his fellow patients, look grey and dispirited. There is nothing more that can happen, it seems. Doc's face is thin, and he worries that his old TB might be wasting him. "I don't know what it is. I'm havin trouble doin every little thing," he says. "I start reading, but I can't go more than a page or two. I start lookin at the girls, but I wonder if it's to stop readin. I still can't walk too tough. An now I been bed-wettin." Back in the hotel, Doc spoke with a gravelly Red Foxx vibrato, but here his voice is faint, like the sound of a radio program at the most distant reach of its transmitter. "I been through this bed-wettin stage before." He fixes his gaze on the TV set mounted high on the wall. "It happens for a while, then all of a sudden it stops. I wish it wouldn't happen here. ... It's — there's this nurse. She wakes the room up in the middle of the night — 'Oh my, Mr. Young!' She's a mouthy little motherfucker, lets the whole world know — 'Why, you've wet your bed again! Just like a four-year-old!' I'd love to pop her in the mouth! I may just do that!" he says with a trace of his old familiar growl. "Yeah!" He looks right at me, eyes twinkling. "Wait up for her tonight an pop her fat mouth. That'd be one hell of a way to celebrate my birthday!"

CHRISTMAS

It is the quietest day of the year. Empty hallways. Silent rooms.

Lloyd Smith has dinner with his AA group at Trinity House. Muriel and a few others are fed at a church on Ninety-third Street. Bobby and Doc get hospital turkey — and Doc gets a blue Hanes tee-shirt from some do-good group. "I can use it, too," he says. By his nightstand is some red wrapping paper with frolicking animals in holiday costumes. He keeps it folded neatly along with the cellophane shirt bag, as if both were separate gifts. Everyone else — Doug, David, Ralph, Buffalo, Fat Edna, Sugar Blue, Mr. Winslow, Benny, Ironsides, Youngblood, Elaine, pot heads, winos, methadone tasters, coke and dope poppers, epileptics, diabetics, hustlers and hard-working people, schizos, manic-depressives, psychotics and scared hallucinating crazies, runaway kids, abandoned wives, queens, whores, transvestites, number runners, and forgotten old-timers — all fall out of sight today.

"Christmas is for children," David says. "It's all right when you're young, but it don't mean nothin when you gotta face life on your own."

Quietest day of the year.

Unsettling peace.

ONE LAST THING

Youngblood's sitting awkwardly on a folding chair, legs crossed, arms drawn close to his body as though he's afraid he might be punished for taking up too much space. "People dyin," he cackles. "Geech went to bed and didn't wake up. And this new guy, a whitey, he got drunk or high or somethin and fell out his window. Some people go to a whole lotta trouble to be stupid. This whitey, he hadn't been here long enough to unpack his bags. . . . And Buffalo — yeah, he's gone. Didn't get to his pills on time." Youngblood cackles again, but there is no mirth to it. It is more a kind of filler, something to plug up the silence while language catches up with feeling. "Yeah, Buffalo was comin apart. Walked around like he was drunk, but it was his boxin days that messed his body up. BOOM! — your spine. BOOM! — your kidney. BOOM! — your brain. Helluva way to make a living. Yeah, they say he was a contender. In fact, we got another guy here — hey Willy! tell him how you went in there with Sugar Ray Robinson."

Willy looks up from the TV. He's wearing a grey suit over a wool shirt buttoned to the throat. His shoes are old but neatly polished. He takes good care of himself. "I fought him, all right," Willy says. "Some club in Detroit."

"Tell him what happened," Youngblood cackles. "Tell him how good he was."

Willy doesn't move. "Yeah, he was good." His voice seems to come from somewhere else.

"Family Feud" is on the tube. The studio audience is roaring as a black family hugs the MC, while bouncing wildly, as if mounted on pogo sticks. Youngblood watches for a moment or two, perhaps to reassure himself that the world is indeed as bizarre as he believes it to be. "Yeah, and the cops came and took Sugar Blue away. He stopped takin his medication and that violent shit came up on him. Got in a big fight right in this room. Broke up a couple of chairs; knocked a hole in the wall. They grabbed Sugar and sent him up to the psychiatry hospital, but he slipped out and come back for Christmas. Cops come this mornin and took him off again." Youngblood stretches and unfolds his legs. For the first time, he seems to feel entitled to the space he occupies. "Sugar was always surprisin you," he adds. "Few years ago he robbed a store and got the whole block high. Set up a table right in front of the buildin — I'm not bullshittin. You seen them kids sellin comic books and lemonade an shit — well here's Sugar Blue with his little table, givin away wine and whiskey, turnin on the whole neighborhood! Cocksucker! He'll be back."

Youngblood falls silent for a moment and stares at his feet as if the next words were written on his shoes. "Yeah, Sugar'll make it back every time, but I don't give too many of the others much of a chance. I'll tell you one last thing," he says as he raises his eyes to meet mine in a sharp glance, "It's not the buildin that's the problem, it's the people. You tell me if I'm right. You got people in here don't know whether it's day or night. Don't clean their clothes, brush their hair, don't have no respect for themselves. Walkin up and down the halls, everything hangin out — droolin down their face, pissin in their pants. They're lost. Be better dead. Listen, you know how many of these people wake up every mornin miserable? You know what they're thinkin? They're sorry to face the day; they're wishin they could die in their sleep and not go through no more of this. Thurman, Gerry, Geech, Buffalo, Arthur Moore — they didn't wanna kill themselves. That is, they didn't set out to do it — but they didn't wanna live. They had nothin goin for em except wakin up scared an worryin how to get through the day. There wasn't nothin for em here but more time to feel bad. They're better off. They checked out the scene and got out, understand?

"Now how you gonna fix all that? You think paintin their rooms and hirin on more psyches gonna change anything? Give em pork chops instead of macaroni for lunch? You dealin with the trash in here, and they didn't get to be no trash overnight. I'm bein realistic. You may not like what I'm sayin, but people ain't used to hearin the truth. Most of these people, they already had their chance — they had a hundred chances. They been through the prisons, had their alcohol program, their drug program, all kinds of psyches workin on em — an they're worse, they're not better. You can do what Hitler did with the Jews an put em all away, or you can hire more social workers an more psyches an fix up a game room an set up work programs an spend all kindsa money we ain't got. Or you can be realistic. You gotta look through what you got in these hotels an forget about all that bullshit about savin everyone. There's a few people like David — he could be all right. He's livin clean; he's tryin to learn things. You give him lotsa supervision and he might make somethin of hisself. But the others — you gotta cut em loose. You throwin good money after bad. They had their chance. They ain't livin. Not really.

"Who's makin em live like that? It ain't the buildin. It ain't Reagan — they don't know who's president. Maybe they don't even know we got a president. You hear what I'm sayin? They been in the jungle too long. No one's gonna change em now. You tell me this — you wanna train a wild animal for a circus or somethin — now are you gonna go out an get yourself some old lion that's been runnin loose for twenty years? You sure ain't! You gonna find yourself a young one, somethin that ain't got so wild an ornery, so you can teach it to respect you. You get one of them old lions been goin off on its own an huntin all them years, you gotta kill it or cut it loose cause you sure ain't gonna teach it to listen to you or get it to jump through no hoops."

GRADUATION

Muriel answers her door in a threadbare sweater and raggedy blue wool tights. She was sleeping, dreaming, when I knocked, and even now she seems uncertain as to whether she can sort interior visions from recollected experience. "I don't feel bad remembering my past," she says. "It kind of amazes me to see all the things that happened to me. I'm really much more interesting than I thought I was. My life has taken some strange routes — like taking a left turn when you should've gone right. Like taking the elevator — I push one to get down and wind up on the seventh floor."

"HELP ME! HELP ME!" a voice screams in the courtyard. "THEY'RE BEATING ME! HELP! GET THE COPS! PLEASE HELP! SIXTH FLOOR!" No phone in Muriel's room. No phone in the hallway. I could race downstairs to the lobby and call the police, but an odd paralysis takes hold — I don't budge from my rickety chair. There is too much going on. Too much. This cramped space, these green walls, the two little "Thinking of You" cards taped above Muriel's bed — this small room holds me. "This happens all the time around Christmas," Muriel says. "Every night the place goes wild."

Later, as I'm about to leave, Muriel hands me a folder with "MURIEL BERRY" neatly printed in big block letters. It's her graduation materials from her first months in SPOP. She's very pleased. "Who can say where this will lead?" she tells me. "It's not every day you get to graduate. . . ."

Muriel's Graduation Folder

MURIEL BERRY

FUNCTIONAL ASSESSMENT UNIT
CASE COORDINATOR: James
DATE ENTERED: 9/4/80
DATE GRADUATED: 12/23/80

[Then — as in a high school yearbook — scribbled words of encouragement from the staff:]

> Good luck Muriel
> Enjoy your new interests
> and have a good life!   Gina

> Muriel,
> We are all going to
> miss you! We wish you
> only happiness & peace of
>   mind   Richard

> Keep your head to the sky
>   and lots of luck   Ricardo

Muriel,
    It took a little
extra time and prodding, but
you did it. Good show!   Mr. B.

Muriel, you made lots & lots of progress, congratulations
                    Dr. Gilman

Muriel
    GOOD LUCK
always and
congratulations
on completing
THE PROGRAM   Cora Beth

[Inside the folder is a Functional Assessment Unit Recipe Booklet with nine cooking class recipes:]

1. **Cake from a mix**
    1 box any cake mix
    1 egg
    water
    Follow directions on box. This recipe requires
    an oven.
    Serves — 6 people
    Cost — approximately $1.25

[Other recipes include spaghetti, tuna and cheese casserole, meat loaf, tuna fish salad — and on the last page "Helpful Hints":]

1. Never handle hot pot or pan without potholders
2. If a pot lacks a cover, use some aluminum foil to cover it.
3. Lemon juice perks up tuna when added.
4. When draining spaghetti from boiling water always put cold water in pot first
5. Try to eat balanced meals . . .

[All this, and two typewritten pages — Muriel's autobiography:]

MURIEL BERRY

I was delivered by a "country doctor" in Gray Gables, Mass. on November 13, 1924, (A Friday)! My mother graduated from High school and my father was a mechanic (both deceased). My brother was training to be a pilot — crashed — sent home in a sealed casket. My mother was in constant mourning; the social life was at an end. Taken to a specialist in Boston — I was sent to join relatives in Kansas City, Mo. — nothing but bridge games. I returned to Cape Cod and was introduced by a schoolmate to newspaperman who I married at the "Little Church around the Corner."

I worked as a night manager for Western Union until the birth of my son. I had a nervous breakdown (shoveled coal for the Doctor's fee). I've been in and out of hospitals ever since.

My mother was a "book-worm" and my father concentrated on providing for the family. His brother — my uncle William Berry notified me of his death and took care of the funeral arrangements some years ago.

I enjoyed living in Greenwich Village and worked for Trio of interior decorators. I attended two art schools after recouperating from "Dilemas" (spent several months in Manhattan State and Pilgrim State.) Placed here from women's shelter — temporary welfare automatic switch to SSI — on "speaking" terms with most tenants. I admire the staff — experiencing a "please! I'd rather be left alone attitude." I dislike being "pushed"!, prodded into surroundings — situations that displease me. I realize that most of these events have, left me with a rather inferior self-confidence. Therefore I would rather try to "bury the past" and build a more constructive life for myself.

I wish to emphasize "bury the past" — I feel a refreshing self-confidence. I further realize that I without doubt have not taken a real good look at myself!

I suppose that actually I have not been honest with myself therefore have given a false impression to others as well as myself — which leaves a huge area for reconstruction — perhaps this indicates a hope for reincarnation — which in truth has no bearing on the reality of my present state — emotionally as well as pyhsically — facing facts as they are.

I find it a relief to unburden myself — however I do not feel these apologies are sufficient to warrant my somewhat erratic behavior patterns — Either you do or you don't do as you claim to be beneficial to oneself as a member of our society.

Rereading has made me more fully realize that I have not been as truthful with myself and probably others as well — too much of the "escapist" perhaps which constitutes a rather weak apology.

I find also that I am too easily distracted therefore have difficulty concentrating on the pertinent matters that I should most of all be concerned with.

Excuses wear out — either to oneself or to others concerned about my welfare.

Not meaning to assume what logically can be considered an egotistical attitude since I do realize that many of my "failures" are of my own so-called making — that is I enjoy being stimulated — a sort of awakening — which is sometimes shocking — at other times gratifying (not to "pat myself on the back" version — which can quite easily become decieving!)

(Frankly at this point I feel rather confused and wonder if I am really seeing things clearly). (Another excuse? — perhaps!), leaping either before (or perhaps without) looking.

To begin with life is a prize that we have been blessed with and not necessarily expected to gamble with.

A priceless possession!

Possibly I am too much of a "private person."

Also I am tired of making excuses for my failures — serious reflection has given me pause to re-evaluate all circumstances leading up to my present state of being.

Perhaps this all adds up to inferiority complex — which I quite sincerely wish to dispel.

More later.

REUNION

"I was smokin pot," Ralph says, "and I had this friend here, so maybe he's the one that did it." He bursts out in a wild cackle. "Yeah — ha! — he musta been the one who set my mattress on fire. I was thinkin Bishop Ralphie did it, but I'll bet it was my friend." He laughs all over again. "Mattress fires are the worst. You gotta keep throwin water on em or they'll burn you up while you're sleepin. I know about that from a dream I had . . . unless that's what someone told me. I stuck my blanket under the sink and put it down the hole in my mattress to make sure it was out. Hard to sleep after that cause everything was pretty wet." He shakes his head disconsolately and shrugs at the charred mattress. It looks like someone fired a cannon through it. "Ha!" he says, "Now I don't got to worry about no one takin it!"

He steps out into the hallway just in time to catch Sugar Blue racing up the stairs two and three at a time. "Sugar!" Ralph throws his arms around him. "Sugar, I love you!"

Sugar Blue grins sheepishly. He's wearing a blue seersucker suit, checked shirt, and a yellow tie with leaping horses. He returns Ralph's hug; Ralph holds on tightly, urgently, long after Sugar Blue has dropped his arms. "He broke out!" Ralph shouts down the empty corridor. "Ha! You broke right outa the hospital, didn't you?"

Sugar Blue fiddles with his tie. "I *got* out. I didn't knock down no walls or beat on no guards." He sounds tired, subdued. "They let me go. Yeah, they *made* me go cause I was gettin it on with this chick."

"You still got your room?"

"Yeah, they locked it up and took the rent from my SSI. You gotta come up and see the cockroaches. I got some now the size of your shoe."

"An I can show you my mattress. Ha! I had a great fire last night. Up half the night throwin water on it. My room's gettin to be a real dump."

Sugar Blue's digging through his pockets, pulling out scraps of paper. He grins from time to time while Ralph keeps talking, but he looks like he's got other things on his mind. "I love you, Sugar!" Ralph says again. "I been thinkin about you all mornin."

"Yeah," he shrugs. "Well, here I am."

FRIENDS

I haven't seen much of Lloyd Smith since his summer drinking binge. All autumn and winter he's been busy lugging lumber and supplies for the neighborhood hardware store. At night he keeps to his room. This evening he's standing halfway up the eighth-floor stairs, stoned and wobbly. Just standing, as if going up or down is more than he can handle right now. "They paid everyone but me," he says. "The boss told me I gotta come in on Friday because there's — hey, man, you know any two-room apartments?" I've never heard any "Hey, man" stuff from Lloyd. I feel rotten. "Like I can go up to $250 a month, man. In a pinch maybe $300. . . . My boss — I only get one-week vacation. He gives everyone else two. What kinda bullshit is that?" Familiar alert face, but tonight his pupils are little pinpricks. "One-week vacation, man! No time to relax. And these bastards here, they're gonna pick us off one by one. Gonna knock down all the walls and make this a condominium." His anger abates and he smiles warmly. "So how you doin? Where you been? Hey, tell me this, tell me this one thing — you ever been to Paris, man?"

"Yes," I tell him.

"That's great! That's really somethin!" He leans towards me, purses his lips. "Listen, man, you got a two-bedroom apartment, right?"

"Right."

"So now what if I gave you $200 a month and took the small room?"

"That's where I work. That's where friends stay when they're in town." I hope that will be enough of an answer.

"I understand. Hey, I *do* understand. But I'm talking about $200 cash up front."

"Thanks, Lloyd, but I like having some extra space."

His features sag. "You surprise me! You really surprise me. I thought we were friends. Friends! You know? And here you are, lettin me down."

"We are friends, but you asked if you could move in with me. That's a pretty big — "

"Two hundred dollars up front. I'm not asking for nothin I don't pay for."

It's futile. There's no way I can let him down easy. It's futile and sad. This rich and terrible year churns inside me. I've lived too close to too much need. So many people buffeted by their own fragile feelings. *Love* is a word rarely uttered in these hotels. But friendship — choosing roommates, borrowing and lending money, shooting up, sharing a bottle, putting together a hustle — friendship founded on being high on the same thing at the same time, on a common dislike for someone, or a shared obsession with gambling, soap operas, numbers, or cats — friendship is the ruined currency of daily life here.

Lloyd wobbles and grabs the railing to steady himself. Stoned and hurting. Feeling and put-on all tangled. There's nothing I can say. "I can't do it, Lloyd. I just don't want to."

"I gotta get outa here. I need a place near my job."

"It's gonna be rough," I say. "But if you start looking now you can find something before the hotel closes."

He leans against the banister and begins staggering downstairs. "That's not a friend talking," he mumbles. "They want us outa the neighborhood. You got a room. You got a room you could rent me if you was my friend. You surprise me, man. I thought you'd come through for me. I thought you cared."

SAFE

Ralph sits cross-legged on the stairs. Blank expression. Meditating. Earlier, he was praying — *Please, Lord, please, dear Lord, don't let me punch this nigger in the mouth.* He was angry at Sugar Blue he explains. But when I ask him what the trouble was, he can't remember. "This is the best thing I can do," he says. "I feel safe meditatin. Long as I can keep the power in my forehead, nothin can hurt me."

I wish him a happy new year. He's already back in his trance.

YEAR'S END

Smoke billowing across Broadway, up past the hotel. As if these littered streets coughed up one last breath to die with the dying year. Sidewalks fill with people heading home from work. Some yank scarves over their mouths; others step out into Broadway to look for fire engines. But there is no fire. Nothing but furry grey smoke rolling in great gusts. Street lamps and headlights blur and spread. Bad air. Bad night. Bad year. Unreal city . . .

"I'm coming! I'm coming!" Fat Edna says to no one. A man on the Broadway island stumbles from the curb blowing a party-favor trumpet at onrushing traffic. In this strange smoke, he could be standing on a cloud. "Shut up!" she yells. He aims his instrument at her and blows a raspberry. "FUCK YOU!" she bellows. "IT AIN'T TIME, YOU FUCKIN SPIC!"

A crowd of passers-by gathers to watch, fascination mixed with contempt. The man raises his horn again: B-R-A-A-A-A! B-R-A-A-A-A! B-R-A-A-A-A-A-A-A-A-A-A-A!!!

"FUCK YOU!" Fat Edna shrieks at the crowd. "FUCK THE FUCKIN NEW YEAR!" Her anger snaps. She shrinks away, mumbling to herself, lurching through the vile smoky night toward the hotel. "Room," she says; the very word seems to calm her. "Home . . . home . . . soup . . . my room . . ."

EPILOGUE:
THE FOLLOWING YEAR

The workers don't speak. Strong angular faces of Eastern Europe. They step aside politely as the agent leads me down the corridor to the room Doug and Bobby once shared. The old linoleum has been torn off the floor, leaving bare concrete. Bundles of wire run over-

head, poking from holes, then dipping back into the unfinished ceiling.

The apartment is small and cheap-looking with ugly red carpeting that smells of industrial freshness, like the vinyl interior of a new car. The shiny bath and kitchen appliances look false as any movie set. The walls are fresh and white. There are new windows, each with a little yellow sticker, not yet removed. Only the old radiators remain untouched, still covered with layers of cracked paint. Now, they seem the one substantial thing left in Hotel Walden.

"Free gas and electricity," the agent tells me. "Seven-fifty for the one-bedroom, five-fifty for the studio/efficiency. You know, they don't make buildings like this any more. Sixty years old, and it's good for another sixty. They tell me it used to be quite a place — they say the Yankees used to stay here." Five or six of the former tenants are hanging on. They've refused management's offer of a handsome bonus to move them out of their SRO squalor. "We got our lawyers working on it," the agent says, "Those welfare people will be gone before too long."